The ALLURE
of
TOXIC LEADERS

ALSO BY JEAN LIPMAN-BLUMEN

Hot Groups:
Seeding Them, Feeding Them, and
Using Them to Ignite Your Organization
Coauthor, with Harold J. Leavitt

The Connective Edge:
Leading in an Interdependent World

Gender Roles and Power

Sex Roles and Social Policy:
International Perspectives on a Complex Social Science Equation
Coeditor, with Jessie Bernard

Step Wars:
Overcoming the Perils and Making Peace in Adult Stepfamilies
Coauthor, with Grace Gabe

The ALLURE
of
TOXIC LEADERS

*Why We Follow Destructive Bosses
and Corrupt Politicians—and
How We Can Survive Them*

Jean Lipman-Blumen

OXFORD
UNIVERSITY PRESS
2005

OXFORD
UNIVERSITY PRESS

Oxford   New York
Auckland   Bangkok   Buenos Aires   Cape Town   Chennai
Dar es Salaam   Delhi   Hong Kong   Istanbul   Karachi   Kolkata
Kuala Lumpur   Madrid   Melbourne   Mexico City   Mumbai   Nairobi
São Paulo   Shanghai   Taipei   Tokyo   Toronto

Published by Oxford University Press, Inc.
198 Madison Avenue, New York, New York 10016

www.oup.com

Oxford is a registered trademark of Oxford University Press

Library of Congress Cataloging-in-Publication Data
Lipman-Blumen, Jean.
The allure of toxic leaders : why we follow destructive bosses and corrupt politicians—
and how we can survive them / Jean Lipman-Blumen.
p. cm. Includes bibliographical references.
ISBN 0-19-516634-5
1. Leadership—Moral and ethical aspects.
2. Leadership—Psychological aspects.
3. Power (Social sciences)
4. Immorality.
I. Title.
HM1261.L56 2004 303.3'4—dc22
2004012520

2 4 6 8 9 7 5 3 1

Printed in the United States of America
on acid-free paper

To Hal
entwined in life, in heart,
and in work.

Contents

Part IV: Liberating Ourselves from the Allure of Toxic Leaders

Preface

Toxic leaders cast their spell broadly. Most of us claim we abhor them. Yet we frequently follow—or at least tolerate—them, be they our employers, our CEOs, our senators, our clergy, or our teachers. When toxic leaders don't appear on their own, we often seek them out. On occasion, we even create them by pushing good leaders over the toxic line. That paradox of ambivalence ticks at the core of this book. Exploring that paradox, plus the strategies we might use to recognize, avoid, reform, overthrow, or escape from destructive and corrupt leaders, is the challenge of *The Allure of Toxic Leaders*.

In this book, I examine why toxic leaders—from Enron's Ken Lay and Jeff Skilling and the Catholic Church's Cardinal Bernard Law to the Italian media mogul and prime minister Silvio Berlusconi, as well as junk bond king Michael Milken, automotive giant Henry Ford, and Tyco International's L. Dennis Kozlowsky, for starters—fascinate and attract followers. I trace how employees, voters, parishioners, fans, board members, and often the media remain in the thrall of toxic leaders, even when they clearly recognize the cynicism, corruption, and cruelty those leaders display.

How are we to understand that paradox? This book raises questions about the imprints from our childhood and our shared human condition that leave us vulnerable to destructive leaders, to the Maos and Hitlers who stride the international stage, as well as to everyday organizational tyrants.

Many internal and external forces are at play in this dynamic. They include our own human psychological and existential needs; political, social, and economic crises; cultural and historical norms and traditions; technological innovations and scientific discoveries; and the immense global dilemmas of our era. Working together, in a complex, constantly changing world, these forces render us exquisitely susceptible to leaders who, again and again, leave us worse off than they found us.

This book does not blame the victim, but it takes a serious look at followers' ordinary human needs: the yearning for certainty in an uncertain world, for self-esteem, heroism, access to centers of action, opportunities to engage in noble enterprises, and the promise of immortality. These are just a few of the forces that make us easy prey to toxic leaders—ruthless bosses, unscrupulous politicians, and other tyrants, petty and profound.

Even toxic leaders without military might or brutish police forces can easily intimidate and corral followers. Curiously enough, they don't really need to intimidate us to make us acquiesce. We followers regulate our own behavior through a set of control myths, intertwined with our own hierarchy of needs. The followers' unwitting self-regulation leaves toxic leaders free to go about their destructive business as they see fit.

The book, however, does not stop there. In fact, the final section focuses on pragmatic strategies for liberating ourselves from the traps that toxic leaders lay for us and that we set for ourselves. In those chapters, I also expose whatever fragile silver lining there may be to enduring toxic leaders, since many people caught in the most threatening circumstances do manage to learn and grow from them.

Before we can free ourselves, however, we shall have to make hard choices, both individually and collectively. These options range from confronting and counseling the leader to prodding the leader to reform and, if that doesn't work, facing up to the bitter task of unseating the leader. For in the end, we may need to organize our colleagues and marshal still other resources to overthrow a destructive leader.

This book describes the importance of setting limits on the tenure of leaders to prevent their turning toxic. It also suggests ways to repair the process whereby we select leaders, so that we can identify effective and decent albeit reluctant candidates who will assume the burdens of leadership for the sake of the group, not their own power. In addition, the book examines respectable departure possibilities for leaders who have overstayed their usefulness and still other scenarios for keeping current leaders on the straight and narrow.

Once we fall under a toxic leader's spell, escape is likely to be painful, sometimes nigh impossible. In this instance, too, prevention is worth a thousand cures. Thus, recognizing the early signs of toxicity in leaders and their seductive visions can be potent preventive medicine. Detecting the undercurrents of destructiveness and evil before they draw us into the riptide of toxic leadership can be our lifeline.

The problems toxic leaders pose for their followers are escalating. To address them, we must take a long, hard, but useful look at ourselves, at the world in which we live, at the leaders who seduce us, and at the possibilities for surviving, perchance succeeding, despite the allure of toxic leaders.

Acknowledgments

On the journey that one takes in writing a book, many people offer guidance, sustenance, and cheer. Each person's contribution has been unique.

My husband, colleague, and intellectual co-conspirator, Hal Leavitt, is without peer. He has challenged my thinking, encouraged my efforts, edited clumsy sentences, and even cooked dinner when I seemed completely tethered to my computer. I have been blessed, indeed, to have Herb Addison from Oxford University Press as my very own Maxwell E. Perkins, who gently and always so respectfully made valuable suggestions about substance and style. Helen Mules, Sue Warga, Dino Battista, Tim Bartlett, Jordan Pitcher, and Peter Harper were a spectacular Oxford team, without whom most assuredly this book would have gotten lost along the way. Denise Marcel, my agent, has been a stalwart and indispensable companion throughout the entire journey, from the time this book was merely a cinder in my eye to its completion.

Many colleagues who feel more like friends and family have accompanied me in mind and spirit on this journey. At the Claremont Graduate University, David Drew, Mike Csikszentmihalyi, Dick Ellsworth, Stead Upham, and Wes Balda have been particularly great sources of inspiration. Grace Gabe and Warren Bennis have never ceased to encourage me in a thousand ways even when this book interfered with other important happenings.

Colleagues at other institutions, too, have also cheered me on during this trek. Neil Elgee has been an ardent supporter since we first discovered our joint respect for the incandescent work of Ernest Becker. So have Robert Kramer and Sheldon Solomon, from whom I have learned much. Georgia Sorenson, Joanne Cuilla, and Gil Hickman provided long-distance renewal that reminded me of the cups of water that, as a child, I used to hand to the exhausted Boston Marathon runners at the peak of Heartbreak Hill.

Friends and family have offered essential succor and cheer, as well as invaluable counseling. My friend since adolescence, Connie Martinson, has the endearing habit of acting in loco parentis, proffering the deeply honest and caring advice that only a mother or sister would dare give. She has been a generous font of wisdom on every aspect of publishing, from book titles and covers to the very substance of the work. Leslie Martinson also brought his brilliant director's eye to the cover, thereby immeasurably improving it. Alice and Mike Stein have been friends for a lifetime. Their kindness and support were emotional vitamins that buoyed me along the way. Bonnie and Robert Fisher have been in my corner all the way, with trenchant questions and deep friendship. Len Comess has put a wise, compassionate, and steadying hand on my shoulder, helping me keep to the path. My children, Lorna, Lesley, and Peter, and my sister Claire have been loving, patient, understanding, and reassuring, particularly when my spirits flagged. Their calls, e-mails, and instant messages have cheered me along the way. John Leavitt, my son by marriage, also has been a source of gentle camaraderie. My grandchildren have often put a smile on my weary face. Other people's children—my many students—have given me pause for thought with searching questions that I have struggled to answer.

Heather Fraschetti deserves thanks of a very special and immeasurable sort. It was Heather who chased down a thousand Web sites, expired URLs, and library books; who had the patience to insert all my undecipherable handwritten corrections to the manuscript; who worried over the persnickety formatting of the entire book; who extracted the references from the endnotes; and who was there at every moment, overworked but endlessly cheerful.

Finally, the many people whom I have interviewed for this book, who generously shared with me both the wisdom and the pain of their experiences with toxic leaders, must perforce remain anonymous heroes. Although I shall always honor their privacy, I shall never forget their immense contributions.

Without each and every one of these wonderful people in my life, there would have been no journey; there would have been no book. Thanks are simply not enough.

Pasadena, California   J.L-B.
May 2004

Unhappy the land that has no heroes.
No, unhappy the land that is in need of heroes.

—*Bertolt Brecht*

I

THE BIG PICTURE

1

Toxic Leaders: They're Plentiful

I am bewitched with the rogue's company. If the rascal have not given me medicines to make me love him, I'll be hanged.
—Falstaff in Shakespeare's *Henry IV*

Ah, mon cher, for anyone who is alone, without God and without a master, the weight of days is dreadful. Hence one must choose a master, God being out of style.
—Albert Camus, *The Fall*

Falstaff is not the only follower who has ever felt bewitched by a toxic leader. Many of us succumb to their allure. Falstaff, for his part, was openly besotted with Prince Hal, the rebellious, youthful leader-in-waiting.[1] More often, however, we followers deny how truly enchanted we are. We may grouse about toxic leaders, but frequently we tolerate them—and for surprisingly long periods of time.

Tolerate, in fact, may be far too weak a word to describe the complex relationship between toxic leaders and their followers. These intriguing leaders first charm but then manipulate, mistreat, undermine, and ultimately leave their followers worse off than they found them. Yet many of these followers hang on. I do not speak merely of the leader's immediate entourage—the leader's close-in staff and advisors. I am speaking also of the larger mass of supporters (employees, constituents, volunteers) who only glimpse their toxic leader through a glass darkly—perchance through a window of the executive suite or on the television screen. More surprisingly perhaps, even those groups charged with keeping leaders under the microscope and on the straight and narrow—the media and boards of directors—fall under their sway.

Followers of toxic leaders often do much more than simply

tolerate them. They commonly adulate, abet, and actually prefer toxic leaders to their nontoxic counterparts. That astonishing choice occurs everywhere that leaders strut their stuff—in business, politics, the nonprofit world of education and religion, athletics, the family, and all the other arenas of human action. During their heyday, Enron's Kenneth Lay and Jeffrey Skilling, WorldCom's Bernard Ebbers, ImClone's Samuel Waksal, Tyco International's L. Dennis Kozlowski, Sunbeam's Al Dunlap, HealthSouth's Richard Scrushy, Adolph Hitler, Boston's Roman Catholic cardinal Bernard Law, TV evangelist James Bakker, and Texas Tech basketball coach Bobby Knight, for starters, enjoyed—and many still enjoy—enthusiastic support from their followers.

One historical example from the corporate world: Not long after a jury convicted Michael R. Milken, the "junk bond king" of investment firm Drexel Burnham Lambert, of securities fraud, a large group of former DBL employees appeared on Phil Donahue's TV talk show. To a person, the still unemployed stockbrokers and administrative assistants spoke glowingly of their former boss, despite the fact that Milken's illegal actions led to the closure of the firm and the loss of their jobs.

Another historical example from the political arena: In 1904, while serving a sixty-day jail term for impersonating a constituent at a federal postal exam, Boston's Ward 17 boss, James Michael Curley, won an alderman's seat.[2] According to the *Boston Irish Reporter*, Curley explained, "I felt I had done a charitable thing for a man who needed a job, so he could support his wife and four children."[3]

Then in 1945, after decades of a "colorful career" and while under indictment for mail fraud, Curley was handily elected mayor of Boston.[4] In 1946, a jury convicted the "rascal king." The day the verdict came down, the middle-aged saleswomen in Filene's Basement, a venerable Boston institution for bargain hunters, wept disconsolately. Curley ran the mayor's office from his jail cell for five months, until President Harry S. Truman commuted his sentence in 1947. In 1950, Truman pardoned him.

Here's a more recent example: When I first began this book, Vincent "Buddy" A. Cianci Jr., the mayor of Providence, Rhode Island, for twenty-one years, was on trial for graft. Cianci was accused of "heading a criminal enterprise [whose purpose] was to enrich himself personally and politically," according to prosecutor Richard W. Rose.[5] Nonetheless, the *New York Times* reported that the six-term mayor "remains popular despite the charges." Subsequently a federal jury found Cianci guilty of a felony. In December

2002, Cianci began serving a five-year, four-month sentence in a federal penitentiary in Fort Dix, New Jersey.[6] Following Cianci's sentencing, one female constituent wistfully complained, "I wish he'd get away with it."[7] Robert Barrera, a businessman from North Smithfield, lamented, "This is an event that people will remember like 9/11 and when Kennedy was shot. [Cianci] was such a positive influence you hate to see this."[8]

Where Are the Saints?

Do not look for saints among formal leaders. Saints rarely seek elected or appointed office. They seldom enter the rough-and-tumble of politics or the corporate world. Nor are we likely to encounter saintly leaders in the spit and polish of the traditional military. And, certainly, we'll be hard pressed to find them in the more arcane halls of academia. Oftentimes they are even absent from the sacred assemblies of the church, as the sexual abuse scandal within the Catholic Church has so poignantly revealed.

If saints did frequent such locales, there would be little need for this book, which considers why followers knowingly tolerate, seldom unseat, frequently prefer, and sometimes even create toxic leaders.

We are more likely to discover saintly leaders outside of formal organizations, taking up the burdens of unsung leadership. We might spot such leaders in the streets feeding the homeless or on the hustings among the voiceless, where social movements are fomented.

Still, formal organizations are not totally devoid of decent leaders. You can find them in steady, sometimes little-known companies that provide an honest service or produce a dependable product, or in the clinics that treat the undernourished and the impoverished, or in schools that care about knowledge, truth, and integrity. For example, by all accounts, Aaron Feuerstein of Malden Mills, whom we'll meet later, brightens the corporate firmament, even as he suffers financial setbacks.

Not everyone, of course, will agree on the saintliness of these leaders. In fact, their opponents frequently perceive them as rabble-rousers or worse. For example, when Mohandas Karamchand Gandhi left South Africa after two decades of organizing the poorly treated Indian minority into a nonviolent political movement, "his greatest Afrikaner adversary, General Jan Smuts, was relieved enough to write to a friend, 'The saint has left our shores, I hope, forever.' "[9]

So we can all see at the outset that the topic of toxic leadership is vexing at best, given that my toxic leader may be your hero and vice versa. Even Hitler, most reviled of twentieth-century leaders, still has admirers. Historian Robert Gellately reports an interview with a survivor of the Nazi era:

> One . . . woman, wife of a prominent historian of Germany, neither of whom incidentally were Nazi Party members, . . . remembers . . . [that] "there were certainly eighty per cent who lived productively and positively throughout the time. . . . We also had good years. We had wonderful years."[10]

Even Exemplary Leaders Have Some Toxic Chinks

Nor are leaders who are widely applauded as exemplary necessarily without their occasional toxic chinks. Numerous corporate leaders whose missteps were visible only to those in the inner circle have led their businesses to great financial success. Sometimes the toxicity is an act of commission, at other times one of omission. Lee Iacocca, as CEO of Chrysler, revived that nearly moribund company, yet stumbled into several ill-advised actions, including subsequent harsh treatment of the unionized employees who had contributed mightily to the automaker's resuscitation.

Some exemplary not-for-profit leaders have stepped over the line in their zeal to reach their laudable goals. Political leaders, too, some among the most admired—such as Franklin D. Roosevelt, Harry S. Truman, and even Abraham Lincoln—occasionally have acted in ways that we'd be hard pressed not to label "toxic."

Even the saints are not completely "toxic free." According to Christopher Hitchens, Mother Teresa blithely accepted a donation from financier Charles Keating, of the savings and loan scandal. Subsequently, the founder of the Order of the Missionaries of Charity wrote to presiding judge Lance Ito, attempting to intercede on Keating's behalf in the sentencing phase of his trial.[11] So let's be realists and remember that even beloved icons of leadership can display human frailties.

Public, Private, Not for Profit: Indulgence Reigns

In the last few years, the corporate stage has been littered with tattered integrity, limitless greed, lust for power, corrosive cynicism, and deliberately peddled illusions of the leader's omnipotence. From Victor Posner of corporate raider infamy to Dynegy's Chuck Watson, Sotheby chairman A. Alfred Taubman, Warnaco's

Linda Wachner, and Gary Winnick of Global Crossing—and this far from exhausts the list—the corporate world has produced a bumper crop of toxic leaders.

The not-for-profit world boasts its own mother lode of candidates, including William Aramony of the United Way, who served seven years in the federal prison camp at Seymour Johnson Air Force Base in North Carolina. Aramony was convicted on twenty-five counts, including "conspiracy to defraud, mail fraud, wire fraud, transportation of fraudulently acquired property, engaging in monetary transactions in unlawful activity, filing false tax returns and aiding in the filing of false tax returns."[12]

The U.S. Olympic Committee, too, has had more than its fair share of toxic leaders. (We'll come to the International Olympic Committee shortly.) Some, such as former president Sandra Baldwin, who admitted lying on her resumé, have been forced to resign. Others, including CEO Lloyd Ward, who failed to disclose his conflict of interest in promoting his brother's and a childhood pal's firm to supply backup power for the Dominican Republic's games, received a genteel tap on the wrist from the board. In another toxic twist, the board ousted Baldwin's replacement, president Marty Mankamyer, after she revealed Ward's conflict of interest. The board of directors "blam[ed] her for infighting within the organization and claim[ed] she conspired with a staff member to try and force CEO Lloyd Ward from his job."[13] Through all this, Ward seemed to be hanging on. Not until after Mankamyer's ouster did the media drumbeat finally force Ward's departure.

Across the religious spectrum as well, we witness toxic leaders: TV evangelist James Bakker, convicted of twenty-four counts of fraud and conspiracy; Bishop Thomas O'Brien, former head of the Roman Catholic Diocese of Phoenix, involved in a deadly hit-and-run accident as well as the cover-up of child molestation by priests; the faceless ranks of pedophiliac priests in the United States and abroad; the late Rabbi Meir Kahane, New York urban terrorist turned member of the Israeli Knesset; and the 1930s demagogic radio priest Father Charles E. Coughlin.[14] The list goes on.

Toxic Leadership Crosses Geographical Borders in a Single Leap

Geographical borders do not impede the appearance of toxic leaders—political and corporate—who undermine, manipulate, terrorize, sabotage, diminish, and even eliminate their followers. From Josef Stalin in the Soviet Union to Augusto Pinochet in Chile, Richard Nixon in the United States, Indira Gandhi in India, Pol

Pot in Cambodia, Ferdinand Marcos in the Philippines, Alberto Fujimori in Peru, Saddam Hussein in Iraq, Slobodan Milosevic in Yugoslavia, and Charles Ghankay Taylor in Liberia, we see that toxic leadership offers a multicultural, multiracial, multiethnic equal-opportunity career path.

Nor should we interpret all these political examples to mean that the political arena has a headlock on toxic leadership. In fact, media mogul Silvio Berlusconi, subsequently the prime minister of Italy, adroitly managed to plant a foot in both camps. As sitting prime minister, Berlusconi, the wealthiest man in Italy, was put on trial for allegedly attempting to bribe judges eight years earlier. With the trial nearing a verdict, Berlusconi convinced his political allies in Italy's lower house of parliament to pass an immunity bill suspending the trial until after his term of office. That move cleared the way for Berlusconi to assume the presidency of the European Union, which was imminently scheduled to rotate to Italy.

During the trial, in a scene worthy of Woody Allen's directorial genius, Berlusconi testified that he had engaged in the shady business deal on which the trial centered at the urging of then Italian prime minister Bettino Craxi, who "urged him to do so for the good of Italy."[15] "I had no direct interest, and Craxi begged me to intervene because he believed that the operation damaged the state," Berlusconi insisted.[16] According to Berlusconi, his political adversary Romano Prodi intended to allow a state-controlled food company to be sold at a fire-sale price to one of Berlusconi's corporate competitors. (Incidentally, at the time of the trial Prodi was president of the European Commission.)

Moving unequivocally into the corporate arena, Jean-Marie Messier, chief executive of French media group Vivendi Universal, finally stepped down after a whirlwind tenure that left the shell-shocked company with an 80-percent decline in its value. The media had repeatedly predicted the departure of the former "darling of the Paris financial community" as he made one dramatic misstep after another. Nonetheless, the cosmopolitan CEO seemingly managed to keep his balance on that tightrope, at least until the major North American shareholder maneuvered his ouster.[17]

Across international borders, the not-for-profit world wallows in its own problems. Although some observers have diagnosed the Catholic Church's sexual abuse scandal as an "American affair," reports from other parts of the globe belie such oversimplification. A cover story in the *National Catholic Reporter* noted that in Sicily, Father Margarito Reyes Marchena, a Honduran immigrant, came under fire for allegedly abusing four Italian children. Father Vincenzo Noto, vicar general of the Diocese of Monreale, where Reyes had subsequently moved, declared, "The true victim is this 59-year-old priest." To aid the accused cleric, Father Noto started a collection and initiated a petition supporting Reyes.[18]

Let's consider one last set of international examples from the not-for-profit world of amateur athletes. First, the 1998 Tour de France earned the gold medal of scandal when Grenoble police arrested racers, trainers, and officials in a series of raids that "uncovered systematic use of the banned endurance-boosting hormone EPO."[19] The authorities detained Willy Voet, Festina team assistant, for "smuggling a carload of drugs across the Franco-Belgium border."[20] In addition, "authorities arrested the squad's manager and doctor."[21] That these toxic leaders had misled their charges was demonstrated by the fact that the Tour disqualified France's premier team and its top rider.

Second, in the 2002 Winter Games in Salt Lake City, Marie-Reine Le Gougne, a French Olympic skating judge, allegedly "favored a Russian couple in [the] pairs skate to ensure a gold medal for the French in the [subsequent] ice dancing competition."[22] In this winter wonderland soap opera, Le Gougne claimed that French figure-skating federation president Didier Gailhaguet had insisted that she vote for the Russians, but later retracted her confession.

The third example involves none other than the president of the International Olympic Committee, Juan Antónío Samaranch. Samaranch was accused of numerous improprieties, from indulging in an overly opulent lifestyle on the committee's tab to turning a blind eye to the Salt Lake City "gifts for votes" effort to become the site of the 2002 Games. Add to that Samaranch's nepotistic maneuver: The IOC president proposed his son for life membership in the IOC. These charges did not prevent the IOC from awarding Samaranch the IOC's most coveted honor, the gold Olympic Order, and honorary life presidency of the IOC when he stepped down after twenty-one years at the helm of the beleaguered organization. Presumably because that didn't say it all, more than one hundred IOC delegates voted to rename the Olympic Museum, in Lausanne, Switzerland, the Samaranch Museum. To put the cherry on the banana split, the committee then voted to invite Samaranch to all future meetings of the ruling executive board. Clearly, Falstaff was not the only one enamored of a toxic leader.

Toxic Leadership Proves Historically Durable

Nor is toxic leadership a recent historical phenomenon. As the Old Testament suggests, it has been around since King David bedded Bathsheba and sent her husband to certain death in battle. It probably also figured prior to recorded history, along with the wooly mammoth. Wherever we look, we see ample evidence of toxic leaders, some more extreme than others. Many nevertheless manage to retain both their followers and hagiographers for a surprisingly long time.

From one historical period to another, more often than we might want to admit, we accept and applaud leaders who exhibit various degrees of toxicity—some simply incompetent, some cowardly, others morally myopic, some cynical and venal, still others downright evil—while occupying formal leadership positions. Centuries apart, British monarch Henry VIII and American industrialist Henry Ford wielded toxic power.

Sometimes we recognize leaders' toxicity only *after* they leave their institutions in disarray and their hapless followers in despair. Worse yet, we frequently perceive the inadequacies of toxic leaders in real time but do little to stop them. These toxic leaders too often have their way with us and depart in their own good time under their own steam. Not until J. Edgar Hoover, director of the FBI for nearly half a century, died in office was his malignant leadership revealed to the public, yet many Washington insiders had long been aware.[23] During his lifetime, however, presidents, the press, and ordinary citizens lionized Hoover, even as he perpetrated some of his most reprehensible acts, including blackmailing presidents and railroading innocent people to protect FBI informants.[24] At this writing, the FBI building in Washington, D.C., still proudly bears his name.[25]

Enter the Whistle-blower

Even when whistle-blowers, such as the FBI's Coleen Rowley, WorldCom's Cynthia Cooper, and Morton Thiokol's Roger Boisjoly, step forward at great risk to name and career, rarely do their courageous efforts result in punishment of the toxic leaders they unmask.[26] True, the general public and the media often acclaim whistle-blowers. To wit, *Time* magazine anointed Cooper, Rowley, and Enron's Sherron Watkins "Persons of the Year" in 2002. (Sherron Watkins acknowledges that she inadvertently became a whistle-blower only after "a Congressional investigator for the House

Committee on Energy and Commerce stumbled across her memos [to Enron CEO Ken Lay] among thousands of subpoenaed documents."[27] Nonetheless, FBI director Robert Mueller commended Marion "Spike" Bowman, who headed up the FBI's National Security Law Unit, for "exceptional service." Bowman's unit was the very division that, in August 2001, denied the request of Rowley's Minneapolis office to search the apartment and computer of Zacarias Moussaoui, a suspect in the September 11 World Trade Center attack. Moreover, despite public recognition, Rowley and her co-whistle-blowers have been pushed aside in their own organizations. According to *Time*, one of Rowley's colleagues at the Bureau informed her that "high-level FBI agents in Washington had been overheard discussing possible criminal charges against her."[28] Once identified, whistle-blowers predictably suffer various forms of backlash in their organizations.

Although it is hard to believe, we tend to *prefer* toxic leaders for a host of tantalizing reasons that we shall explore in this book. When we don't have them, we go to great lengths to create them. The staggering numbers of such leaders in every arena, documented in the daily news, give ample evidence of our predilection for these problematic figures.

The Paradox of Cynicism: The Leader's Longevity

Paradoxically, at the same time that we yearn for them, we also feel deeply cynical about toxic leaders. In fact, a recent poll suggested that the American public's expectations for the morality of congressional leaders fell markedly below those for ordinary citizens. Following the Enron, Andersen, and Global Crossing debacles, the public image of corporate leaders is probably not much better. Still, our cynicism is often tinged with just enough fascination to keep us from casting them out altogether.

Sometimes we ignore toxic leaders' obvious faults because their charisma blinds us, at least until the leader is publicly unmasked. One former assistant to the charismatic but corrupt president of a small private college, who eventually retired on his own schedule, confided to me, "I know our new president is an honest, intelligent, and kind man, but I really miss Dennis's charm. He was so much fun to be around."

True, a few toxic leaders, such as Buddy Cianci, have been overthrown, imprisoned, or otherwise done in, but they tend to be the exceptions. Most toxic leaders achieve surprising longevity, even those without armies or secret intelligence forces to intimidate potential dissidents. Overthrowing such leaders is no mean feat. As we've just seen, Juan António Samaranch headed the International Olympic Committee for twenty-one years.

Let's also remember that Ferdinand Marcos, Slobodan Milosevic, and Saddam Hussein are only three among the more recent toxic political leaders who held on for years, notwithstanding considerable opposition. And Hussein's ouster came not at the hands of his own citizens but through an external coalition. A jobless Yugoslav lawyer interviewed in the final days of Milosevic's administration dejectedly described how both she and her husband had simply "kept their heads down" during the previous ten years because "the time was not right" to resist the leader's abuses.

Prominent supporters, from political parties to boards of directors who help catapult the leader into office, assiduously protect their leaders' power—tied, as it is, to their own self-interest. Many influential supporters collude willingly, others follow blindly, and still others are drawn unwittingly into compromising actions that hand the leader a club to hold over them.

As for the great mass of rank-and-file followers, despite their complaining around the copy machine, they, too, routinely accept the domination of poor leaders, even when they greatly outnumber them. The multiple reasons that prompt followers to put up with and even seek out toxic leaders stem from many sources—our psyches and those of the toxic leaders, the complex world in which we live, and the experiences followers have in that world, as we shall explore in the pages to come.

The Media's Myopia

Even the media have difficulty resisting the seductive appeal of wily leaders. For example, historical accounts of Fidel Castro's early presidential days exemplify how enthralled the media worldwide can become with an intriguing leader, notwithstanding signs of nascent toxicity. In the corporate sector, ITT's Harold Geneen, Henry Ford and his grandson Henry Ford II, and arbitrageur Ivan Boesky held center stage as media superstars, despite their clearly noxious impact.

Business Week's cover story of the downfall of Tyco's L. Dennis Kozlowski made a rare admission of media myopia. In its analysis of how and why Kozlowski raided the Tyco coffers without restraint for close to a decade, the analysts candidly shared the blame they attributed to lawyers, accountants, executives, and the board of directors: "The press, including *Business Week*, also bears some blame for generally portraying Tyco as a lean and mean profit machine."[29]

In many cases, corporate leaders who ravage their companies, along with thousands of employees, become the darlings of the media and financial analysts. Such was the case with former Enron CEO Kenneth Lay. At least that was so before he openly displayed strong poster boy credentials for toxic leadership by urging Enron employees to purchase company stock even as Enron was imploding.

Al Dunlap's earlier performance at Scott Paper, which markedly increased shareholder value, made him downright irresistible to Sunbeam's board. No matter that the human costs were great. No matter that Scott Paper ultimately ceased to exist. During Dunlap's tenure as Sunbeam's CEO, dozens of fawning articles appeared in the press. In fact, echoing Falstaff, John A. Byrne described Dunlap's appeal:

> The bewitching power that Al Dunlap exercised over Wall Street came from an embellished track record as a corporate tough guy. . . . Dunlap, his record showed, did not shy from either conflict or adversity. . . . If Wall Street could have invented an executive that perfectly suited its style and its preferences, it would have created Al Dunlap. In a way, it did.[30]

Rather sadly, at the peak of Dunlap's rampage *Fortune* magazine reported a poll of Cornell MBA students in which 60 percent said they admired the self-labeled "Chainsaw Al" for his slash-and-burn strategy. They saw it as "results oriented."[31] Eventually Sunbeam was forced into bankruptcy proceedings. Later the Securities and Exchange Commission accused Dunlap of directing a "huge accounting fraud" during his Sunbeam heyday.[32] Subsequent investigations revealed he had engaged in similar illegal behavior in previous posts.

As long as these corporate titans paint the bottom line black, the media as well as boards of directors, not to mention eager stockholders, generally remain in their thrall. Unfortunately, the media's assessment of these leaders as "rising stars," "gurus," or "fallen angels" infiltrates the public consciousness, significantly shaping the attitudes of impressionable leaders-in-waiting, who mistake them for role models.

Not all toxic leaders behave toxically all of the time. Like Ken Lay in his civic philanthropist's role, they can act nonmalignantly, even constructively, in some contexts and in a toxic way in others. Sometimes, however, the apparently benign behavior simply creates a smokescreen or serves as the means to other toxic action. Of course, when leaders hang out their incompetence, moral myopia, corruption, or unmitigated evil for all to see, the media have no trouble flip-flopping almost instantaneously from fawning to feeding frenzy.

Corporate leaders are not the only ones who catch the media's eye. Leaders in all sectors—religious, political, and educational, for starters—are fair game once they expose their toxic colors. In the Roman Catholic Archdiocese of Boston, Cardinal Bernard Law's long-term devotion to social causes, as well as his efforts to reach out to Israel and Cuba, led many observers to predict he would become the first American pope. Yet this much-admired cleric eventually found himself in the eye of the sexual abuse hurricane within the Church. Once the media exposed his thirty-year cover-up of pedophiliac priests, they kept the story on the front burner.

Clearly, this was a scandal long in the making. For three decades, His Eminence had continued to reassign priests accused of molesting young parishioners to new parishes where they preyed (no pun intended) on other unsuspecting victims. Amid calls from angry Catholics for Law's resignation, a substantial segment of the Boston laity nonetheless continued to support the beleaguered cleric. In this case, the media's late but unrelenting attention ultimately aroused enough whistle-blowers and appalled enough Catholics to bring down the intransigent cleric.

In every arena, we have multiple examples of the media feeding off the toxic behavior of leaders. Two factors—the media's legitimate watchdog function and its profit motive—increase the Fourth Estate's attention to toxic leaders once they are unmasked.

The Distorted Lens on Leaders

Traditionally, many, if not most, books on leadership concentrate on leaders rather than on followers. They view leaders through a distorted lens, emphasizing their strengths and minimizing their failings. These admiring accounts burnish the leader's charismatic facets to blinding brightness and inflate their images to Herculean proportions. It is not surprising, then, that James MacGregor Burns observed in his pathbreaking book, *Leadership*, that "leadership is one of the most observed and least understood phenomena on earth."[33]

This genre of leadership studies commonly softens the dark shadows cast by seemingly superhuman leaders. Then, of course, the autobiographies of leaders paint their authors, like former Sunbeam CEO Al Dunlap and Chrysler's Lee Iacocca, only from their most flattering angle. Such tales of glory inspire us to emulate these grandiose figures or at least to warm ourselves in their reflected glow.

Lest the reader think I am engaging in the countersin—a shortsighted view of good leaders—let me be clear: I do, of course, recognize that positive leaders exist and frequently contribute much to society. Václav Havel, Nelson Mandela, Mohandas K. Gandhi, and Martin Luther King Jr. stand out on the world's political stage as exemplary leaders who led in turbulent times. Warren Buffett of Berkshire Hathaway, Aaron Feuerstein of Malden Mills, Herb Kelleher, former CEO of Southwest Airlines, Anita Roddick, founder of the Body Shop, and Marcy Carsey, cochair and executive producer of the Carsey-Werner Company, come to mind on the corporate side, plus many more unsung business leaders. In fact, the great benefits that *good* leaders can bring make us want to invest *all* leaders, deserving or not, with these constructive attributes.

Yet the topic of bad leaders, particularly as individuals, has its own following. Clearly, there has been no shortage of bad leaders to chronicle. Library shelves groan with such studies. Leadership books that train less distorted lenses on the leader's obvious toxicity appear mostly after their subjects are safely dead. Then we tend to perform psychological autopsies, searching for the disease that poisoned the leaders' lives, along with our own.

For some time now, a sizeable market has flourished in posthumous profiling of incompetent, feckless, and cynical, not to mention evil, political and corporate leaders. These biographies detail their cradle-to-grave exploits. Half a century after his death, Hitler remains the top choice of political biographers. A search of Amazon.com reveals that between 1944 and 2003, biographers churned out no less than 2,067 books about Hitler, evidence of a feverish production schedule averaging more than thirty-five volumes per year.

Toxic leaders in the corporate world have also been subjected to biographical exhumations. John D. Rockefeller, ITT's Harold Geneen, and Henry Ford, founder of the Ford Motor Company, head a long list of business leaders admired in life only to be defrocked in death. During his lifetime Ford was revered as a corporate hero for his innovative assembly line and the unprecedented wages he paid his workers. Only later did posthumous biographies document the otherwise harsh treatment the automobile tycoon meted out to his employees, as well as his antiunion sentiments, his Nazi leanings, and his anti-Semitic activities and writings.[34]

Researchers Examine the Toxic Entrails

Beyond biographical research, the social and behavioral sciences have trained their lenses on human behavior associated with toxic leadership. Deeply affected by invasions in Europe, World War II, and the Holocaust, a small set of social and behavioral scientists— such as psychoanalyst Erich Fromm[35] and cultural anthropologist Ernest Becker[36]—sought to understand how civilized human beings could engage in such despicable behavior.

Experimental social psychologists, including Solomon Asch,[37] Leon Festinger,[38] and Muzafer Sherif,[39] designed experiments to determine how group pressures encouraged or discouraged conformity in group members, but by and large they did not explicitly link their important work to toxic leaders per se. In a major study stimulated by the phenomenon of Nazi leadership, Theodor Adorno and his colleagues developed the F-scale (*F* for *fascism*).[40] They sought to identify individuals with authoritarian personalities, people who were likely both to obey authority and to enjoy exercising it over others. Their focus, however, was largely upon that specific personality type.

Yale University researcher Stanley Milgram studied obedience to authority in a set of infamously disturbing experiments.[41] Indirectly, Milgram was exploring obedience to a toxic leader. Here, the toxic leader appeared in the guise of a "scientist" clad in a white lab coat, who instructed participants to administer what they believed to be electric shocks—some presumably "very dangerous"— to other "volunteers" engaged in the experiment. Milgram's research demonstrated that a surprisingly large percentage of individuals can be intimidated into obeying a malevolent authority, even when all the so-called authority does is wear scientific garb and intone, "The experiment must go on." Milgram's experiments did not, however, focus on *why* the participants were intimidated or why, even *without* intimidation, many of us yearn for, are attracted to, and sometimes prefer toxic leaders.

Some authors have examined why specific individuals or groups carried out the directives of a particular toxic leader. Hannah Arendt's landmark treatise on Adolf Eichmann scrutinized Hitler's notorious henchman, responsible for the murder of millions of Jews in Nazi death camps.[42] In that work, Arendt explored why an individual obeyed the orders of one specific evil leader, causing the implementer, too, to spiral into the "banality of evil." More recently, historians Daniel Goldhagen[43] and Robert Gellately[44] have looked backward to study the masses that supported, even implemented, Hitler's demonic strategies.

Leaders and Followers: Action, Interaction, and Inaction

Biographers and historians have explored the dark psychological spaces of toxic leaders to discern what made them tick. With rare exceptions, some we've already noted, seldom do they plumb the deep forces that make the *followers* tick. Leadership is often treated as *action* by the leader directed toward or against others. More appropriately, we should view leadership as *interaction* between leaders and their followers. What goes on *between* leaders and their supporters is perhaps far more significant for the course of history than simply what leaders do to followers.

Not only do we fail to dissect the interaction between leader and follower, but we often completely ignore the followers. We allow their inaction in the face of toxic leadership to fall below our angle of vision. Thus we rarely investigate what influences followers to tolerate—sometimes for decades—leaders who deceive, denigrate, and even destroy them. That is the task of this book.

Toxic Leaders: How Shall We Recognize Them?

"How do we recognize toxic leaders?" is a question worth a multivolume encyclopedia of its own. I am talking neither about garden-variety incompetents nor about insensitive bosses, whom most American workers love to hate but who don't do much serious damage. Rather, I am concerned with leaders who have toxic impact.

The dictionary defines *toxic* as "acting as or having the effect of a poison." Toxic leaders do indeed have poisonous effects that cause serious harm to their organizations and their followers, but the multiple toxins they can dispense create varying degrees of impairment. (And, of course, let's not forget that beyond individual toxic leaders, organizations qua organizations can yield their own toxins. They do so through detrimental policies and practices— including setting unreasonable performance goals, promoting excessive internal competition, and creating a culture of blame—that transcend any individual toxic leader.) In this volume, however, we want to limit our focus to the *followers* of toxic leaders, rather than considering toxic leaders or toxic organizations per se.[45]

To capture the complexity of toxic leaders, we need a multidimensional framework, one that delineates their actions, their character, their intent, and their impact on followers. It is not always easy to separate the actions of toxic leaders from their character. For example, when leaders consistently deceive their supporters, where do we draw the line between the act of lying and the embedded character flaw that sees no problem with misusing the truth? Intent and impact are similarly intertwined.

Followers suffer poisonous effects when leaders place their own well-being and power above their supporters' needs. Followers and the organizations they inhabit also endure great harm when leaders act without integrity by dissembling and engaging in various other dishonorable behaviors. Corruption, hypocrisy, sabotage, and manipulation, as well as other assorted unethical, illegal, and criminal acts, are part of the poisonous repertoire of toxic leaders. And, of course, in admittedly rare instances, toxic leaders move to the furthest point of the toxic spectrum and perpetrate downright evil. Nor is this the whole of a very complex picture.

Crafting even a rough definition of toxic leaders is a major challenge. Nevertheless, let's take a stab at it to help followers recognize harmful leaders before they allow themselves to be done in by them. Yet defining the gradations of toxic leaders or creating a primer on toxic leaders per se is not my central concern. In fact, toxic leaders provide only the backdrop for the focus I wish to keep on their followers.

Although I want to fasten our attention squarely on followers, still, it's important to define early on what we mean by "toxic leaders" so that we can appreciate the dimensions of the problem their followers confront. Let's undertake this critical task so that we may also understand exactly what kinds of leaders and what types of behavior the followers are willing to endure. In this context, the term "toxic leaders" covers a multitude of leadership sins.

Here, we shall use "toxic leaders" as a global label for leaders who engage in numerous *destructive behaviors* and who exhibit certain *dysfunctional personal characteristics*. To count as toxic, these behaviors and qualities of character must inflict some reasonably serious and enduring harm on their followers and their organizations. The intent to harm others or to enhance the self at the expense of others distinguishes seriously toxic leaders from the careless or unintentional toxic leaders, who also cause negative effects.

The degree and complexity of toxic behavior may differ among individual leaders; so may the range of their undesirable personal qualities. My goal, remember, is not to calibrate a given leader's thermometer of toxicity or to compare degrees of toxicity exhibited by different leaders. Nor do I want my readers to get hung up on how much of which behavior or characteristic constitutes toxicity. That would only distract us from our primary purpose.

Instead, this book's focus is specifically on the dynamics that entrance the toxic leader's followers or at least help keep them in line. I want to explore what prompts us to accept and promote bad leaders and what often renders us lethargic, intimidated, reluctant, and inept at overturning them. To do so, however, requires first that we share a common general understanding of how toxic leaders act and what they are like.

Toxic Behaviors: How Toxic Leaders Act

For purposes of this book, let us categorize as toxic those leaders who engage in one or more of the following destructive behaviors. These behaviors range from deliberate, conscious engagement in despicable acts to unintentional, unconscious toxic behavior, such as failing to recognize their own or others' seriously harmful incompetence.

The characteristic *destructive behaviors* of toxic leaders include:

- Leaving their followers (and frequently nonfollowers) worse off than they found them, sometimes eliminating—by deliberately undermining, demeaning, seducing, marginalizing, intimidating, demoralizing, disenfranchising, incapacitating, imprisoning, torturing, terrorizing, or killing—many of their own people, including members of their entourage, as well as their official opponents

- Violating the basic standards of human rights of their own supporters, as well as those of other individuals and groups they do not count among their followers

- Consciously feeding their followers illusions that enhance the leader's power and impair the followers' capacity to act independently (e.g., persuading followers that they are the only one who can save them or the organization)

- Playing to the basest fears and needs of the followers

- Stifling constructive criticism and teaching supporters (sometimes by threats and authoritarianism) to comply with, rather than to question, the leader's judgment and actions

- Misleading followers through deliberate untruths and mis-diagnoses of issues and problems

- Subverting those structures and processes of the system in-tended to generate truth, justice, and excellence, and engag-ing in unethical, illegal, and criminal acts

- Building totalitarian or narrowly dynastic regimes, including subverting the legal processes for selecting and supporting new leaders

- Failing to nurture other leaders, including their own succes-sors (with the occasional exception of blood kin), or other-wise improperly clinging to power

- Maliciously setting constituents against one another

- Treating their own followers well, but persuading them to hate and/or destroy others

- Identifying scapegoats and inciting others to castigate them

- Structuring the costs of overthrowing them as a trigger for the downfall of the system they lead, thus further endanger-ing followers and nonfollowers alike

- Ignoring or promoting incompetence, cronyism, and corruption

As you can readily see, this list starts at the intentionally negative end of the spectrum, where toxic leaders set out to dominate, even eliminate, their own followers, as well as people and groups beyond their own constituencies. At the other end of the spectrum, where incompetence becomes salient, the leader's toxicity is not necessar-ily deliberate. Yet the threat that *unintended* harm poses to followers is no less real, since followers may be in danger of losing their jobs, their homes, their life savings, and sometimes their very lives.

There are still other toxic behaviors by which we can recognize toxic leaders. For example, some toxic leaders use scarce resources to build monuments to themselves, rather than to meet their followers' basic needs. Some use corporate jets, decorate opulent executive suites, and draw multimillion-dollar salaries as their firms undergo serious downsizing. Saddam Hussein maintained a multibillion-dollar palace construction program while his people went hungry and sick.[46] Another measure of toxicity is the shabby treatment accorded those at the bottom of the followers' heap, while the elite receive white-glove treatment.

Not infrequently, some leaders who live exemplary public lives act privately in ways that evoke even their followers' disdain and undercut their own moral authority. Former U.S. president Bill Clinton, for example, would earn high marks for his brilliance as a policy analyst and political strategist in the first term of his administration. Nonetheless, Clinton's private behavior so lamentably lacked a moral compass that its consequences virtually immobilized him during his second term.

Toxic Qualities: What They're Like

There are numerous dysfunctional personal qualities or characteristics that feed toxic leadership. For example, some leaders earn their toxic stripes through their cynicism, greed, corruptibility, moral blind spots, and stupidity. Narcissism, paranoia, grandiosity, and megalomania drive still other toxic leaders. Then there are leaders whom we recognize as toxic because their actions spring from malevolence, even evil intent. Still other leaders may be toxic through sheer cowardice.

High on this list of qualities are the following dysfunctional personal characteristics of toxic leaders:

- Lack of integrity that marks the leader as cynical, corrupt, hypocritical, or untrustworthy[47]

- Insatiable ambition that prompts leaders to put their own sustained power, glory, and fortunes above their followers' well-being

- Enormous egos that blind leaders to the shortcomings of their own character and thus limit their capacity for self-renewal

- Arrogance that prevents acknowledging their mistakes and instead leads to blaming others

- Amorality that makes it nigh impossible for them to discern right from wrong

- Avarice that drives leaders to put money and what money can buy at the top of the list

- Reckless disregard for the costs of their actions to others as well as to themselves

- Cowardice that leads them to shrink from the difficult choices

- Failure both to understand the nature of relevant problems and to act competently and effectively in leadership situations

Worst of all, perhaps, there are toxic leaders who combine several, or occasionally all, of these negative attributes and behaviors.

Readers probably have their own favorites that would augment this less-than-exhaustive inventory. Still, this varied set of behaviors and personal qualities exhibited by toxic leaders paints the background against which we can view the larger forces that make us suffer them.

Range and Levels of Toxicity Factors: How Much Is Too Much?

Sometimes these toxic behaviors and qualities cluster in groups. For example, Michael Milken, wunderkind leader of the junk bond operation at now-defunct Drexel Burnham Lambert, didn't reserve his brutal avarice and aggression for his competitors. He also undermined many of his own staff through terror tactics.[48] Moreover, Milken held his clients financially hostage when he needed to leverage their resources to complete whiz-fast megadeals. Nonetheless, former employees remark upon Milken's sincere devotion to children—his own and others'.

At other times, however, the leader's toxic behavior is far more circumscribed. In such cases, the leader may exhibit only one or two toxic behaviors and perhaps some less lethal ones, along with a more limited set of toxic qualities.

Even essentially effective nontoxic leaders, as noted earlier, occasionally engage in the milder forms of toxicity, but without causing great or enduring harm. Perhaps a substantially effective leader is the most we can reasonably expect from our fellow human beings. Let's remember, I am not prescribing a plaster-saint model of leadership. We shall simply slide down the theoretical rabbit hole if we are unwilling to recognize that leaders are human, like the rest of us, with their own reasonably limited sets of unsightly but nonmalignant warts.

To complicate matters, leaders may exhibit higher or lower *levels* on any of these qualities. Just how much deceit, cynicism, corruption, or ineptitude a leader must demonstrate to qualify as toxic is difficult to specify. Context, too, introduces an important muddying agent. In some historical moments, such as major crises, the same arrogance and ego that we commonly associate with toxicity can goad the leader to seemingly heroic efforts. During Britain's bleakest days in World War II, Winston Churchill's immense ego and unflagging ambition helped fuel his monumental success as the faltering nation's leader. In his earlier career, however, from the Dardanelles fiasco right up to World War II, these very same qualities made Churchill the butt of his political rivals' scorn.[49]

Thus under certain circumstances, even seemingly toxic leaders can either deploy those negative behaviors and qualities for more positive purposes or transform themselves to lead in a more constructive fashion. Clearly, context counts. As James Allen remarked, "Circumstance does not make the man, it reveals him to himself."[50] I would add, "and reveals him or her to others." Later, we'll consider how one generic context—crisis—can change our leadership needs and views.

With respect to leaders' toxic *behavior*, the same issues of range and complexity apply. Some leaders behave badly from start to finish, while others behave pretty well at the outset but eventually lose their way. And, as the Churchill case illustrates, some grow from toxicity to grandeur or find themselves and their strengths in times of crisis.

At what point does the nontoxic leader step over the line into the toxic or even highly toxic zone? Let's not forget that President Franklin D. Roosevelt saw little wrong with packing the Supreme Court or herding Japanese-American citizens into internment camps during World War II.

What part do needy followers play in pushing nontoxic leaders over the boundary into toxic territory? New York mayor Rudolph Giuliani, egged on by anxious followers grateful for his stunning leadership performance following 9/11, almost crossed the line by attempting to extend his administration beyond the legal two-term limit.

Can we identify those forces or combinations of circumstances that move followers to downgrade their opinion of the leader from acceptable to unacceptable? Or vice versa, for that matter? Can we determine what conditions and what level of toxicity will finally goad followers into action?

Sometimes it takes damning public revelations about leaders for enraptured followers to pry the scales from their eyes. I recall a colleague from the former Soviet Union describing the deep disillusionment of her parents, both ardent Communists, which set in only long after Josef Stalin's death. Not until official documents unequivocally confirmed the whispered horrors of the Stalinist era, which they had steadfastly refused to believe, did the shaken parents finally recognize the Soviet dictator's toxicity.

Clearly, the nature of toxic leadership per se is both complex and compelling. Nonetheless, toxic leadership is not the focal point of this book. Rather, it is simply background to our major concern.

The Central Question

That brings us to our central question: *What are the forces that propel followers, again and again, to accept, often favor, and sometimes create toxic leaders?*

Isn't it high time to come to grips with why we usually let toxic leaders mistreat us and depart when it suits *their* purposes? With the recent revelations about toxic corporate leaders, our patience seems to be ebbing, at least temporarily. True, there are the occasional whistle-blowers, such as WorldCom's Cynthia Cooper and former Morton Thiokol engineer Roger Boisjoly (of O-ring fame), who risk their careers, if not their very lives, to expose toxic leaders. At some tipping point, followers may revolt and attempt to bring down bad leaders. Still, the majority of followers stay the course, many because the barriers to escape seem much too strong, be they financial, political, social, psychological, or existential—or, worse yet, some overwhelming combination of these formidable obstacles.

Let me be very clear: Blaming the victim is *not* my intent. Rather, my hope is to liberate entrapped followers by laying bare the web of forces that tempts us to accept leaders who play havoc with our businesses, our governments, our schools, our communities, our societies, and possibly our lives. By exploring why and how toxic leaders entice us into seeing them through Falstaff's eyes, I believe we can take a giant step toward extricating ourselves from their grip. Then, perhaps, we can select better leaders and face up to the challenge of confronting our own leadership potential.

Overview of the Book

This book comprises four sections. Part I, consisting solely of this chapter, laid out the central problem: why we tolerate, even prefer and sometimes create, toxic leaders.

Part II, which includes Chapters 2 through 6, explores the powerful forces within ourselves and society that prompt our continuing search for leaders despite their propensity to disappoint us. Chapters 2 and 3 examine two deeply-seated internal needs: our psychological needs, rooted within our psyches; and our existential needs, driven by the awareness of our mortality and our yearning for enduring life—real or symbolic. Chapters 4, 5, and 6 explore external influences that make us receptive to toxic leaders. Chapter 4 considers how the paradoxical coupling of external chaos and stability increases our anxiety. Chapter 5 analyzes how crises, by unleashing our anxieties, send us scrambling for omnipotent, omniscient leaders to "keep us safe." Chapter 6 probes three key psychosocial forces—self-esteem, the achievement ethic, and the call to heroism—that influence our quest for immortality.

Part III, consisting of Chapters 7 through 9, moves beyond the forces that drive us toward toxic leaders and inquires into how we might liberate ourselves by confronting, reforming, or unseating them. Chapter 7 focuses on the rationalizations we use to lull ourselves into tolerating, sometimes preferring, toxic leaders. Chapter 8 describes how even nontoxic leaders can be pushed into toxicity by their followers, both well-meaning and malevolent. Chapter 9 explores how the media and boards of directors often engage in a mutual seduction with the very leaders they are charged with keeping honest.

Part IV comprises four chapters. Chapter 10 asks a rather surprising question—can any benefits come from tolerating toxic leaders?—and offers some positive answers. Chapter 11 considers pragmatic strategies for resisting, reforming, and, if need be, removing toxic leaders. Chapter 12 focuses on detecting the warning signs of toxicity in leaders and their visions. Chapter 13 presents some down-to-earth approaches for diminishing our need for leaders stronger than ourselves.

Throughout the book, we'll meet real-life women and men who have seen it all. They've suffered under, struggled with, caved in to, strategized about, and sometimes changed or unseated toxic leaders. I invite you along on this challenging, poignant, tragic, sometimes funny, and now and then uplifting journey.

II

LEADERS, LEADERS, WHY DO WE ALL WANT LEADERS?

2

Within Ourselves: Psychological Needs That Make Us Seek Leaders

An intricate cluster of psychological needs sparks our search for leaders. Together, those deep-seated forces impel us to find a safe and meaningful place in the world. They also seduce us into believing toxic leaders' unfulfillable triple promise: to keep us safe, anoint us as special, and offer us a seat at the community table.

Six Psychological Factors

Let's start with six potent psychological factors:

- Our need for reassuring authority figures to fill our parents' shoes

- Our need for security and certainty, which prompts us to surrender freedom to achieve them

- Our need to feel chosen or special

- Our need for membership in the human community

- Our fear of ostracism, isolation, and social death

- Our fear of personal powerlessness to challenge a bad leader

In this chapter, we'll see how these psychological needs and fears drive us into the arms of leaders, some good, some bad. We'll consider, too, the role of whistle-blowers, valiant figures who struggle to transcend these needs, often with tragic consequences for themselves and those close to them.

Replacing Our Parent Figures

The yearning to fill the vacuum left by a parental authority figure commonly prompts adults to accept controlling leaders. Our childhood experiences with authoritarian, even punitive parents, who also loved and protected us, may condition us, as adults, to accept difficult, hostile authority figures: teachers, bosses, spouses, police, clergy, judges, presidents, and many more. Note how the popularity of TV's Judge Judy only increases as she metes out abusive, quasi-parental advice. As adults, some individuals experience the absence of an external authority, benign or toxic, as a serious psychological void. For them, leaders who act as parental replacements offer great relief. By the process of transference, we project on these parental surrogates all the unresolved conflicts, fears, longings, expectations, ambivalence, and even love that our parents provoked in us. Consequently, we readily dance to the rhythms of a somewhat familiar—if disturbing—melody, quite unaware of the crucial differences.[1]

We are, every one of us, molded and fired in the kiln of infancy and early childhood. We are shaped, sculpted, twisted, colored, and baked by our parents, our teachers, and, for most of us, a wide set of other caretakers. These caretakers can and do inculcate the culture's values and norms. They do so by exercising benign and sometimes not-so-benign power that socializes children to conform to society's expectations in order to avoid punishments as well as to garner rewards.

These caretakers can do all that for one obvious reason: We are dependent on them. Relative to us, they have immense power. As infants and young children, we depend upon them for our very survival. Most of us, therefore, do what the big folks want us to do, when they want us to do it. We comply *most* of the time, or at least until the rumblings of adolescence begin to fragment that innocent acquiescence.

Children, however, are hardly passive sponges. They soon discover the asymmetry of the parent-child relationship. As one of my grandchildren asked his mother at age three, "How come you have all the rules and I don't have any?"

Usually parents exercise their power buoyed by believing they have the children's "best interests at heart." Usually—with the exception of child abusers and other sociopaths—they do. That would be fine, of course, except for one disquieting fact: Even the most well-intentioned parents are not always very astute judges of their children's best interests. That is particularly true as children try on the partial independence of adolescence, when their peers' approval assumes far more importance than their parents'.

Following the dictates of parents wiser, experienced, and more powerful than we has its advantages: We are more likely to grow up reasonably safe, loved, and financially and emotionally supported. We'll probably climb more easily the path that society, through our parents, will reward. Yet learning to mind our parents has its own high costs.

Such early training—mostly by parents—conditions us to replicate childhood behavior in adulthood. The parental replacement—the boss, the CEO, even some spouses—willingly provides guidelines, albeit festooned with prizes and punishments. This ingrained need for authority figures is difficult to root out, despite our childhood fantasy of making our own decisions. The resulting ambivalence creates a vacuum that can be filled only by another demanding individual who inspires awe peppered with occasional terror.

As adults, we frequently continue to obey authority figures just because they are authority figures. You may recall from Chapter 1 the disheartening results of the controversial "obedience" experiments conducted by Stanley Milgram.[2] An astonishingly large percentage of adult participants willingly inflicted what they thought were painful, even life-threatening electric shocks to another adult simply because an authority figure in a white lab coat insisted, "The experiment must go on."

Despite such findings, children, as we've noted, are anything but passive sponges, mindlessly soaking up authority's rules. Like other seemingly powerless groups, they are far from powerless. They can develop multiple forms of countervailing power to offset, if only partially, parental authority.[3] Early on, children learn to "read" their parents' faces, hearts, and minds, to anticipate their needs and circumvent impending anger. They become adept at micromanipulation, that is, the skill of offsetting their parents' greater power via the well-timed use of tears, tantrums, charm, intelligence, good grades, avoidance, and occasionally guile.[4]

Still, the bottom line stubbornly remains the same: Parents' power far exceeds the power of their young children. And, early on, children learn to accept authority obediently. Despite the ambivalence and hostility that accompany dependency, children—with some bizarre exceptions—rarely do in their parents.

Dependency on early caretakers thus instills in us a deep-seated ambivalence toward authority. We learn both to desire and to disdain it. As adults, we are likely to transfer that ambivalence to other powerful figures—bosses, spouses, ministers, therapists, presidents, and kings. The consequences are immense. They lead to psychologically convoluted relationships with all leaders, benign and toxic, which, sadly enough, commonly bear bitter fruit.

"Getting It Right"

If we have come to terms with authority early in life, we become better able to deal with authority figures, good and bad, whom we meet later. We need neither to reject them out of hand nor to kiss their feet. We also have a better chance of recognizing when their behavior is inappropriate.

If, in our youth, we haven't worked through those issues with authority figures and developed the ego strength to stand up to a bad leader, we are likely to go on repeating that behavior. Again and again, we may seek out bad authority experiences to prove to ourselves that this time we can do it. Yet when the latest repetition slips into familiar acquiescence, our tolerance for bad leaders only increases, convincing us that we are truly helpless against them.

Someone I shall call Alton Jones, whom I interviewed for this book, described a difficult childhood that led to total estrangement from both parents. By any standard, his needs for parental support had been poorly met. So I was hardly surprised when Alton described four toxic bosses from whom he had serious difficulty extricating himself.

We don't necessarily repeat good experiences, because we have already resolved the issues they represent. There is little need to revisit success. Been there, done that. Rather, in our desperate efforts to "get it right," we tend to seek out and repeat *un*resolved conflicts with authority figures. Unfortunately, we don't necessarily work these issues through any better the next time. So we just keep reexperiencing the pain and anxiety that come from these negative encounters with authority. Sadly enough, that repetition may convince us that we are destined to be trapped in dysfunctional relationships with toxic leaders.

Negative Role Models: The School of Toxic Leadership

Research abounds on positive role models, those individuals with whom we identify and who teach us how to behave and which values to adopt.[5] Although we complain when positive role models don't live up to the standards we hold for them, we tend to pay less attention to the effects of consistently *negative* role models. For some people sandpapered down by the psychological abrasives of negative role models, the result is a masochistic acceptance of toxic behavior. For others, what most of us would call negative role models become positive role models, teaching them exactly what they need to know in order to become toxic leaders themselves. No additional instruction is required; the model is sufficient.

The controversial Stanford prison experiment, conducted in the summer of 1971 by psychology professor Philip G. Zimbardo and his colleagues, provides intriguing insights into the complex impact of toxic role models.[6] Twenty-four American and Canadian male college students volunteered to participate in what was planned as a two-week study of prison life.

Within a simulated prison, the student volunteers very quickly began to act as if the situation were real. In short order, some "guards" turned sadistic, exceeding the requirements of their experimental roles, while "prisoners" actually became depressed and fearful. Even members of the experimental team, such as the head of the "parole board," began to enact their roles with surprising verisimilitude. Only one "prisoner" objected to the guards' hostile treatment. That prisoner, we should note, had joined several days into the experiment as a replacement for one who had been excused because of psychological symptoms. The other prisoners viewed this individual as a troublemaker despite the fact that he was protesting on their behalf as well as his own. Even the "good" guards felt helpless to intervene.

One unanticipated result that has serious implications for toxic role modeling was that even without direct orders, "prisoners" emulated the sadistic behavior of their "guards" toward other "prisoners." As tensions among participants began to careen out of control, the worried researchers called a halt to the experiment after only six days.

Abusive parents, teachers who demean students, and threatening clergy can stamp the footprint that sadistic bosses and tyrannical leaders later fill. Dysfunctional caretakers create negative role models, teaching us to accept and follow their examples.

Early negative role models can condition us to seek out actively, albeit unconsciously, others who exhibit such familiar behavior. Most adults raised by an alcoholic parent recall their fantasies of escaping the daily traumas of those childhood years. Nonetheless, as adults, many of these same folks reconstruct similar painful conditions by marrying, presumably unwittingly, alcoholic spouses.[7]

The negative role models of our childhood drill a deep well to which we too often return to drink. How often we drink from those noxious waters depends on many factors, including our level of self-esteem, reconditioning, therapy, and education. But one thing we know: For some uncounted number of us, the negative role models of childhood attract us to toxic leaders throughout our lives.

Negative Role Models Can Also Generate Positive Behavior

Escaping the shackles of negative role models is not easy. Much painful emotional work of confronting ourselves and others must be done before we can move beyond their harmful scarring. Nonetheless, some individuals subjected early on to negative role models learn to use them as psychological weight training, to prepare themselves to resist such toxic behavior.

Julian Lennon, whose father, Beatle John Lennon, left him behind when he divorced Julian's mother, insists that his famous parent taught him "how *not* to be a father." According to the young Lennon, "He walked out the bloody door and was never around."[8] In later chapters, we shall consider how we can transform the negative role models of toxic leaders into positive object lessons for freeing ourselves from their allure.

Exchanging Our Freedom for Security

When we emerge from the family cocoon as independent adults, finally free to be ourselves, our euphoria may soon evaporate. Freedom from primary relationships and childhood roles may leave us feeling isolated, lonely, and powerless.[9] As we become more individuated, we may sense we are increasingly adrift.

Many of us experience this new freedom as an "unbearable burden," rendering us directionless, foundering in a meaningless sea.

We then begin to search for replacements—someone or something with authority—to replace the security and meaning that really never existed.

When our freedom unnerves us, we tend to gravitate toward any leader who will make us feel safe, protected, and good about ourselves. Toxic leaders, who promise security and assure us that we are special or "chosen," become particularly powerful magnets for our unmoored egos. We may find them so compelling that we willingly relinquish some, if not all, of our newly found freedom. This process sets us up to tolerate the toxic leadership that we ourselves have inadvertently sought out.

While autonomy fulfills the yin of ambivalence toward authority, liberating individuals to think and act on their own, independence also generates the countervailing yang—a great sense of isolation and smallness. That reactive response to freedom is hardly a new phenomenon, but just how does one cope with that yang, that frightening freedom?[10]

One remedy is to join a group and huddle in one another's warmth. There, we can also find comfort via submission to someone we perceive as stronger than ourselves, a powerful, broad-shouldered leader.

Another alternative when we feel anxious and alone is to pledge allegiance to something—an organization, a religion, a political ideology, a social movement, or the state. Those, too, can offer safety and comfort in times of fear and loneliness.

Today, even in democratic societies, we witness the desire to escape from freedom.[11] For example, one might expect that contemporary adolescents, recently sprung from the prison of parental controls, would relish commanding their own fate. Yet no sooner do the doors swing open to the semi-independence of adolescence than teenagers eagerly bow to the peer group's authority. Baggy pants, blue spiky hair, or whatever other fashion statement the group demands is law to males and females alike. Despite the constraints, being part of the chosen is too precious a gift to refuse. It is the irreplaceable gift of belonging, safety, and direction.

The Need to Feel Chosen

Historically, the Calvinist doctrine of predestination, the idea that we are chosen before birth for God's grace or eternal damnation, was a powerful force.[12] From it, a lost and uncertain middle class gained a fresh sense of direction and meaning of life.

The Calvinists of the Reformation were not the only ones to

draw strength from feeling chosen. In fact, the concept of belonging to the chosen group, regardless of its specific character, even now has a powerful grip on humans. The promise of a special place both here and in the hereafter can make us forgo our freedom and follow the dictates of a toxic leader. Later we'll see how the power of this promise increases when we explore its link to even deeper existential concerns about our immortality.

The Dangerous Illusion of the Chosen

While the illusion that we are chosen is both potent and comforting, it is also one of the most dangerous dogmas leaders can offer. Many religious and ethnic leaders have fed their followers' hunger for security with the belief that they alone are the "chosen people." From Moses to Calvin and right through the beginning of the twenty-first century, religious leaders have assured their followers that they are unique, maybe even called to special holiness by a higher power. To protect their uniqueness, the leader usually insists, the chosen must distinguish themselves from the nonchosen, that is, the Other.

Many toxic leaders have used this perilously uplifting belief to prompt the chosen to close ranks, to distance themselves from the Other. In fact, toxic leaders may propose annihilating the Other to demonstrate the chosen's power and worthiness. Annihilating the Other—literally, economically, or politically—performs another worthy feat. It cleanses the world of the impurity of those who don't belong or believe in the chosen's product, market strategy, political ideology, religion, or gang norms.

Leaders, too, fall victim to the same reassuring illusion. Frequently, they are the first to confuse the fantasy with reality. CEOs who perceive other firms only as competitors to be destroyed, rather than as collaborators, exemplify this pitfall. So do the ideologues of political parties. So do the elders of various fundamentalist religions.

Belief systems—commercial, philanthropic, political, or religious—that anoint us as the chosen have a magnetic pull. The chosen group can be Calvinists, Muslims, Jews, Catholics, Lutherans, Buddhists, or any one of thousands of other religious sects and subsects. Nor must they only be God's chosen. They can also be society's chosen—Harvard grads, Microsoft or Enron employees, Navy Seals, or Nobel laureates. Only one element remains constant: Leaders with God (or God's equivalent) on their side have a mandate to dominate or eradicate the nonchosen (alias the "evil ones" or the "infidels").

We perceive heroes (we often fail to distinguish between heroes and leaders) as favored by the gods, and we are loath to cross those whom the gods have chosen.[13] Joining ranks with the chosen's crusading leader consequently becomes a route not simply to safety but to victory and glory.

Here, we can detect the embryo of ultranationalism and ultraorganizationalism, the credo that our group is the best, the only one that deserves supremacy. Particularly when a group has experienced a humiliating defeat, be it a near bankruptcy or a political failure, a savior's promise of rebirth is appealing. The rebirth occurs through purification, distilling the group into a chosen fragment. Believing we are part of the chosen reinvigorates our pride. We feel a righteous determination to convert, take over, outdo, dominate, or eliminate those outside our select group.

When we feel we are the chosen, that our company or our idea deserves top billing, how do we convince others? Two related possibilities present themselves: absorb or convert the nonbelievers. Absorbing smaller cults or killing them off has a long history within the world of religion. In the 1990s, business publications described, sometimes in graphic detail, the commercial counterpart: a feverish drive toward mergers and acquisitions, in which many bodies were left by the corporate wayside.

The drive to convert those who don't agree with us is hardly new. The pages of history the world over are rife with tales of conversion efforts. Accepting the mantle of the chosen often sparks a readiness to do battle against those who don't see things the same way. The chosen take as their opponents those who don't concur with the chosen's self-determined mandate to dominate, be it the commercial market, the neighborhood, or the world.

Cultural anthropologist Ernest Becker and psychoanalyst Otto Rank warn us that convincing others of the truth of our beliefs, the rightness of our position, even the superiority of our products is of the utmost importance—in fact, literally a matter of life or death:

> In each historical period . . . man thought that he lived absolute truth because his social life gave expression to his deepest innate hunger. And so Rank could say, "Every conflict over truth is . . . just the same old struggle over . . . immortality." . . . [T]ry to explain in any other way the life-and-death viciousness of all ideological disputes. Each person nourishes his immortality in the ideology of

self-perpetuation . . . ; this gives his life the only abiding significance it can have. No wonder men go into a rage over fine points of belief; if your adversary wins the argument about truth YOU DIE. Your immortality system has been shown to be fallible, your life becomes fallible.[14]

These scholars provide a lens for viewing the fierce competition within the organizational world, where conversion to this or that strategy can cause corporate heads to roll. Some corporate warm-up exercises include collective vows to outdo or do in any and all relevant Others. Usually that means external competitors. Sometimes, however, those Others may simply be the guys down the hall in the bean counters' department. When the group the corporate leaders wish to convert is the client or the consumer, then marketing and flooding the airwaves offer familiar, less lethal methods.

Nor does derision by the nonchosen deflate the chosen's belief in themselves or their products. In fact, the contempt of outsiders is often turned to the chosen's benefit, to bind them ever more closely not only to one another but to their leaders.

Not unexpectedly, those excluded from the ranks of the chosen often react with anger and enmity. This merely ratchets up the chosen group's internal cohesion, "proving" that they represent something special that the nonchosen envy and desire. Ironically, the chosen's provocative claim and stubborn resolve to defend their special status can lead to *their* becoming the despised outsider, the Other to the nonchosen.

Differentiating ourselves as the chosen, however, often leads us to forget William Faulkner's profound insight: "Apprehending the other in terms of mutual humanity is the task and the trouble."[15] We'll return to the concept of the chosen later, when we see how it is linked to our deepest yearnings for meaning, for achievement, even for immortality.

Our Need for Community

Although we like to feel special, we also have an intense need to belong. In fact, part of feeling chosen usually means membership in an elite group. Two additional psychological forces are intricately linked not only to each other but also to our readiness to tolerate and even seek out toxic leaders:

- Our deep, positive, human need for membership in a community

- Our dread of community's opposite face, ostracism and "social death"

Let's be clear: Our fear of physical death is not the sole cause of our anxiety. In fact, the anxiety we feel in the face of *social* death may be just as great, possibly greater, than our dread of physical death.[16] Social belonging is a powerful drive for which we are willing to sacrifice much. Without it, many individuals feel that life itself is drained of its meaning.[17]

That need for community runs deep. Plato, in *The Republic*, characterized humans as "social animals," incapable of living alone.[18] We need to live in a group to become human, despite the obvious drawbacks that some groups can entail.

Our community provides security and meaning as well as sanity. For, even as each community twists and distorts our human natures to fit its specific standards, that community also protects us from our inner dreads and the dark dangers that lurk outside our group.

Bolstered by the group, we become part of something. We gain meaning and worth. Banished from the group, our lives become devoid of sense and value. It is no wonder that the community reserves its severest punishment—exile—for those who violate its most cherished norms.

Nor is it any surprise that we social animals soon learn—from experience and example—that it is worth sacrificing almost anything just to maintain our membership in the group. We often give up our independence, our individuality, our associates, our beliefs, and sometimes even our integrity to guarantee our social belonging.

Another interviewee, whom we'll call Mary Anton, described her experience with a toxic leader at work:

> I could see she was really a dysfunctional leader, but I didn't want to leave the other people I worked with. We were a great team, and I loved working with them. We often made fun of her behind her back. But we all stayed.

And consider the next step: If, in the best of all worlds, we should "learn" (usually from the leader of our group) that ours is the chosen group—*the* group of *all* groups—then we will bear all manner of privation and eagerly obey all manner of outlandish commands just to remain a member of this select aristocracy.

Fear of Ostracism and Social Death: The Sorry Fate of Most Whistle-blowers

Silent dissenters who believe they are alone—that no other soul shares their opinion—commonly fear the ostracism of their peers. So they swallow the bile of dissatisfaction and join the toxic leader's wave of followers. In the Hitler Youth, many boys who didn't endorse the Nazi agenda nonetheless were swept along by their more ardent peers.

The fear of ostracism—or social death—at the hands of a group that appears to support the leader also keeps discontented followers from protesting. Subdued by their fear of isolation, followers commonly hide their dissent and console themselves with the belief that the devil one knows is preferable to the unknown Beelzebub.

Occasionally, some stalwart individuals feel strongly enough to speak out, like Coleen Rowley, who took on the entire superstructure of the FBI in the wake of 9/11. After the publication of her critical memo to the director of the FBI, Rowley found herself stigmatized by many colleagues, as well as by Charles George, who at the time served as president of the Society of Former Special Agents of the FBI. George "compared her to convicted spy Robert Hanssen, calling her behavior 'unthinkable' in the society newsletter; instead of going to the Russians, she went to Congress."[19]

Rowley's colleagues sent her signed paraphrased copies of an essay on loyalty by Elbert Hubbard that had hung prominently at the FBI in Hoover's regime.

> If you work for a man, . . . speak well of him and stand by the institution he represents. . . . [A]n ounce of loyalty is worth a pound of cleverness. . . . If you must growl, condemn, and eternally find fault, why—resign your position and when you are on the outside, damn to your heart's content.[20]

Unfortunately, confronting toxic leaders too often amounts to professional or social suicide. For example, in an earlier time, when the FBI sagged under the insidious reign of J. Edgar Hoover, William Sullivan, a longtime top aide to Hoover, finally wrote a personal letter to the director urging him to step down. The following day, when Sullivan reported for work, he discovered he no longer had an office. Sullivan's name had been removed from the door, and the locks had been changed.[21]

The sorry fate of so many whistle-blowers—loss of jobs, families, friends, professions, and sometimes their very sanity—offers little motivation for would-be resisters to follow suit. Few turn out as successfully as Erin Brockovich, chronicled in film. More commonly, whistle-blowers share the lot of Roger Boisjoly, an engineer formerly with the Morton Thiokol Company. Boisjoly protested against launching the ill-fated space shuttle *Challenger* because he feared the O-rings were faulty. In the aftermath of the 1985 shuttle explosion, Boisjoly not only lost his job; he also lost his professional standing as an engineer.

Such wholesale rejection of an individual is tantamount to social death, and, of course, the threat of social death, like the danger of physical death, evokes profound anxiety. In some ways, social death, with its known or imaginable suffering, can sting even more than physical destruction. After all, we have a harder time envisioning the aftermath of our physical death. If we do, we often see it as a permanent eviction from some Garden of Eden.

Sociologist Judith Lorber describes "outsiders within," those individuals who are inside "but not part of the insiders, and so feel alienated and isolated."[22] C. Fred Alford argues that such individuals are "unassimilated to the organizational culture."[23] Other research emphasizes their imperviousness to the social cues that teach "insiders" to march in step with the culture. There are many grounds on which one can feel isolated and alienated, beginning with differences based on gender, education, ethnicity, age, religion, and so on.

Feeling estranged because you differ on the core values that the group embraces can move you to action, since values, perhaps more than demographics, serve as a powerful basis for action. Whistle-blowers Coleen Rowley of the FBI and Cynthia Cooper of WorldCom clearly experienced the "outsider within" phenomenon as they observed their organizations moving to different ethical drummers than their own. Perhaps, that sense of alienation is the necessary first stage an individual must experience en route to becoming a whistle-blower.[24]

Oftentimes, whistle-blowers are brutally cast in the role of scapegoats. The leader's supporters then refocus their public relations blitz on the whistle-blower's "shocking" betrayal of the great leader and the magnificence of the leader's cause.

Standing Alone

While sensible whistle-blowers may expect a virulent response from the leadership group, most, like Rowley, are quite unprepared for a hostile reaction from those they believe secretly agree with them. Surprisingly, coworkers, friends, and sometimes even family commonly reject what they perceive to be the whistle-blowers' obsessive or quixotic pursuit of their own agendas. Alford's study of whistle-blowers who have been broken in mind, spirit, and occasionally in body is enough to give most would-be resisters serious pause.[25] Rather than being heralded as heroes who dared to speak "truth to power," those who protest may find themselves rebuffed, avoided, and maligned as "crazies" or worse, even by those who privately concur.

Douglas Durand, vice president for sales at TAP Pharmaceutical Products in Lake Forest, Illinois, worried about the effect his whistle-blowing would have on his family. The unsavory practices TAP used to promote its new drug for prostate cancer, Lupron, among doctors greatly troubled him. TAP allegedly cheated the government out of $145 million as it pushed its annual sales of Lupron to $800 million by "fraudulent drug pricing and marketing conduct" during the 1990s. Durand objected to TAP's practice of giving urologists large waiting-room TVs, VCRs, and other small office equipment to prod them into prescribing Lupron. TAP even considered giving doctors who recommended Lupron a 2 percent "administrative fee." Still, Durand seriously weighed the potential consequences of suing TAP under the provisions of the federal Whistleblower Protection Act. Under that statute, insiders may file a civil lawsuit against their organization for committing fraud against the government. Durand described his concerns:

> I wanted to leave a trail showing I was on the side of the Government, not working to cover up fraud. The idea of suing as a whistleblower intimidated me. Nobody likes a whistleblower. I thought it could end my career. . . . I asked myself all the time, is it worth taking Liz [his wife] and the kids through this? . . . In the end, I always found myself believing that it was the right thing to do.[26]

Ultimately, Durand did choose to engage in the harrowing process, involving years of secret documentation and arduous testimony for the government. After two years of negotiation with the government, TAP agreed to a fine of $875 million, of which $77 million went to Durand.

Not all, or even most, whistle-blowers end up like Durand. Almost unbelievably, as we have seen in tragic real-life experiences and experimental research, when whistle-blowers complain, those individuals may actually suffer punishment at the hands of their peers. Even though their fellow sufferers know the whistle-blower is courageously speaking the truth on their behalf, they fear that the wrathful recrimination of the toxic leader may spill over onto them.

In short, the fear of retaliation by toxic leaders, their staffs, and organizations acts as a powerful deterrent to those who would resist bad leaders. Coupled with this, the anger and ostracism by peers, friends, and even family map out a clear road to social death. These terrifying consequences must make any potential protesters think twice before speaking out against the excesses of the leader.

Our Sense of Personal Weakness Helps Toxic Leaders Maintain Control

Another psychological driver that makes us susceptible to toxic leaders is our sense of personal impotence vis-à-vis such powerful figures. Many of us feel perfectly confident about our own worthiness. We're good at our jobs, as well as at relationships with colleagues, friends, and family. Yet we feel quite impotent when it comes to challenging toxic leaders or altering the dysfunctional systems they have put in place. "After all, I'm just *one* person. I have no power. How can you expect me to change the whole world?"

So we often passively surrender to such leaders. We just don't challenge them. Instead, we change ourselves, adapting to the world they create. Or we try to escape from it, leaving it to others to change.

Perhaps, just perhaps, a new wind is beginning to blow. For the last few years, the Aspen Institute has been polling American business school students about their attitudes toward ethics. In their survey of seventeen hundred MBA students, the institute found a 34-percent drop between 2001 and 2002 (53 percent versus 35 percent) in the number of students who said that they were "very likely" to look for other employment if they discovered that their values conflicted with the company's. In the latest survey, more students than in the previous year said they would "advocate alternative values or approaches," "speak up about [their] objections," and "try to get others to join [them] in addressing [their] concerns."[27]

We commonly accept toxic leaders because we fear that we are incapable of overthrowing such strong figures all by ourselves. Oftentimes, followers are completely unaware that others share their wish to unseat the leader and, given the proper encouragement or safeguards, would join forces with them.[28]

Mary Ellen Quite, another pseudonymous interviewee, discovered that several of her coworkers shared her wish to confront the boss, but only *after* she had changed companies. She recalled:

> I wish I had known it at the time. I probably would have pulled up my socks and gone to my boss's boss. Or, at least, gone with a few others to complain. But I thought I was all alone on the surfboard, so I just decided it was better to leave.

The awareness that others share your opinion can make a powerful difference. Experimental research suggests that when a single individual holds one position and the larger group unanimously holds another, the psychological pressure on that individual to agree is enormous. The likelihood that the lone holdout will cave in is also very great. But if the "deviant" individual finds a single ally, or possibly an individual who disagrees with both positions, the holdout is psychologically rearmed, ready to fight on for what he or she believes. Even a splinter of perceived support may be enough to turn silent objectors into outspoken dissidents.[29]

Beyond the experimental laboratory, however, things do not always work out so neatly. How often have we seen one participant at a meeting declare her objection to a delicate situation, while others who silently agree do just that—silently agree—and nothing more? After an uncomfortable pause, the meeting takes a different turn. If another group member, particularly an influential one, supports the dissenter, things can break wide open.

The role of the group can be key to shifting our own behavior. Le Bon argued that when individuals become part of a group, they give up responsibility for exercising their own conscience, which would ordinarily guide their actions if they were alone.[30] The 1964 case of Kitty Genovese, where thirty-eight bystanders just watched as the twenty-four-year-old was repeatedly stabbed, is emblematic of this behavior. Thus, in a group, individuals often act irresponsibly when they see bad things happening. They just let others take responsibility for objecting to bad, incompetent, or evil leadership.

When we belong to a group, we compare ourselves to the other members. They commonly seem far more competent or experienced than we are. As one member of a group, it's quite easy to say, "Let somebody else take on the leader. I'm not the strongest or most senior person in this group."

When the people we perceive as stronger than ourselves don't act, their inaction may further undermine our confidence to challenge single-handedly a toxic leader. If *they* are not challenging the leader, how can *we* hope to succeed in such a bold move?

So it seems that we often feel it is only reasonable to wait for the smarter, stronger, more experienced, and wilier group members to step forward and take on the leader. If, in addition, we feel the pressure of other pragmatic concerns, such as our son's college tuition, we may slip back into the shadows, waiting for others to step forward to challenge the leader.

How Toxic Leaders Play on Our Fears

Toxic leaders are likely to exploit these group dynamics by isolating and spotlighting "traitors," "troublemakers," and individuals who "aren't team players." They may resort to multiple forms of intimidation to make sure that others don't support those "bad guys." Sometimes they seduce potentially dangerous members with various rewards. When objectors are cut down, tamed, or separated from their supporters, they may not feel quite so strong—and vice versa with regard to supporters.

Another interviewee, whom we'll call Carol Sosan, was a straightforward, outspoken project director in an aerospace plant. She was infuriated at the brutal treatment received by her boss at the hands of his boss. She convinced a coworker, Louise, to go with her to the chief personnel officer to state their complaints. This is her story:

> We went to the personnel office to present our concerns very calmly and objectively. We got absolutely nowhere. The personnel officer said there wasn't anything she could do. She suggested we go directly to our boss's boss. Several weeks later, it was clear that John [their boss] was being pushed out and only because his outstanding work made his boss jealous. Everyone could see what a great job he was doing. It was sickening. People who didn't do their jobs got raises, and John was not too politely shown the door. Not actually fired, you know, but made miserable every minute of the day, embarrassed in front of us and the rest of his staff.
>
> Finally, Louise and I decided we couldn't live with ourselves unless we did something about this. So we went to John's boss and told him what we thought. Again, we tried to be very professional about it. We talked about the importance of morale and a standard of integrity. We also told him what an outstanding leader John was for our entire team. Well, he told us, "Get with the program or find yourselves some other company where you'll be happier." When we told the others in our group what had happened, they were scared for their own jobs. Eventually, we both left.

Toxic leaders often isolate the objectors by an ingenious strategy. They seek the acquiescence of each member of the objector's group through assuring him or her that all other members of the group are in total agreement with the leader's position. Then they present the objector with a "solid front" of opposing colleagues.

Some years ago, an economist who worked at the World Bank, whom I'll call Dillon Jones, protested certain procedures that he thought unethical, if not outright illegal. Dillon, a stalwart Englishman with a finely honed sense of integrity, went right to the top to voice his concerns. He was quite certain he would be received positively, probably thanked for his candor and courage. Instead, Dillon suddenly found himself with a desk but no assignments. At first he couldn't believe it. He carried on for another six months, waiting patiently for the winds to change, and then he left.

Toxic leaders frequently use dramatic exhibitions of power as object lessons for all would-be challengers. Sometimes they fire objectors outright. Other times they do it gradually, by depleting the offender's organizational oxygen and responsibilities, as in the case of Dillon Jones.

Toxic leaders with more massive institutional resources use other means—parades, mass demonstrations, and the expertise of TV producers—to portray them as invincible. From simple shows of force, such leaders may move to more direct toxic action, such as physical deprivation and torture, to intimidate any potentially resistant followers. In some cases, physical exhaustion, hunger, and poor health, brought about by the abusive action of bad leaders, reduce the capacity of individuals to oppose them.

In addition to these methods, Hitler's Holocaust and Mao Zedong's Cultural Revolution used brutality to gain submission. Their victims—and most of those who watched from the sidelines—soon learned to lower their heads and stifle their objections. Besides, the leader need not resort to physical repression. Some others, unable to bear the dissonance between what they see and what they believe is right, crumble into believing the leader is right. The means of intimidation are myriad.

J. Edgar Hoover had a favorite method for keeping objectors and whistle-blowers at bay: he compiled dossiers of their indiscretions. In the later Hoover years, many insiders were aware of the director's toxic excesses, but most felt too cowed to challenge him. Even his bosses, the presidents of the United States, one after another had shrunk from facing down the powerful director, fearful of what he held in his infamous "private files." For example, President Richard Nixon, who summoned Hoover to lunch with the intent of easing him out, couldn't bring himself to confront the longtime director. In that Kafkaesque case, one toxic leader successfully trumped another.

Even in death, the FBI director cast a deep shadow of terror over many, including President Nixon, who, on learning of Hoover's death, quickly dispatched Louis Patrick Gray III to the FBI to gain control of Hoover's private files. Nixon worried that those files contained incriminating information about him, plus a host of other political figures and celebrities. While the president's initial private response to the news of Hoover's death was "Jesus Christ! That old cocksucker!" he immediately ordered a full state funeral for Hoover (the first ever for a civil servant). Publicly, Nixon described Hoover as a "truly remarkable man" who was "one of [his] closest friends and advisers."[31]

How We Fight Back: Organizing Ourselves and Others

As children, all of us learned ways to defend ourselves—at least partially—against the power of parents. Later, as adults, we have also developed ways to exercise countervailing power against leaders, an issue we'll return to later. Here, let's simply note that counterbalanced strength was the basic insight behind the creation of trade unions. They emerged to fortify the single, downtrodden worker against the dictatorial boss. The famous union ditty sung by Pete Seeger captures this idea very well:

> The boss won't listen when one guy squawks,
> But he's got to listen when the union talks . . .
> 'Cause . . . he looks out the window and what does he see
> But a thousand pickets, and they all agree:
> He's a bastard . . . [32]

Perhaps one of the most undervalued aspects of American society is our propensity to organize ourselves, voluntarily and spontaneously, without the help of formal leaders. Alexis de Tocqueville noted this tendency as a special and remarkable feature of American democracy in 1835.[33] It remains an enduring trait of contemporary American life.

Of course, this strategy also feeds our need for belonging. We Americans are probably the most self-organizing society in all of history. And that may be, along with our Constitution and Bill of Rights, one of our most potent weapons against toxic leadership.

Sometimes, of course, even vast numbers—particularly when

people are beaten down by poverty, hunger, and ignorance—don't help. History is replete with toxic governments, from tsarist Russia to Saddam Hussein's Iraq, that terrorize their citizens.

In sum, our individual psychological needs, drawn from experiences with parents and other early caretakers, can leave us vulnerable to toxic leaders. The disproportionate authority and power of our parents, as well as our teachers and clergy, set us up to respond almost robotically to other authority figures.

Though we yearn for independence, when we achieve it we often feel isolated and adrift. Paradoxically, that anomie may send us scurrying back into familiar, comforting submission to an authority figure.

Early experiences with negative role models—be they dysfunctional parents or other caretakers—teach us to accept abuse or become abusive ourselves, to tolerate or practice deception, manipulation, and destruction. Our need for membership in a community also makes us think carefully before challenging the toxic leader, lest we evoke not only the leader's anger but also the group's disapproval and ostracism. The dubious fate of whistle-blowers serves as further warning to all but the most valiant or obsessively foolhardy that defying the toxic leader is no small feat.

All of these powerful individual psychological factors gain added momentum from other deep-seated forces: our existential fears and anxieties. Buried in the deep waters of our unconscious, these motives usually remain undetectable and thus beyond our control. In the next chapter, let's reel them up from the depths of our unconscious and examine them more closely.

3

Deeper Within Ourselves: Angst and Illusions about Life, Death, and Immortality

Existential anxiety ticks at the very core of the human condition.[1] It stems from the convergence of the known and the unknown: the certainty that death awaits us, welded to the uncertainty of its exact time and circumstances. We know we cannot reduce that uncertainty, except by taking deliberate action to bring about our own death, a grim course few elect. Thus existential anxiety, common to us all, galvanizes a relentless search for security and certainty.

John O'Hara's allegory *Appointment in Samarra* captures that existential dilemma: A servant returns from the market, profoundly shaken. His master asks the cause of his terror. The servant replies that he noticed the Angel of Death beckoning to him, and so, horror-stricken, he sprinted home. He then asks his master for a horse so that he might ride to distant Samarra to hide from the Angel of Death. The master agrees, and the relieved servant gallops away.

Later that day the master goes to the market, where he, too, encounters the Angel of Death. He asks the angel why he made that threatening gesture to his servant. Death allegedly replies, "That was not a threatening gesture, simply one of surprise. I didn't expect to see him here today, since I had an appointment to meet him tonight in Samarra."[2]

Awareness of Our Mortality and Toxic Leadership

The profound existential anxiety O'Hara describes adds another piece to the toxic leadership puzzle: We know we are mortal, that each of us will have to keep our own appointment in Samarra. Only the particulars of our death remain unknown.

This sensibility of our fragility, limned by our inescapable mortality, arouses our profound anxiety. How and when shall we die? That haunting question fills us with existential angst that could easily overwhelm us. Confronting our anxiety without letup could lead to paranoia and paralysis, making us certified basket cases. So we tend to drown our existential dread in the sea of our unconscious. There, unnoticed and silent, it gnaws away at us, exerting an even more powerful force on our behavior.

Our intense self-awareness nonetheless has major benefits. Unlike the ambulatory ant, we recognize that infinite opportunities await us. We can envision sublime, heroic destinies.[3] That same awareness drives us to reach for the heavens, to attempt superhuman feats of creativity, intelligence, bravery, athleticism, leadership, and moral singularity. Much of that effort is designed to outwit death, at least symbolically.

The infinite possibilities of life, lashed to the finite limitations of inevitable death, induce two profound emotions: exhilaration and desolation. This fundamental contradiction in our human condition frames our behavior, our yearnings, our vulnerabilities, our dreams, and our strengths. The need to reconcile these contradictory forces creates an enormous tension. From that same seedbed grow many of our expectations for ourselves and the leaders we choose to follow.

Leaders Offer Illusions: Our Lifeline in an Uncertain World

The real tragedy of the human condition is not that we must die but that we choose to live by illusions. Sadly but mercifully, these illusions blunt our experience of reality. We trade off the sting of actuality for the comforting cocoon of illusions, insulated from fear.

Yet just as the world creates fear, it also provides ways to cope with it. One powerful way beckons us: leaders who vow to protect us. Leaders offer us various reassuring illusions. The most seductive illusion of all promises escape from death, either physically or symbolically, but only if we follow those leaders.

Freud noted that groups seek illusions and that humans "constantly give what is unreal precedence over what is real."[4] The illusion that life is both controllable and meaningful allows much of social life to proceed. The unpalatable truth that we are quite small and powerless in a world roiling with chaos and uncertainty is simply too much to bear.[5]

Illusions are the umbilical cord linking leaders and followers. Leaders understand their followers' need for illusions. So do their entourages, who promote illusions about the leader's omnipotence and omniscience.[6] In addition, the media feed the followers' thirst for information about potential saviors, corporate and otherwise. To boot, we followers weave our own illusions about leaders.

In a terrifyingly uncertain world, the illusions that leaders spin offer us a lifeline. They free the other side of our natures—the creative, thoughtful, spiritual side—permitting even us small, short-lived creatures to become significant figures in the grand universe. But to achieve such glory, we must constantly patrol and repair the protective dike of our illusions, particularly our illusions about our leaders: that they really know all the answers, really have our best interests at heart, and really can keep things on an even keel.

Creating Godlike Leaders

Heroic leaders, whom we invest with divine grace, seem to fill the bill. For example, in the central Himalayas of India, bards call upon gods either to fix or to prevent sickness or bad luck by telling stories about the life of the god believed responsible. The stories are considered so important that a god would "come in person to hear his own divine story and act it out again. . . . [T]his happens through gods coming into human bodies and being immediately present there, available, accessible to the human world."[7]

If gods or human leaders—and we see how difficult it can be to distinguish between them—promise us safety, we are only too quick to accept. We rarely consider the price we eventually may have to pay for such insurance.

It is no coincidence that we attribute divine powers to those individuals whose mission is to stave off death, since in many cultures the definition of "hero" turns on surviving a confrontation with death. In our own culture, we frequently play this game with physicians, investing them with godlike prescience and skill. Rationally, we know medical and scientific uncertainties abound. Still, we attribute divine capacities to these quite fallible mortals. When they reassure us that our symptoms do not spell our imminent demise, we respond gratefully, as if they were the celestial judge commuting our death sentence.

At other times, in the face of a grim prognosis, we still look for that guru physician who must be out there somewhere with a miraculous cure. When the godlike healers fail us, we frequently take legal action against them to vent our disappointment in our shattered illusions. Sometimes, of course, if patient after patient insists upon treating Dr. Bones as God, Dr. Bones comes to believe it, too, with still more alarming consequences.

The Impossible Search for Security, Perhaps a Savior

To cope with our existential dilemma, to minimize that potentially overwhelming anxiety, we do more than simply look for leaders. Sociologist Elemér Hankiss proposes that "existential fear and anxiety are among the major forces that generate and maintain human civilization."[8] He argues that we build homes, communities, religion, science, and art to keep our anxiety at bay. In fact, culture and civilization are designed partly to "offer us relevant answers to the 'ultimate' questions of human life: the human condition, the fragility of the human being, the absurdity of death, the meaning and meaninglessness of human life. These questions obviously arise from existential anxiety."[9]

We also search for the meaning of life, our own in particular. Followers respond to leaders who promise to help them bear life's inevitable heartbreaks by lending meaning to what they do. Cultural anthropologist Ernest Becker insists we need reassurance that we live in a meaningful and orderly world in which we play a significant role.[10] Small wonder that we resonate to corporate leaders who grandly claim, "Our product will change the world forever" or "Our product will make us all heroes and millionaires."

Occasionally these illusions become self-fulfilling prophecies. Despite its ups and downs, Apple Computer certainly changed computing with its introduction of the Macintosh. More often, however, extravagant illusions don't come true. Enron is only the most recent example of the worst-case scenario, as it struggled to become the "world's leading company."[11] And in the end, "the people who had won and the people who had lost through their associations with Enron would ask themselves the same question: Had it ever been a real company? Or had Enron been, from the very beginning, just a brilliant illusion?"[12]

We also impute godlike powers to humans in the desperate hope that they can help us cope with our existential anxiety. We look to bosses, parents, therapists, and other transference objects, on whom we can project our unresolved emotional conflicts.[13] Many of us look to leaders who project an aura of certainty—real or imagined—that we lack within ourselves. And if they are not *actually* knowledgeable and in control, we convince ourselves that they truly are, to satisfy our own desperate need. In the process, we sometimes push leaders into believing in their own omniscience. Some, of course, don't need much of a push.

Italian prime minister Silvio Berlusconi, whom we met earlier, provides a clear case. On trial in 2003 for bribing judges in the mid-1980s, Berlusconi spoke in an interview with *New York Times* correspondent Frank Bruni:

> [H]e portrayed himself as . . . the savior of Italian democracy, willing to attract undue legal persecution and unwarranted vilification to protect Italy from the clutches of the left.
>
> "It's a great sacrifice to do what I'm doing," Mr. Berlusconi, who is also Italy's richest man, said.
>
> "I have a sailboat, but in two years, I've only been on it one day. . . . Do you understand?" he asked. "My life has changed. The quality has become terrible. What a brutal job." He added that he worked constantly and was "always alone, always alone here."
>
> Asked why he endures it, he said that he entered politics in 1993 and remains in politics today to keep Communists and other leftists from undermining Italian democracy.
>
> "Otherwise," he said, "there would be no freedom in Italy." "If I left political life right now, Italy would fall into the hands of Communists," he added later. . . . He said he alone had the ability to prevent that. "There is no one else in Italy today," he said, as two aides, flanking him at the dinner table, chimed in simultaneously: "Who else? Who else?"[14]

When, in the most dangerous sequela to a leader's grandiose dream, the leader begins to mistake the illusion for the reality, the disoriented leader then has a difficult time charting her course in a sea of illusions. Sometimes, as we saw in the Enron case, after the dust has settled, neither the victims nor the victors can distinguish illusion from reality.

Not long ago, I dined with a very thoughtful friend who kept asking me who I thought was the "single best, most authentic, most effective, most honest" leader in the world today. When I asked why he felt the need for a specific person, he replied with some exasperation, "I guess I'm looking for a savior."

My friend is not alone. Clearly, the business media are on the prowl as well, with featured cover articles such as "How A. G.

Lafley Saved P&G,"[15] "Can Stan O'Neal Rescue Merrill?"[16] "Can Ford Save Ford?"[17] "Steve's New Act: How He Plans to Save the Music Biz and Make Apple Rock,"[18] and "Can Dick Parsons Rescue AOL Time Warner?"[19]

If we are to live our lives and "do our thing," we must somehow maintain the illusion that life is both meaningful and under control —if not under our own, then under someone else's. So we seek meaning and a controlled world from leaders, whom we agree to obey in exchange for this reassuring gift.

At times, when we think we can fulfill that promise for others, we assume the role of the powerful. Perceiving ourselves as omnipotent beings can intoxicate us. If we can keep others safe, surely we can do so for ourselves. When we believe we can't, we look for someone who can. Along the way, we commonly encounter toxic leaders, who, sensing our vulnerability, promise that security and meaning. Some, we know, even believe they can do it.

How Leaders Mislead: Beware Leaders Bearing Gifts

The gift of safety that heroic leaders promise, mostly through smoke and mirrors, usually comes at the cost of our freedom. Leaders who offer us this illusion have taken the first dangerous steps toward toxicity. Identifying with such leaders may temporarily reduce our anxiety, but it also predisposes us to tolerate even more pernicious behavior.

Consider, for example, one group of toxic leaders, the Taliban. In May 2001 the international press reported the Taliban's authoritarian edict to eliminate the farming of opium poppies, Afghanistan's largest cash crop. Before the November planting season, Mullah Mohammed Omar, the Taliban's supreme leader, issued the governmental ban and

> augmented it with a religious edict making it contrary to the tenets of Islam . . . The Taliban enforced the ban by threatening to arrest village elders and mullahs who allowed poppies to be grown. Taliban soldiers patrolled in trucks armed with rocket-propelled grenade launchers. About 1,000 people in Nangarhar who tried to defy the ban were arrested and jailed until they agreed to destroy their crops. . . . Mullah Amir Mohammed Haqqani, the Taliban's top drug official in Nangarhar, said the ban would remain regardless of whether the Taliban received aid or international recognition.[20]

The international community and the media applauded. Outlawing poppy farming was a monumental feat, considering that Af-

ghani farmers were growing 75 percent of the world's opium poppies. This announcement "just coincidentally" occurred the day
following the Taliban's decree that all minority Hindus must wear
yellow identification patches on their shirts. (The Taliban insisted
the Hindus had *requested* the identifying patch to "protect" them
from beatings like those the Taliban inflicted on their *own* Muslim
compatriots whose beards were too short or who didn't attend
prayer services.)[21] Within days, the Bush administration announced
additional foreign aid to the Taliban. All this occurred four months
before 9/11. Incidentally, despite both the governmental ban and
the religious edict forbidding poppy cultivation, in October 2003
the United Nations Office on Drugs and Crime reported that
197,000 hectares of poppies were blossoming once more in
Afghanistan.[22]

That scenario clearly reveals how toxic leaders seduce both followers and outsiders by the illusionary gift of safety, insured by a
policy of authoritarianism. They introduce authoritarianism to
keep things under the very control we desire. Let's examine this
scenario more closely. Note first how the Taliban imposed a severe
punishment, segregation, for the weakest among them. Then they
diverted potential critics' attention from that toxic act by presenting them with a grand gift, the elimination of opium—protecting
potential objectors from a danger they fear even more. They
offer a gift the critics can't refuse, a gift that also silences them.
When world attention shifts elsewhere, however, the gift quietly
disappears.

Perhaps if we had not been lulled by the Taliban's illusionary
elimination of opium poppies, we might have recognized the warning signs of leaders misleading and more lethal outrages to follow.

Being at the Center of Action

In Chapter 2, I introduced the notion of the chosen versus the
Other, or the nonchosen. There, I emphasized how feeling we are
the chosen not only meets our needs for security and belonging
but also signals our membership in the elite.

Belonging to an important group, like the chosen, offers other
intriguing advantages as well. For one, it means being at the center
of action, where leaders hang out. Being at the very center of
everything makes us feel alive and meaningful. Important action
takes place in *centers*, in places where, as anthropologist Clifford
Geertz suggests, "leading ideas come together with . . . leading

institutions to create an arena in which the events that most vitally affect its members' lives take place."[23]

Leaders who create (or from whom *we* demand) larger-than-life illusions of their power and knowledge seem to connect us to the deepest aspects of life. Linked to omnipotence and significance in this way, we believe we have touched the very epicenter of meaning. That is where followers experience the leader's power and thereby feel vicariously powerful. If Microsoft is where the action is, that's where we want to be. If Enron is the corporation of the future, then we'll choose that instead. Followers have still another reason for yearning to be at the nerve center of action, for that is where charisma throbs, the spot where the leader's mana touches us.

When I served on special assignment to the domestic policy staff in the White House, I witnessed the euphoria of White House staff, ecstatic to be working at what they felt was the power center of the universe. They believed what they did had immense impact on the world. Staff members toiled twelve or more hours a day, some on a volunteer basis, just to be among the chosen, where they could feel the pulsating heartbeat of the planet. Weighing in on policy decisions that affected millions of lives or writing action memos and "talking points" for the president convinced staffers they were shaping momentous events.

Being at the center of things, where important action occurs, ensures our own meaningfulness. If our life has real significance, then even physical death cannot take that away. That is a powerful lure for some followers. Enduring a toxic leader costs less than social death and isolation, both of which lead to meaninglessness. Small wonder that dictators resist exile. Exile from the center brings an unbearable pain that only readmission to the community can relieve.

The Center: Where Knowledge Resides

The center also represents what is known. There we reduce our fear by increasing our control over the unknown. So, quite naturally, people want to be where the known is, where control over the unpredictable resides. Working at the center of corporate life, with access to institutional resources and power, gives us a strong sense of power. The folks at the core of the dot.coms of the 1990s felt they were "where it was at." Sadly enough, so did many employees at Enron, Tyco International, WorldCom, and—well, you know the list by now.

As science reduces the unknown and technology increases our tools for action, we feel we have more control over our lives, less need to fear the unknown, the unpredictable, possibly even death. If we are not the discoverers of new knowledge, we still want to share the illusion of increased safety and power by staying close to those who are. That yearning to remain at the center, from which safety, power, and meaning emanate, where leaders hold sway, can sorely tempt us to close our eyes to the price we may be obliged to pay: enduring the toxic action of the leader.

What the Center Means to Leaders

Leaders want to be at the center, too. Being at the center provides them with a raison d'être, a sense of being vitally alive, of fulfilling their destiny. Micha Popper's fascinating book on hypnotic leadership describes the parallels between certain actors' need for a life-sustaining audience and charismatic leaders' obsessive need to be at the center of things. According to Popper,

> although the motivation of actors and leaders does not necessarily come from the same sources, the need to be in the center of the stage, to be the object of attention is cardinal. Hitler wrote about this explicitly. He saw struggle, in general, and the struggle for leadership, in particular, as a source of life . . . it is a feeling shared by many others, including leaders who are not necessarily destructive. Churchill described it, so did Woodrow Wilson, and even superficial observation of the behavior of leaders cannot fail to show the level of energy and vitality they display when they are at the center of attention.[24]

Popper and others attribute such longings to the lack of love during childhood that leaves such individuals desperate to gain attention, to prove themselves worthy of adoration, and to acquire a sense of control over their own lives. Commanding center stage lends meaning and immortality to such leaders' lives.

> What are the sources of this desire to be at center stage, to be admired and adored, to have influence and power? This desire, this need, is so overpowering in certain people that it seems to be the only thing that gives meaning to their life. It seems as if the position of leadership offers the only salvation and without it, death, which is forever knocking on the door, is the only alternative.[25]

New Knowledge, Leadership, Power, and Immortality Projects

Thus leaders, good and bad, gravitate to the center of things, for their own reasons. There, they push new ideas, new information, and new processes. These fresh ideas and knowledge may simply be the latest illusion, since the current new knowledge is often displaced by subsequent, more "correct" knowledge. For example, the revolutions in knowledge stimulated by Copernicus, Galileo, Newton, Darwin, Freud, Einstein, Planck, Schrödinger, and Bohr all unmasked previous knowledge as simply downright wrong, somewhat illusionary, or only partially correct explanations of reality.

New knowledge often threatens our security because it destroys the old ideas that gave structure and meaning to our world. Consequently, we often resist new explanations, vilifying the bearers of new knowledge, such as Galileo. Gradually, additional pieces of confirming information fall into place, creating the paradigm shift that Thomas Kuhn so aptly described.[26] The new knowledge provides better illusions, at least until the next cycle occurs.

Not everyone rejects new knowledge and ideas. In fact, some eagerly seek out fresh knowledge and innovation in business, science, technology, literature, and the arts. Many devote their lives to that search. These seekers understand that new knowledge can enshrine the discoverers as leaders in their field.

Craig Venter, former head of Celera Genomics, participated in a private-public partnership with Francis Collins, of the National Institutes of Health, and Ari Patrinos, of the Department of Energy, in the Human Genome Project. Their mind-boggling project involved "a thirteen-year effort to identify all the approximately 30,000 genes in human DNA and determine the sequences of the 3 billion chemical base pairs that make up human DNA."[27] Then there is Bill Gates, who dropped out of Harvard to found Microsoft, where so many computer gurus congregate to exchange ideas and develop new knowledge. Gates clearly relishes the process of discovery per se. He proudly wears his corporate title of "chief software architect." From all appearances, including his picture on the cover of *Fortune* magazine with his pal Warren Buffett, he also savors the role of corporate leader.[28]

Society endows such knowledge seekers and innovators with considerable power. The power that comes from such immortality projects commonly bleeds into areas in which that leader actually has scant expertise. The media treat Nobel laureates as if they were omniscient, asking their opinions on topics far afield from their competence. Albert Einstein's and Thomas Edison's views were sought on virtually every serious matter of the day. The opinions of athletic heroes, who break physical records, count, too. Note how *MAD Magazine* lampooned Joe DiMaggio's appearance in a Mr. Coffee ad:

> In the course of his 16-year career with the Yankees, Joe DiMaggio hit 361 home runs, had a lifetime batting average of .325, and hit safely in 56 consecutive games. Which of these accomplishments qualifies him as an authority on coffee makers?[29]

Pushed by their needy followers, some leaders fall into the trap of believing in their own wisdom. Some foolishly pontificate on subjects about which they know very little more than the rest of us. That doesn't necessarily stop the followers from believing them and actually acting upon their advice.

Henry Ford, the innovative automaker, stumbled headlong into that trap. Ford used his immense fortune to spread his anti-Semitic take on world politics and myriad other issues. Ford acquired a national voice by purchasing the *Dearborn Independent*, a weekly newspaper. He also published the *Protocols of the Learned Elders of Zion*, an infamous anti-Semitic tract of dubious authorship. During World War I, Ford organized the ill-fated peace ship with many willing followers aboard.[30] Sadly enough, Ford had crashed through the looking glass of megalomania, accepting his needy followers' belief in his omniscience.

Tantalizing power thus can be both a motivator and a consequence of new knowledge and technology. Nor is power necessarily the most important factor. Some seekers of new knowledge are simply burning with curiosity. Inventor-industrialist Edison's endless curiosity led him to develop the incandescent electric lamp and 1,092 other patented inventions. If there is a puzzle to be unlocked, the curious can't help but try to solve it. Other knowledge seekers are on a quest to accomplish something that will go down in history, even if their theory is subsequently supplanted.

We see such individuals hard at work—consciously or not—on what Otto Rank called their "immortality projects," the accomplishments that will make them live on in other people's minds long after they die. For that is exactly where immortality resides. Napoleon understood it: "There is no immortality except memories left in the minds of men." Ernest Becker wrote:

> [M]an wants what all organisms want: continuing experience, self-perpetuation as a living being. But . . . man—alone among all other organisms—had a consciousness that his life came to an end here on Earth; and so he had to devise another way to continue his self-perpetuation, a way of transcending the world of flesh and blood,

which was a perishable one. This he did by fixing on a world which was not perishable, by devising an "invisible-project" that would assure his immortality in a spiritual rather than a physical place. . . . [W]hat people want in any epoch is a way of transcending their physical fate, they want to guarantee some kind of indefinite duration.[31]

In a strange twist to the Human Genome Project, in May 2002 Craig Venter, the controversial former CEO of Celera Genomics, admitted what other scientists had suspected: Venter had used his own DNA in that major scientific quest. Informed of this serious ethical and scientific breach, an Australian scientist who had participated in the project's public component commented wryly, "Looking at the bright side, it will definitely help in the search for the megalomania gene—clearly Venter's got it."[32]

As individuals and as organizations, these seekers of new knowledge and novel approaches are striving to gain control over the unknown, the ultimate unknown being death. Science seeks to reduce the unknown and thereby exert control over health, life, and possibly death. The yearning for eternal life is a large part of what motivates Larry Ellison, CEO of the software company Oracle, to underwrite the research of molecular biologists to the tune of $50 million a year. For some followers, immortality is a symbolic transcendence of death. For others, it is the hope of eternal life, without debilitation and decay. Ellison, who is clearly hoping for this, admits, "I guess I'm a scientist groupie. They are so successful, so accomplished, so credentialed."[33] "A fitness buff, Mr. Ellison says he would love it if one of his researchers discovered the fountain of youth. He says he'd happily give away all his money to find a cure for cancer, which he watched kill his mother, as well as his Oracle co-founder, Bob Miner. 'It is absolutely true that I don't want to die,' he says."[34]

These motives, of course, are not the only ones that prompt our efforts to reduce the unknown, but they count among the most powerful drivers.

New knowledge creates an illusion of increased safety, reassuring accepters they have more control over the previously unknown, the misunderstood, and the unpredictable. It eases our transition from a crumbling faith in current knowledge, now exposed as illusory, to belief in emerging knowledge, even if that, too, eventually will suffer the same fate.

The emergent knowledge then structures a new center of power and action. It creates new meaning. Simultaneously, new knowledge injects greater meaning into the lives of leaders and their followers, who like to be among the cognoscenti, the chosen few who are up on the latest architecture, films, theater, music, even travel destinations, and food.

Being at the center can put us in touch with authentic existence, an ideal described by philosophers Søren Kierkegaard, Karl Jaspers, and Martin Heidegger.[35] The excitement of new ideas provides yet another facet to the attraction of leaders, even if these new ideas ultimately turn out to be wrongheaded or, worse yet, destructive— even if their immortality projects, in which we participate, go down in flames.

The Danger at the Center

Still, that epicenter where the chosen congregate is also danger- ously unstable terrain. It can easily drag us into the quagmire of toxicity. Employees at Enron have reported that in its heyday En- ron was just such an invigorating place, the place to be. Enron executives rubbed shoulders with heads of state, senators, and ce- lebrities, tolling the bells of political power, making potfuls of money, living the good life. Who would want to be ejected from such a Garden of Eden? So if the price of staying is to shred some documents or "slightly bend the rules" when the leader justifies the action as "necessary for the cause," we might be tempted, despite our own misgivings.

Consider this case: Betty Vinson, a forty-seven-year-old ac- countant and senior manager at WorldCom's accounting division, which imploded in an $11 billion fraud, found herself in an awk- ward spot. Vinson was initially shocked at her bosses' request to make false entries. At first

> Ms. Vinson balked—and then caved. Over the course of six quarters she continued to make the illegal entries to bolster WorldCom's profits at the request of her superiors. Each time she worried. Each time she hoped it was the last time. At the end of 18 months she had helped falsify at least $3.7 billion in profits.[36]

But Ms. Vinson was *not* alone. In a report issued in June 2003,

> investigators hired by the company's new board found that dozens of employees knew about the fraud at WorldCom but were afraid to speak out.[37]

In Vinson's case, she reported to Buford (Buddy) Yates, a col- league from a previous job at Lamar Life Insurance in Jackson. That small detail probably is not totally inconsequential, since we tend to respond to people whom we've grown to trust. So beware: Even our long-trusted associates, sometimes family and friends, can lead us down the garden path.[38]

For some followers, enduring a harrowing culture is not too great a price to remain in the magic circle of the chosen. In fact, if you made it in such a competitive environment, that is only further proof that you have the right stuff, that you count. Enron managers sorted people into two groups: winners, who were promoted, and losers, who were unceremoniously dumped.

The Enron milieu was cutthroat, aggressive, and competitive. Cutting corners was no big sin.

> The culture at Enron was treacherous, but that was the point. Enron hired the best and the brightest, so fighting your way to the top was tougher. But once you got there, you knew—it was incontestable, incontrovertible—that you were a winner.[39]

If you didn't participate actively in questionable practices, at a minimum the culture required looking the other way if you wanted to remain in the charmed circle. After Enron lay in shambles, Sherron Watkins recalled her wavering assessment of her former boss at Enron's Capital and Trade Division, Andy Fastow:

> Sherron was ambivalent. [Fastow] had made her laugh, but he'd also asked her [to] do some things that had made her uncomfortable. After a few years she'd had enough, and transferred to Enron International. But in her current [shaky][40] situation Fastow looked pretty good. He wasn't exactly popular at Enron—he had evolved into a brat and a bully, famous for his tantrums—but he was a Skilling favorite, and therefore untouchable.[41]

Enron is only the most recent poster organization for this scenario. "At Enron it was always the future that mattered: inventing it, shaping it, ruling it."[42]

The chosen must often tolerate all manner of suffering to protect and maintain their special standing at the center of the world. The chosen draw considerable ego strength and resolve from believing that their status makes them unique and places them at the sacred center. Yet historically the chosen have frequently paid with their lives for that privilege.

Another oft-ignored danger exists at the center: Sometimes the people at the center don't know what they are doing. And, given their exclusionary proclivities, they are unlikely to take counsel or correction from those outside the charmed circle. If groupthink, that premature rush to consensus described by psychologist Irving Janis, begins to invade a power center, emperors may very well parade without clothes and proceed without counsel.[43] They may even begin to bend and reshape warnings from others, several circles out and with less power, to suit their own beliefs.

The Desire to Identify with a Noble Vision

Not least among the existential factors that make us susceptible to toxic leaders is the yearning to identify with a grand and noble vision. Most humans long to be part of something pure and beautiful, or at least seemingly so despite a festering malignancy. Such was the case with Jim Jones's followers, who fled with him, in 1977, to what they believed to be an utopia in Jonestown, Guyana.

Participating in a noble enterprise brings many benefits, from increased self-esteem and community membership to a sense of meaning and direction in our life. If that noble vision also elects us to the ranks of the chosen and perchance opens the door to immortality, then so much the better.

Nietzsche wisely said, "He who has a *why* to live can bear with almost any *how*."[44] Finding or, better yet, creating the meaning in our lives provides the central task for most healthy humans. For many, meaning comes through relationships with family and friends; for others, it flows from achievements in their careers; for still others, it emanates from a selfless commitment to a cause greater than themselves. For some, it takes all of these, woven together into a complex tapestry, to satisfy their desire for meaning.

Noble visions often call for dedication to make the world a better place. Committing ourselves to an altruistic cause is indeed exhilarating. Participating in such a vision gives us clear direction, a rationale for our lives, and a path to its meaning. For some, it is nigh impossible to reject such an opportunity, particularly when it may also be pointing the way to immortality.

Paradoxically, noble visions can also easily send us down the primrose path to toxic leadership. Beneath their seductively sweet coating of nobility lie some of the greatest dangers. Particularly when we feel undervalued and insignificant, a leader's noble vision may offer a tantalizing route to grandeur. Signing on to the leader's lofty vision enhances us. Almost immediately life takes on new significance.

One problem with noble visions is that my noble vision may well be your worst nightmare. The terrorists who rejoiced at transforming New York into an inferno on 9/11 were guided by their leaders' "noble vision" of destroying the "infidels." How achingly familiar that language seems!

Obviously, not all noble visions are that divisive or contentious. Besides, some look sterling at the outset, only to degrade later into base metal. Yet, regardless of the eye-of-the-beholder problem, visions defined as noble radiate immense magnetism. President John F. Kennedy's goal of putting a man on the moon, Steve Jobs's desire to put a user-friendly computer on every child's desk, and even the company sales manager's call to double your numbers next year can stir the blood and make the heart beat faster.

Some visions move only the primary followers, who are called to action. More enduring visions speak not only to the original followers but also to nonfollowers and future generations. Four decades after Martin Luther King Jr. spoke from the steps of the Lincoln Memorial, urging his fellow Americans to eradicate racial hatred, his "I Have a Dream" speech continues to stir our souls.

When Noble Visions Go Awry: A Trip or a Trap

Noble visions, however, can draw us into dangerous waters. They can go seriously awry, shattering into poisonous shards. Enron's promise of a new business model, intense excitement, and great wealth ended in ashes. WorldCom's vision met the same fate.

Unfortunately, distinguishing between the noble visions put forward by good leaders and those that toxic leaders set before us is not always easy. At the outset, both may promise glory. These grand enterprises—revamping a dying industry or eliminating disease—feed our hunger for immortality, for leaving something permanent and glorious after we are gone. During our lifetimes, such worthy enterprises confer on us membership in an exceptional community, exceptionally good or bad. These are not inconsequential attractions, tied, as they are, to our deeply rooted yearning to be part of a meaningful world.

Sometimes we fully comprehend the negative core of a noble vision only after it has gained a galloping momentum that is hard to shut down. Early on, the Enron vision with its "new business model" enthralled its followers. By the time some employees caught on to the duplicity of Enron's "creative financing," they were too enmeshed, too addicted to the high stakes, to let go or blow the whistle.

At Enron's Management Conference 2000, under gathering storm clouds, soon-to-retire CEO Ken Lay, his anointed successor Jeff Skilling, and Harvard Business School professor Gary Hamel all pumped the employees with the Enron vision. Skilling, renowned for his intellectual muscle, was particularly gifted at charging up the troops.

> It was Skilling who had made the stock price ascend to the heavens. So, it was Skilling who made Enron's troops frantic to live in fast-forward mode, who made them anxious to prove that they could deliver any concept he could dream up, who made them desperate to tag along. . . . Because if Jeff Skilling thought you "got it," you really did.[45]

Each year at the management conference, Skilling predicted with amazing accuracy next year's stock price. When Skilling took the podium,

> he stood before his faithful and bowed his head, as if he had to think about what he had to say. When he looked at the crowd again, he was beaming. Enron stock, he told them, would hit $126 a share in 2001. There was just a second of stunned silence before the crowd burst into applause. No one quite knew how the stock was going to increase another 30 percent, even with the success of Broadband, which was not exactly a sure thing. Neither was Enron Energy Services, the company's foray into the management of power needs for large corporations. And a few people in the crowd had heard of problems in Fastow's finance group. But no one was that worried. They reminded themselves that they worked for Enron, and, no matter what, Jeff would find a way.[46]

Only management guru Tom Peters, scheduled to speak following Skilling, offered a more wary message:

> "That's the scariest thing I've ever heard," Peters said to Skilling, his former colleague at McKinsey. What, exactly, had Enron done that was so novel? he asked. . . . The company had taken a model and replicated it in other fields—Enron had created markets where none had existed. . . . Other businesses were already copying Enron, and the novelty would soon wear off. And then where would Enron be? Where were the company's new ideas? "An excess of self-confidence kills companies," Peters warned. . . . When Peters stopped speaking, Skilling . . . thanked him, and repeated himself: Remember, he said, Enron had found the one successful business model that could be applied to any market.[47]

The Enron debacle is only one example of how noble visions can be both a trip and a trap.

Learning to differentiate between the noble visions that are pure to their core and those that hold the seeds of toxicity can be difficult but not impossible, as we shall see in a later chapter. The attraction of participating in the noble enterprise envisioned by the leader is magnetic. In fact, that road to immortality often proves exquisitely hard to resist.

L. Dennis Kozlowski's vision for Tyco International also caught the corporate world's imagination. So esteemed was Kozlowski for his daring nonstop acquisitions strategy that *Business Week* included him in its 1998 list of the twenty-five top executives of the year.[48] In 2001, when the M&A Group promoted its CEO Academy as a "boot camp" for new CEOs, Kozlowski was among the much-touted faculty. This is how *Business Week* described him then:

> [T]he course will be taught by professors from elite business schools, top professionals, and such executive suite veterans as . . . Tyco International's Dennis Kozlowski. . . . And in an era when more than half of all mergers founder—often bringing down the CEOs who attempted them—Tyco's Kozlowski will discuss "the dark side of acquisitions."[49]

Eighteen months later, Kozlowski met a similar fate. The Tyco CEO later made the cover of *Business Week* in a story entitled "The Rise and Fall of Dennis Kozlowski: A Revealing Look at the Man Behind the Tyco Scandal."[50] That time, however, the authors (one of whom had written the 2001 article) wrote:

> With every passing month, Tyco International Ltd.'s Leo Dennis Kozlowski looms larger as a rogue CEO for the ages. The story of Dennis Kozlowski's rise and fall . . . is a tragicomedy for our times. The history of American business contains few figures who were unhinged by greed as theatrically as was Tyco's burly ex-boss. But perhaps because Kozlowski is so apt a symbol of Bubble Era excess, the question of why he did what he did has gone unanswered and, in fact, has rarely been raised in print. Egged on by insatiably de-manding investors, admiring analysts, and fee-hungry investment bankers, Kozlowski had become irrational exuberance personified by the late 1990's.[51]

Kozlowski's vision endured for a decade, while his theft from the company continued unabated and ignored. His vision had infected and enriched his supporters within and beyond the company.

Nor are the noble visions of corporate leaders the only ones to come apart at the seams. Political and religious visions frequently suffer the same fate. The 9/11 catastrophe provides a vivid religio-political example. After the attack, a handwritten letter found in the hijackers' effects gave dramatic testimony to a misguided quest for immortality. The letter exhorts the terrorists to conquer their fears by remembering that "infinite paradise" will be their reward.

It reads, "You will be entering paradise. You will be entering the happiest life, everlasting life."[52] The fresh wound of 9/11 undoubtedly still seems an exalted victory to the perpetrators' leaders and supporters. Viewed through another lens, it appears diabolically twisted.

Rank and Becker have analyzed brilliantly the compelling force of "immortality projects," particularly those that explode into evil acts.[53] The perpetrators draw motivation from what they believe to be good, even noble intentions. With the 9/11 terrorists, the immortality-promising vision described in the letter led to unspeakable evil, killing and physically wounding more than twenty-seven hundred people and emotionally scarring millions more.

What are the limits of the noble vision? Where and how does it bleed from nobility into demonic ambition? When and how do the leader's goals of positive victory mutate into a pernicious debacle, ultimately destroying both leaders and followers? What are the costs to friend and foe, the chosen and the Other, alike? These are bedrock questions that followers of a noble vision must answer for themselves.

The Not-So-Heroic Leader's Vision

Savvy leaders have long known that identifying an enemy—usually external—is a surefire method for uniting a group. That enemy, of course, must be distinctly different from the regular insiders, or at least be defined that way.[54]

With mind-numbing regularity, the visions of toxic leaders point to enemies and scapegoats as the wellsprings of all their followers' problems. Expunging those poisons, these leaders promise, will restore our well-being and purity. It will also calm our existential angst. By eliminating that contamination within, by transcending that evil, we shall prove ourselves worthy. Besides, if we know ourselves to be truly worthy, we can virtually guarantee our own immortality. Every example of ethnic cleansing follows this rationale.

The heroic leader's promise to eradicate the polluting enemy relieves the group's insecurities and its projected guilt. Human beings, as Becker, expanding on Nietzsche, explained, are always beset by dissatisfactions and guilt, from the trivial to the monumental. The quest for purity helps to dissipate this powerful mix of dissatisfaction and guilt.

> This is what drives them to a search for purity where all dissatisfaction [with themselves and authority] can . . . be wiped away. Men

try to qualify for eternalization by being clean and by cleansing the
world around them of the evil, the dirty. In this way, they show that
they are on the side of purity even if they themselves are impure.
The striving for perfection reflects man's effort to set some human
grip on his eligibility for immortality, and he can only know if he
is good if the authorities tell him so; this is why . . . he will do anything the group wants in order to meet its standard of "good," his
eternal life depends on it.[55]

By pointing to the "source" of impurity, the heroic leader opens
the gate to the Trojan horse of power. Nietzsche reminds us that
all morality is a matter of power. Once made aware of those inferior, impure outsiders, the insiders are magically transformed from
huddling followers into superior beings. Now, clothed in Sir Gal-
ahad's armor, sustained by pure and noble zeal, they can ride forth
to eliminate those contaminating Others.

The genius of this strategy is that anyone can be selected to fill
the role of the Other. Simone de Beauvoir masterfully demonstrated how women historically have been assigned that part.[56] Yet
women are not the only ones designated for that role. Any corporate competitor, any ethnic or racial group, any political party,
any nonheterosexual group—any of those and more can be cast as
the defilers. The list is endless.

The visions of heroic leaders frequently promise to restore the
purity of society by removing whatever blight tarnishes it.[57] Scapegoating and sacrificing are central to this process. Becker, drawing
on Mumford, noted that scapegoating and sacrificing are themselves sacred acts.[58] The spilled blood can be human or organizational, real or symbolic. The corporate goal of destroying Big Blue
or Microsoft can be as satisfying as cutting down a battalion of
wartime enemies.

When toxic leaders succeed in distracting their dissatisfied followers into "holy wars," several bonuses accrue. First, the agitated
followers don't notice the more local, pragmatic economic and political problems that constitute the true root of their anguish. Second, this affirmation of clout over death soothes the followers' existential angst.

From the followers' viewpoint, participating in such glorious enterprises surely warrants immortality. Besides, an additional trio of
tempting side dishes accompanies the prospect of eliminating the
contaminating enemy. Righteous anger replaces riveting anxiety,
allowing the rush of emotional adrenalin sorely needed to confront
the enemy. Anger obscures danger, and the perceived righteousness
of the cause ensures the followers that a higher power, usually God,

is on their side. (At the same time, of course, God is busy issuing denials.) Finally, joining a crusade lifts the spirit and braces the ego. Self-esteem, previously deflated by anxiety, revives.

On occasion, the heroic leader suggests magical solutions—sometimes utopias—in which we can lose our fears and regress to childlike passivity and dependence. Cult leaders Jim Jones and Charles Manson enticed their followers with that strategy. Belief in the heroic leader's noble vision can turn more deadly than heroic.

Thus do heroic leaders calm our existential anxiety. Not only do their visions promise us safety, sanctity, and sense; they also offer us the key to immortality and other miracles. The final price, however, is sure to be much higher than the advertised price.

In this chapter, we have examined how our existential anxiety—the warp and woof of the human condition—makes us accept, even long for, leaders, both good and bad. Still, those deep, internal forces are not the only ones that push us toward toxic leaders. In Chapter 4 we'll turn to several powerful *external* forces that threaten to suck us ever deeper into the quicksand of toxic leadership.

4

A World of Uncertainties and Change;
A World of Certainties and Stability

Our human destiny has always been to live in a world of contradictions. On one hand, that world brims with daily uncertainties and endless change. Elemér Hankiss describes it as an "alien" world, full of unknowns and dangers—seen and unseen.[1] Uncertainties and change stream into our lives, spreading a layer of "situational fears" over our deeply repressed existential anxiety.

On the other hand, that same world introduces certainties and stability generated by our history and culture. Sometimes we experience those certainties as so restricting that we can hardly wait to break out of the cultural mold in which we feel imprisoned.

In this chapter, we'll examine two major types of external forces. One set increases both our fears and our wish for someone to take charge; another shapes our particular response to leaders. First, we'll consider the impact of ordinary daily events that pepper our environment with uncertainty and change: natural disasters and "normal accidents," as well as sociopolitical catastrophes, and personal reversals and tragedies.[2] Second, we'll plumb the more stable cultural aspects of our environment. These enduring cultural norms imprint us with many strongly held expectations for ourselves and those we hail as leaders.

We'll also consider the opportunities that change brings.

Change, good and bad, can open the door to new, exciting challenges. And, as we shall see, leaders become relevant here, too.

The Anxiety of Everyday Change

It would be burden enough if all we had to contend with were the existential uncertainties rooted in the core of our human condition. But that existential anxiety is then aggravated by the rat-a-tat changes of everyday life, with their situational uncertainties.

The uncertainty triggered by major social change—wars, epidemics, economic crashes—promotes quite conscious anxiety. Fear barks at uncertainty's heels. While change and turbulence have always been with us, the particularly frantic rate of change in our own times clearly ratchets up the process. Technology—TV, computers, satellites, and much more—accelerates and multiplies the effects. It gives us a ringside seat at the bombing of a nightclub in Bali, an earthquake in Japan, a shuttle disaster over Texas. The fear that attends such unsettling events further compels us to search for certainty and security, however and wherever we can find them.

Leaders are attractive anchors in such periods of distress—a trusted physician when we feel ill, a financial advisor when our bills overwhelm us. In the corporate sphere, when our organization is ailing, we are comforted by the new leader taking the helm. Al Dunlap, for example, received the nod from the Sunbeam board of directors when that home products company found itself in troubled waters.[3]

The terrorist attack of September 11 momentarily pulled aside the curtain concealing our unconscious fear, forcing us to stare at just how close we all are to unexpected death. That inferno at ground zero demonstrated how easy it is for the fabric of our lives to unravel on any cool, clear September morning. The ambiguity that arises from nonstop change in the external world heightens our existential anxiety. Poet Lawrence Ferlinghetti wrote:

> The world is a beautiful place
> > to be born into
> if you don't mind happiness
> > not always being
> > > so very much fun
> > if you don't mind a touch of hell
> > > now and then
> > just when everything is fine
> > > > because even in heaven
> > > they don't sing

all the time . . .
Oh the world is a beautiful place
to be born into
if you don't much mind
a few dead minds
in the higher places
or a bomb or two
now and then
in your upturned faces
or other such improprieties[4]

Just to make things worse, uncertainty seems to increase as we age. The certainty we took for granted as children, confident of our immortality, dissipates with maturity. As children at play, at one moment we could fall to the ground, shot dead by a pal. A moment later we could arise giggling, alive and well. Maturity, alas, has its eye-opening costs. Intensified by the interplay of needs and motives buried in our psyches and the driving forces in our environment, our anxiety seems ever ready to overwhelm us.

The Web of Cultural Certainties

Our everyday world is shaped by myriad certainties that counterbalance our existential uncertainties: the formal and informal institutions of our era, our local culture and norms, our history, our society's beliefs and myths. Together, these certainties create a web of stability.

All these predictable components add balance to our uncertain world. They lead to deep-rooted expectations about how leaders will behave, including the criteria and the processes by which we select and send them on their way. The characteristics of our own society—from its unique history to its current structures of government and culture—shape our assumptions about life. Drawing on its special history and culture, our society determines how leaders will come to power and what constitutes good or bad leadership. It tells us how, if, and when we should oust our leaders.

Born into a democracy, for example, we expect elections and orderly transfers of power. We learn to roll with the wild punches of political campaigns but then join together under the elected leader.[5] In monarchies, kings and queens inherit their thrones based on royal lineage. In some societies where unelected dictators hold sway, leadership may change hands only by more turbulent means—a military coup, a guerilla uprising, or a popular revolution.

Lay analyst Erik Erikson reminds us that "an individual life is the accidental coincidence of but one life cycle with but one segment of history."[6] We enter that singular world—with its unique culture, history, and institutions—already hostage to all the psychological and existential needs and fears we have just explored in the last two chapters.

The specific society in which we live offsets our anxieties by offering tantalizing, if mostly illusionary, options for keeping us safe and sane, for keeping the world spinning predictably on its axis. Culture, created by humans to reduce our existential fears, offers us security through clearly prescribed norms for every aspect of life, from how we learn in school to how we select a mate, how we enter a career, how we become heroes, and how we choose a leader. Faced with a seemingly immutable culture, we commonly respond with knee-jerk reactions dictated by the norms of our particular place and time.

Where Leaders Enter the Picture

Amid contrapuntal certainties and uncertainties, we seek out leaders to help us negotiate the dangers we meet. Ongoing, if sometimes subtle, change frees us to make ourselves over in our own image. For some of us that is not sufficient. The uncertainties we encounter in our daily existence create unfamiliar fears that send us searching for a new anchor in our life. After dreaming about freedom, our first taste may be surprisingly unpleasant. Paradoxically, we respond by reaching for something more familiar, the comfort food of security prepared by a leader who seems strong and clever enough to keep us well fed in this uncertain world.

Constant change, seasoned with ambiguity, increases our vulnerability to toxic leaders. They promise to allay those fears and protect us—despite the fact that they really can't. In the anxiety of such moments, we become only too willing to trade our fears for the sheltering "security" of a strong leader, one with a clear ideology and a clear explanation of the disturbing changes exploding around us, a leader who can bring meaning to our chaotic world. Ironically, our growing independence and autonomy, the very circumstances that can set us free, also increase our vulnerability to the lure of toxic leaders.

Dangers That Come with Change and Ambiguity

Our era is hardly the first to confront dangers that keep company with change and ambiguity. In fact, we humans have always lived in a world of magnificent uncertainty, constantly exposed to myriad hazards.

On any sunny April day, we may encounter a fateful reversal of our personal lives and fortunes. Your parent dies, your spouse is critically injured on the freeway, the boss downsizes you, a routine medical exam reveals a mass in your abdomen, your retirement account at ImClone evaporates, or, worse yet, several catastrophes occur all at once.

At such moments, anxiety floods our consciousness. We feel shaken and diminished. We hardly know what to do next. In a common reaction to personal crises, we turn to others: God, a strong family member, a priest or physician, or maybe the local town leader. From each, we seek reassurance that things will get better, that our world will not spin completely out of control.

In the universe beyond our immediate personal surround, we encounter awesome perils. In the twenty-first century, ambiguity and change seem to wreak havoc faster than ever. This uncertain existence begets anxieties that drive our search for leaders, be they good, toxic, or something in between.

Natural Disasters Come When They Will

Most natural disasters erupt without advance notice, disrupting our lives and forever altering our worlds. Noah, at least, received enough warning to build the ark, but that's not the way things usually happen. Despite scientific attempts to predict earthquakes, floods, and tornadoes, they usually occur without much notification and careen beyond our control. All that most leaders can do is offer some symbolic solace, maybe a stab at interpretation, and limited cleanup help after the fact.

Let's consider an example from October 17, 1989. At 5:04 p.m., during the height of the rush hour on a warm evening in northern California, the Loma Prieta earthquake rumbles up from twelve miles below the earth's surface, sending waves of destruction rippling out sixty miles from its epicenter. The magnitude 7.1 earthquake collapses the elevated section of Interstate 880 in Oakland, along with a section of the San Francisco–Oakland Bay Bridge's upper roadbed. Cars near the collapsed section of the bridge plunge over the edge and smash into the roadbed below, killing their unlucky occupants. Apartment buildings and houses teeter drunkenly before disintegrating into heaps of rubble.

In Candlestick Park, ten miles away, sixty thousand fans await the opening pitch of the third game of the World Series. Twenty-one minutes before the scheduled start, television cameras zoom in on spectators eating hot dogs as they mill about the stadium. Suddenly the TV picture begins to break up.

A distant rumble grows louder. "It sounded like rolling thunder," recalls Peter Rubens, a winery manager, who had seats in the lower deck of right field.[7] The noise deepens to a roar. ABC sports announcer Al Michaels's staccato voice cuts off in midsentence: "We're having an earth—" The TV screen now blacks out completely. The stadium shudders. Remarkably, the sixty thousand people in the stands escape serious injury.

The shaking stops. The crowd lets out a mighty cheer. One relieved fan even holds up a hastily scribbled sign: "THAT WAS NOTHING. WAIT TILL THE GIANTS BAT!"[8]

Former San Francisco mayor Dianne Feinstein, learning later that the "Stick" had withstood the deadly quake, breathed more easily. As mayor, Feinstein had allocated scarce tax dollars to retrofit Candlestick Park to prevent massive damage from an earthquake that might never occur on her watch. So, even in the lopsided struggle with natural disasters, leaders who act in their constituents' best interests can indeed make an important difference.

Unlike the baseball fans, forty-two people on the interstate lost their lives in their mangled cars.[9] An additional twenty-one people died from other earthquake-related causes. Thirty-seven hundred injured people crowded into local emergency rooms.[10] Thousands more counted themselves fortunate to have lost "just" their homes, their belongings, and their lifelong neighborhoods. This time the fragility of human existence came sharply into focus.

The Loma Prieta earthquake, like other formidable disasters, evokes stark images and naked fear. These all-too-real nightmares send us searching for leaders to help us cope and comprehend the incomprehensible. Natural disasters respect no race or social class anywhere across the globe, day or night. In the lull between disasters, the residual fears remain in our psyches mixing silently and dangerously with our existential anxiety.

Scientific and Technological Catastrophes Arrive Without Bidding

Spectacular scientific and technological catastrophes also shake our worlds and lay bare our anxieties. The scientific and technological innovations that we humans cannot keep ourselves from making often carry their own seeds of disaster.[11]

- On February 1, 2003, the world watched in horror as the space shuttle *Columbia* disintegrated eighteen miles above Texas, just sixteen minutes before its scheduled landing, hurtling the seven trapped astronauts to a fiery death.

- On August 12, 2000, 118 young Russian sailors met their death imprisoned in the disabled nuclear submarine *Kursk* in the icy waters of the Barents Sea.

Those were two exceptionally spectacular disasters. Still, we witness somewhat less dramatic but equally deadly events every day: airplane crashes, highway accidents, and hazardous chemical spills. Some of these directly affect us—a colleague is killed in the plane crash reported on the eleven o'clock news. Some we simply watch from afar, grateful that, this time, we have escaped.

Cutting-edge technological ventures are, by definition, fraught with hazards. Sociologist Charles Perrow warns of the inevitability of these "normal accidents," the offspring of complex technological advances.[12] The dangers of landing a man on the moon took away our collective breath as we viewed that landmark event. The disintegration of the shuttle reminds us that immense risks still remain.

Yet leaders who goad us to superhuman accomplishments earn our praise. The success of the dangerous lunar landing only enhanced the legacy of the slain young president who had summoned the nation to a seemingly impossible achievement. Admittedly, the ten-year race for the moon also generated technological by-products that enhance our daily lives. Still, the dangers escalate, and we continue to seek increasingly strong leaders to guide us over these hurdles.

Despite the risks, our human curiosity eggs us on. The vast repertoire of technological advances contains its own frightening possibilities and ethical dilemmas.[13] We search for the leaders who can help us wade through the ethical-technical morass or simply reassure us they can handle it all.

Social and Political Forces Erupt into Catastrophes

Technological catastrophes are not the only kinds of disasters we humans can create. Social and political differences—rooted in political ideologies, cultures, social classes, and religions—drive us to riots, revolutions, and wars. In these humanly contrived disasters, toxic leaders often play a ghoulish directorial role, promising greatness, fulfillment, even immortality to their followers. Osama bin Laden is only the most recent political model.

In the last few years, corporations have not escaped their own disasters. The list is both long and familiar. Corporate scandals have become so routine, they are virtually unremarkable. While Enron may have received the most media coverage, let's not forget the meltdowns of Adelphia, Andersen, Dynegy, ImClone, Qwest, Tyco, Warnaco, Westar, and WorldCom, just to cite the top contenders. By now, we need a scorecard to keep track of the corporate villains and the disasters they unleashed.

The world still reels from the images of September 11, 2001, when millions of Americans awoke to a surrealistic catastrophe. At 8:50 a.m. American Airlines Flight 11, with ninety-two people and thousands of gallons of fuel aboard, slammed into the north tower of the World Trade Center in the New York financial district. Thick smoke and flames engulfed the top floors of the building. Initial reports were unclear. At first we seemed to be watching a cinematic thriller featuring a bizarre accident replete with spine-chilling special effects. Sadly, there was no such easy out. As New Yorkers and a worldwide TV audience stared in numb disbelief, a second jet, this one with sixty-five passengers and crew, flew straight into the south tower.

The TV announced the unthinkable reality: Terrorists were attacking the United States, targeting the twin towers of the World Trade Center, the Pentagon, and possibly the White House or the Capitol, using hijacked domestic planes. The immediate reports estimated that more than 4,700 people were missing, presumed dead. Among them were 377 New York firefighters and more than 80 police officers, who raced into the World Trade Center in a gallant effort to rescue the trapped occupants. As days passed, the numbers climbed, first to 5,000 and eventually peaked at 5,219. Only months later did they settle back to 2,795.[14] Nine thousand people sustained injuries. Deep below ground, fires burned for weeks.

Terrorism had come starkly of age. Ambiguity and chaos rained down; anguish and misery seeped into every crevice. The culture of New York took a sharp turn. The large, impersonal, often surly city molted into a village of solicitous neighbors. The entire nation shuddered in collective grief. Uncertainty, change, and chaos encircled the globe. The images continue to haunt our national memory.

Bad Is Stronger Than Good

Fascinating new psychological research demonstrates that "bad is stronger than good."[15] The findings indicate that, across a broad spectrum of phenomena, bad events stay with us longer than good ones. We are more likely to remember the bad—bad events, bad close relationships, bad feedback, bad first impressions, bad stereotypes, bad parents, bad experiences, and bad decisions by leaders—than the good.

It is not very remarkable, then, that the destruction disasters bring clearly rivets our attention, leaves an interminable mark, and ups the ante for strong leaders. Can any of us forget how we first learned of the attack on the World Trade Center? Can any of us alive at the time not remember where we were when President John F. Kennedy was assassinated?

With so many bad events—wrought by humans and nature alike—journalists despair of calling them to the world's weary attention. The result: Most remain below our angle of vision. Wars rage for years in far corners of the globe while most of the world's inhabitants go about their lives totally unaware. Only the few most disastrous calamities—and sometimes only those most closely linked to us economically or politically—make the news.

Because we cannot put these disasters back in the bottle, we try to suppress or deny them. Yet the interdependence that now tightly corsets the globe only heightens the possibilities for chain reactions of catastrophes.[16] The classic, unchanging call for leaders escalates: the stronger, the better; the more convinced—and convincing—that they know the answers, the better. Or so it seems at first glance.

Still, let's remember that decisiveness, by itself, is not bad. What really undermines us is the belief—by leaders and followers alike—that leaders know best and followers should simply put themselves in their hands. Followers often withdraw into the shell of their anxiety without demanding until later, if at all, the reasoning and facts behind the leader's decision.

The Ironic Outcome of Uncertainty and Change: From Shackles to Freedom and Back Again

A subtle irony links uncertainty with change: Together they create the opportunities for freedom that make some of us rush back into the shackles of certainty. Change and uncertainty free us from ordinary constraints. Thanks to them, we gain new opportunities to escape from society's demands for conformity and become whatever we yearn to be.

Change and uncertainty create our chance to break free, to cast off the constricting beliefs on which we were raised. At that moment we can jettison the rigid roles and the limited relationships into which we have been channeled.

Yet, as psychoanalyst and social philosopher Erich Fromm has warned, "each step in the direction of growing individuation threaten[s] people with new insecurities."[17] Fromm argues, "There is only one possible, productive solution for the relationship of individualized man with the world: His active solidarity with all men and his spontaneous activity, love and work, which unite him again with the world, not by primary ties but as a free and independent individual."[18] As fragmentation, antagonism, and competition escalate around the world, that solution—global solidarity, buttressed by love and work—seems increasingly unattainable for humankind.[19]

For individuals to grow, we need adequate social, political, and economic supports. Otherwise we feel progressively unmoored from life and society as we become more individuated. Freed from customary supports, we find ourselves more anxious than ever, adrift without meaning or direction, sometimes without economic or emotional support. Returning to prison ensures regular meals, even if they're not from the kitchen of world-renowned chef Wolfgang Puck.

A tragic real-life example: Covall Russell, a ninety-two-year-old inmate in the Butte County, California, jail, petitioned the judge to let him remain in jail after the conclusion of his prison term. Having outlived his family and friends, the elderly bachelor finally had found a safe and caring community. In an interview after his release, the "distraught Russell said his remaining options were to . . . violate his parole so he could return to jail, or maybe even take his own life." Shortly thereafter, Russell jumped off a forty-foot bridge into the cold Feather River.[20]

Isolates, those who remain less integrated into social networks provide the extreme case that makes the point. They suffer the pangs of anomie and disconnection. They experience social death. They watch life from the sidelines. They exhibit a special vulnerability to unfreedom, seeing it as the route back to comforting connections.

Thus, marginal individuals, detached from the fabric of social life, are easy targets for leaders who offer a new set of constraints. Cults easily harvest isolates as low-hanging fruit. Intriguing evidence comes from the study of U.S. soldiers taken prisoner in the Korean War.[21] The research of organizational behaviorist Edgar Schein and his colleagues shows that the POWs least embedded in social networks prior to their capture were the ones whom their captors most easily persuaded to defect.

In response to unfamiliar freedom, previously constrained individuals often seek release from the very uncertainty and ambiguity that liberated them to be themselves. The newly unfettered are not consciously trying to abandon their freedom, only the consequences that flow from it. Still, there is no separating uncertainty, freedom, and ambiguity from anxiety and anomie.

The upshot is that willingly, sometimes enthusiastically, many individuals surrender their freedom to any leader who will promise them four things:

- A new, demanding ideology with a clear set of beliefs and rules to replace those shattered by change and freedom

- Unambiguous roles into which followers can button themselves, notwithstanding that the new roles constrict them as much as or more than their previous roles

- A rationale for the new social order and a schedule of costs and rewards, no matter how illusionary

- A continuing, reassuring relationship with—even submission to—a seemingly omnipotent leader, who promises to put the newly freed follower back in a secure box, albeit a different box

The fervor to clarify and distill uncertainty and ambiguity, to rid ourselves of anxiety, leaves us susceptible to—often eager for—toxic leaders, who feed those needs. If, in the process, the leader also holds out an even juicier carrot—a chance for us to achieve greatness, fame, wealth, or possibly immortality through heroic deeds—so much the better.

The Janus Disposition of Uncertainty: Danger and Ennobling Challenges

Like Janus, uncertainty has two faces, pointing in opposite directions. One faces the potential dangers inevitably present in any era.

The other looks toward that era's emerging challenges and ennobling choices.

Both the terrifying perils and the exciting possibilities raise our anxiety and push us toward strong leaders. These leaders reassure us that they can steer us safely through this uncharted terrain. If we're not careful, we won't notice how some strong leaders, who step over the line to toxicity, can urge us toward allegedly death-transcending heroics.

While bad is stronger, the good is not weak. We want strong leaders for more positive reasons as well. Our growing uncertainty is also magnificent, for it holds far more than simply danger and devastation. It offers challenges that promise us growth, creativity, and innovation.

Exciting challenges can entice us with heroic opportunities when they avoid narcissistic heroics. Confident leaders who urge us to stretch ourselves to the limits of heroism soothe our anxieties. They also remind us that we are truly capable of important contributions to a meaningful world.

Challenges stimulate new ideas and technologies that hold the potential for reweaving the very fabric of our lives. The Internet, the Human Genome Project, new miracle drugs, and a host of other amazing technologies will further transform, for better or worse, the landscape of this and future ages. Someone, usually a leader, recognizes the possibilities and urges us to respond. Dr. Anthony Fauci, at the National Institutes of Health, has been a major voice spearheading the drive for AIDS research that has steadily lengthened the lives of stricken patients.

In a world teeming with uncertainties, opportunities abound for committing ourselves to exalting enterprises. These opportunities promise significant benefits for others far beyond ourselves and our narrow circle of family and intimates. The possibilities for improving the world, in small and large ways, provide such ennobling chances. These pursuits, as Rank and Becker argue, also help us to transcend death, at least symbolically.[22] We look to leaders to identify these immense challenges.[23]

The Certainties of Culture: Shaping Our Expectations for Leaders

While daily life unfolds with change and uncertainty, culture, our deliberately constructed defense against anxiety, introduces counterbalances through continuity and certainty. Through its institutions, rituals, norms, symbols, and artifacts, culture shapes our expectations and sets the stage for all human action.[24] We depend upon the culture for assurance that, despite all the uncertainty and chaos, the world is a meaningful, orderly place, and we are significant beings within it. The culture also promises that beneath the disorienting waters of uncertainty lies the hope of stability and meaning.

Through its many institutions—government, schools, the family, religion, the law, science, technology, and art—culture generates a solid sense of continuity and certainty. Yet culture leaves us just enough wiggle room to conduct our lives comfortably and flexibly. While it buffers us against change, culture also performs another crucial service: It pacifies the existential and situational anxieties that threaten to paralyze us. Hankiss, as we saw, takes the argument to the next level, suggesting that we humans have constructed the totality of Western civilization—all our institutions, norms, traditions, art, architecture, symbols, and knowledge—specifically to cope with our fears and anxieties.[25]

Civilization quells our fears by creating the illusion that we are living in a safe, orderly, coherent world. We cling to that illusion, even when our senses tell us it is way off the mark. To keep going, we all seek to live in a culture where we believe we play a central role, where our deeds and thoughts shine with significance. That helps us to make sense of our lives.

Formal and Informal Social Structures

Each culture creates its own social architecture, embedded with visible, formal institutions as well as invisible, informal systems. The visible institutions—governments, businesses, schools, churches, prisons, and families—run more or less in accordance with formal laws and social policies. These, along with the culture's more subtle traditions of behavior and manners, channel our responses in ways we barely notice.

The formal and informal structures of our society bias us toward keeping the current leader in power. In fact, we deliberately design political constitutions and practices, as well as corporate bylaws, to prevent the casual removal of leaders. That way, we believe, societies and organizations may enjoy a reasonable level of stability. Were it not for such obstacles, every overly ambitious "wannabe" leader would be working feverishly to unravel the social fabric.

Social Norms

Social norms also shape our ways of selecting and responding to leaders. But even norms can shift over time or at particular historical moments. For example, some periods of history simmer with readiness to overthrow tradition and rewrite the "rules." Not too long ago, Minnesota voters elected former wrestling star Jesse "The Body" Ventura as governor, largely to signal their dissatisfaction with politics as usual. The protests against the war in Vietnam and the flower children's love-ins marked the '60s. Other eras, like the 1990s, are so suffused with cynicism and apathy that inaction becomes the mode du jour.

Nonetheless, social norms in any era powerfully shape our expectations and behavior. Given the family, the ethnic group, the social class, maybe even the neighborhood into which we are born, we know just what is expected of us: how to speak and dress, the education we should pursue, even which mates, occupations, and residential communities represent acceptable choices. The culture establishes distinct guidelines for how much we must achieve in order to enjoy community recognition. It sets the standards for heroism against which we measure our own and others' achievements. Our self-esteem develops as we meet or fail to meet the culture's expectations.

The illusion of certainty created by the culture is just that—an illusion. As such, it can be punctured. Crises, as we'll see in Chapter 5, can pierce our illusions of stability and certainty. Still, when unexpected events jolt our security, the culture is quick to respond. In fact, it has at the ready various emergency-response institutions—fire and police departments, hospitals, the military, and civil defense units. They rush to our aid and, in most cases, efficiently restore seeming order to our lives.

The Historical Moment

The historical moment that frames each generation plays its own critical role. In fact, it is from the strands of each historical moment that the tapestry of culture is woven. Every historical era spins its own colored threads, different from those of previous times, to weave the fabric of continuity.

Each historical moment is distinctive—the Irish potato famine, World War I, the Great Depression, World War II, the cold war, the Vietnam War, the baby boomer years, the digital era, and more recently the age of terrorism. Each era teaches its generation special lessons: caution, cynicism, distrust, and fear, or alternatively daring, optimism, faith, and ebullience.

One quick example: In the boom years of the 1990s the dot. coms flourished with a brilliance that astounded many Americans. Before the dot.coms crashed and burned, the great fortunes made by many young computer jocks changed the financial hopes of a whole generation. Those who came to occupational adulthood in that historical moment developed—at least for a while—far more grandiose financial expectations than their parents had.

The historical moment grooms us in other important ways as well. The culture and political context of our particular era indoctrinate us with their dominant social and political norms. We learn to value freedom, democracy, equality, diversity, education, truth, rationality, religiosity, and patriotism. Or we learn to value their opposites. Or something else somewhere in between.

Because each historical moment is different, cultural patterns inevitably shift, usually imperceptibly, beneath the illusion of stability. Culture allows for change, sometimes slowing it down but eventually acknowledging if not embracing it in informal as well as formal ways.

When change is gradual and we feel safe, we become preoccupied with our own concerns. We gradually may be tranquilized into accepting toxic leaders.

Large-scale demographic and political trends have their own effects on followers' appetites for challenging bad leaders. Industrialization and urbanization, as well as ethnic and racial ghettoization, poverty, and crime make us worry about our own safety. Only when those forces reach some tipping point, however, do they lead to riots and revolution.[26]

Cultural Myths and Belief Systems: How Leaders Use Them

Belief systems and cultural myths offer all leaders additional conduits for mesmerizing their supporters. Leaders who conform to the patterns of heroism embedded in our culture can develop a strong hold on their followers. Benign leaders, as well as toxic ones, use these aspects of culture; toxic leaders, however, usually misuse them. During World War II, General George S. Patton, an abusive leader, embodied the familiar myth of the great solider. During and after the war, General George C. Marshall offered a nontoxic version of this same myth.

Stronger yet are those leaders who offer a new twist to well-known myths, capturing the followers' imaginations and hypnotizing them into willing, often adoring collaborators.[27] Henry Ford bedazzled his followers with his innovative assembly line and unprecedented wages, burnishing the myth of the genius entrepreneur. He also propagated messages of hate. Alfred P. Sloan Jr., of General Motors, was an imaginative leader who led without resorting to toxic measures. Sloan brought new management ideas to that traditional corporate colossus, winning the admiration of business people worldwide.

Ideologies or belief systems, be they major religions or political philosophies, provide explanations of the complex structure of our world. They help us to understand the differences among various groups. They provide the "reasons" why we find ourselves in our special niche in society. So we are unlikely to give up wanting to believe in the world we inhabit and the leaders who help us understand it. Ironically, when these depersonalized ideologies fragment, we look even more desperately to human leaders for guidance.

The Culture's Role in Selecting Leaders

The culture also comes into play in our never-ending quest for leaders. It creates the guidelines for identifying and selecting them. Corporate culture sets forth its own criteria for leaders.

When the general and corporate cultures mesh, they can create an overwhelming reservoir of power for corporate leaders trying to build a new corporate identity. They also set limits on the leader's behavior, as Jean-Marie Messier, late of Vivendi Universal, discovered. Messier, whose extravagant lifestyle offended the cultural tastes of the Vivendi board and shareholders, found himself unceremoniously booted out of the corporate suite. Perhaps even more lethal in *l'affaire Vivendi* was Messier's seeming rejection of his native French culture—referring to France in one interview as a "small, exotic country."

The Downside of a Strong Culture: When Corporate Culture Leads to a Toxic Organization

Corporate culture can build walls that keep you safe from harm or, alternatively, imprison you. Arthur Andersen, the bankrupt accounting juggernaut, painfully learned that lesson. In its earlier years, the culture taught every new recruit "the world according to Andersen." That meant everything from the kind of hat you wore to where you hung it. Andersen immersed its new, meticulously selected recruits into its corporate culture at the company's "boot camp" in St. Charles, Illinois. This rigorous training earned Arthur Andersen the sobriquet "the Marine Corps of the accounting world."

When the founding father, Arthur Andersen himself, was still on the scene, following the regimented cultural prescriptions meant a company chock full of serious, dedicated, and impeccably honest, incorruptible accountants, just like the CEO. But years later, when the corporate culture changed at the urging of toxic leaders, that robotic cultural obedience turned cancerous.[28]

Barbara Ley Toffler, a former partner in charge of Andersen's ethics consulting group, has described how conformity to company culture can turn the organization toxic: "It was a culture in which everyone followed the rules and the leader. . . . When the rules and leaders stood for decency and integrity, the lock-step culture was the key to competence and respectability. But when the game and the leaders changed direction, the culture of conformity led to disaster."[29]

Despite her disdain for the "Androids," who swallowed and followed orders with "no deviation from the norm, however silly the norm may be," even Toffler succumbed to the corporate ethos of profit and greed. Toffler acknowledges that she "basically went along with the culture," seduced by the opportunity to make more money than she ever earned in her pre-Andersen days consulting or teaching corporate ethics in academia. So we easily see how culture, followed blindly, in organizations as well as in the larger society, can set up followers to accept toxic leadership.

In sum, in a world where uncertainties and certainties layer situational fears over our existential anxiety, we look to leaders, usually strong leaders, for reassurance, guidance, and a sense of meaning in our lives. We are particularly vulnerable when our everyday uncertainty and change escalate into crises.

In the next chapter, we shall consider the ways in which crises rub raw our own need for certitude. Consequently, we don't simply condone the entry of powerful, often toxic leaders. We actively seek them out and anoint them as God.

5

Leadership in Crisis: The Dangers of Creating God

Searching for leaders to guide us through turmoil is perfectly understandable, but we followers tend to want much more than mere guidance. We want leaders who will forthwith slay the dragons that beset us so that we can once again sleep peacefully in our beds. We desire nothing less than leaders who can swiftly whip turmoil and confusion into order and omniscience. In short, we, like the ancient Greeks, want superhuman, divine leaders, albeit in human form.

On September 20, 2001, the *New York Times* ran an op-ed article about Mayor Giuliani, a piece that caught this very human need in its acute state:

> He moves about the stricken city like a god. People want to be in his presence. They want to touch him. They want to praise him. ... On Central Park West, a woman searching for just the right superlative for the man who is guiding New York through the greatest disaster ever to hit an American city finally said, "He's not like a god; he is God." ... He has achieved what political observers would have told you two weeks ago is impossible. He is not only respected, but revered. And not only revered, but loved. This is not hyperbole. If he were running for re-election today, there would be

no need for an actual vote. You could hand him his next term by acclamation.[1]

This is not to gainsay Mayor Giuliani's spectacular performance. We all recall how he rose to the monumental challenge of the World Trade Center attack. We watched Giuliani draw upon strengths, such as compassion and empathy, that were previously undemonstrated, perhaps because he had never before had the opportunity to display them—or perhaps because the situation revealed Giuliani to himself.

Giuliani offered surefooted guidance and support, optimism laced with increasing doses of reality, and resolution alloyed with endurance and sympathy. He calmed an anxious public. He made quick decisions and showed the flexibility to correct initial errors. In the process, Giuliani helped—perhaps more than anyone else—to revitalize the nation's fundamental values and tap into deeply submerged group feelings of patriotism, community, and sacrifice.

Nor is exemplary leadership during crisis reserved for leaders in the public sector. When a fire gutted the Malden Mills factory on a frigid December night in 1995, CEO Aaron Feuerstein watched his life's work go up in flames. Yet his greater concern was for the three thousand employees who would be without jobs. Feuerstein acted quickly to assure his people that they would continue to receive their regular salaries and full benefits until he could figure out the next step. Feuerstein's leadership so heartened a traumatized labor force that within weeks after the fire, the mill was producing 230,000 yards of fabric per week, up from its pre-fire 130,000 weekly high mark.[2] Feuerstein took this decision knowing full well it could lead to overwhelming debt. He rebuilt the factory but eventually was forced into filing for Chapter 11 bankruptcy. At this writing, Feuerstein remains at the Massachusetts mill, no longer in charge of operations, but its spiritual leader nonetheless.

This leadership behavior was not a one-time deal. Back in 1981, when Malden Mills faced bankruptcy, Feuerstein similarly refused to let down his employees and the Lawrence/Methuen community. Instead, he invested millions to develop new fabrics, Polartec and Polarfleece, that would offer unusual protection against cold temperatures and breathe new life back into the company. Refusing to send production offshore to cut costs, Feuerstein reopened the company, paying workers standard U.S. wages.

Four Dangers

Feuerstein and Giuliani were two exemplary leaders who exhibited strength and stuck to their values in the face of serious crises. Nonetheless, in crisis, our propensity to entrust ourselves to leaders to whom we ascribe great powers intensifies. In league with those leaders' reactive readiness to play God, our neediness can breed at least four major dangers, some threatening to us, others to them.

- We cede personal responsibility for our own fates.

- We lay that extra burden upon imperfect humans, who too often can't help but disappoint.

- We risk either blindly manacling ourselves to toxic leaders or, by our neediness, pushing otherwise nontoxic leaders over the line into toxicity.

- We invite authoritarianism to visit as a temporary guest, who, once ensconced in the back bedroom, may be nearly impossible to evict.

New Solutions, New Leaders

When a crisis like the September 11 attack invades our psyches, our repressed existential angst surfaces.[3] Our anxiety escalates dramatically, aggravated by new, quite conscious layers of situational fear arising from the specific features of the immediate crisis we are facing.

At the start of a crisis, most sitting leaders enjoy a spike in their approval ratings. We rather desperately want them to stay in charge. If they can't expeditiously resolve the crisis, however, we soon begin to look for their replacements.

Shaken by fearsome conditions, we transform fallible human leaders into infallible gods—gods for whose protection and guidance we would willingly exchange our freedom, as the Germans did in the decades following World War I. Defeated and humiliated by the war and the terms of the Versailles treaty, Germany experienced a crisis of national identity. That left the German people dangerously susceptible to any Hitler who would promise to restore the nation's pride.

Crises, after all, are not just threatening and terrifying situations. Crises are fires for which we have no firefighters, invasions against which we have no defenses, plagues for which we have no medicines. In fact, they are situations for which our normal coping mechanisms and available resources prove totally inadequate.[4] During crises, we see how roles de-differentiate, losing their sharply defined borders and changing their internal structure. Thus, new roles emerge and existing roles disappear or change internally, taking on new tasks and shuffling off traditional ones.

In crises, roles undergo another shift, with the formal and informal requirements for entering crisis-relevant roles changing dramatically. Consequently, previously unacceptable categories of potential entrants—women, various minorities, youth, and other groups who did not meet the traditional demographic requirements—are now allowed admission. In fact, they may be actively recruited into the very roles from which they were barred in calmer times.

The changes in the entry criteria for roles affect leadership positions as well. And, curiously enough, these far-reaching transformations cannot be attributed simply to a vacuum of eligible role seekers. For example, in every Allied country touched by World War II, the percentage of women elected to the national legislative body rose significantly during that time, despite the availability of sufficient numbers of men who met all the traditional entry requirements.[5]

Crises force us to reconnect with our values and reorder our priorities. In the process, they offer us a finely ground lens through which to gain a sharper, clearer view of our leaders. The hot urgency of crisis melts the superficial layers, revealing the leaders' true grain, knots and all. In crises, we see our leaders as we never before have seen them. This happens for several reasons: first, because leaders have stripped down to their essentials for action; second, because we are viewing them through eyes distorted by fear; and third, because we are responding to them with sharpened priorities and values.

Crises rock the very ground beneath us. At such moments, existing leaders can flourish or fail, flagging leaders can be restored, and new leaders have opportunities to step forward. As a result, crises can provide the opportunity for all kinds of unlikely leaders to emerge. Even relatively unknown leaders can seem attractive to followers, who eagerly respond to their call to heroic action. For example, after four failed presidencies in less than two years, Argentina elected an unusual, low-visibility candidate: Nestor Kirchner, a three-term governor of a sparsely populated province in Patagonia. Elected in the context of an official unemployment rate that stood at 18 percent and an economy that had plummeted 11 percent in the preceding year, Kirchner linked the crisis conditions to his call for far-reaching change. In his inaugural address, Kirchner summoned his constituents to rise to a heroic challenge: "Our past is full of failures, pain, confrontations, [and] energy wasted in sterile struggles. . . . Now is the time for transformation, for the cultural and moral change the moment demands of us."[6]

Crises, however, can also swing the door open for predatory toxic leaders, such as Al Dunlap, CEO of Sunbeam. Dunlap got the nod after Sunbeam missed five quarters of profit and revenue estimates in a row. With few exceptions, Wall Street analysts looked favorably on Dunlap. In fact, the day after Sunbeam's announcement of Dunlap's appointment, the company's stock price, which opened at $12.50, shot up to $18.63, nearly a 50-percent increase, and "the largest jump in the exchange's history."[7]

In critical times, followers tend to look for leaders who are distinctly different from those who presided during the formation of the crisis. That was true in the Sunbeam case as well. Roger Schipke, Dunlap's predecessor, was Dunlap's complete opposite. Schipke was

> a quiet, unassuming man with refined and subtle tastes. He was an executive of integrity and honor, his business judgment informed by his decades at General Electric Co., the academy of Corporate America. He was soft-spoken, well-reasoned, extraordinarily good-hearted, and eminently likable because he seemed so pleasant and agreeable.[8]

By contrast, Dunlap's first meeting as CEO with his senior executives was a bloody debacle designed to bully and insult the assembled staff. In stark contrast to Roger Schipke,

> [t]heir new boss [Dunlap] sat at the table like an imperial demagogue. He cheered his own past accomplishments, reminding the men that he had done eight turnarounds on three continents and Sunbeam would be his ninth. He even urged them to buy his forthcoming book, *Mean Business: How I Save Bad Companies and Make Good Companies Great*, so they would know exactly what he expected from them. . . . "It was like a dog barking at you for hours," Boynton later said. "He just yelled, ranted, and raved. He was condescending, belligerent, and disrespectful." Recalled attorney Fannin: "It was a very, very hostile environment. Everything was a confrontation and a put-down."[9]

And this was just CEO Dunlap's first day on the job!

The Entry of Charismatic Leaders

Charismatic leaders, whose charm frequently outweighs their competence, are apt to come forward when adversity strikes, warned sociologist Max Weber.[10] They present radical remedies that have special appeal largely because they are 180 degrees different from the strategies that have just failed us. That makes sense because crises, by definition, cannot be resolved by our ordinary coping mechanisms and resources.[11] Thus, when we feel threatened, we welcome charismatic leaders with their novel solutions.

Psychologists Sheldon Solomon and his colleagues have demonstrated in laboratory experiments that charismatic leaders are particularly preferred when participants have been made aware of the possibility of their own death.[12] Solomon and colleagues asked 190 student participants, ages seventeen through fifty-six, to read supposed campaign speeches by three candidates—charismatic, task-oriented, and relational leaders—after some students had been asked to ponder their death and others to think about an impending exam. Then the researchers asked the participants to rate each candidate and select the one for whom they would vote. Charismatic leaders did not fare well compared to task-oriented or relational candidates under control conditions; however, when participants were asked to think about their own mortality, the preference for charismatic leaders substantially increased, while affection for relational leaders declined significantly. Under the experimental condition, that is, students thinking about their own death, the appeal of task-oriented leaders remained stable and high. The results suggest our existential angst is at work during crisis, substantially increasing our preference for charismatic leaders.

Uncertainty and anxiety saturate crises, prodding us to look for charismatic leaders, leaders who exude confidence and inspire belief in their seemingly divine capabilities. Weber wrote that our devotion to charismatic leaders is "born of distress."[13] Their followers hold charismatic leaders in awe, wishfully ascribing to them divine gifts or mana. Yet it is in the very mana of charismatics that one senses both great potential and grave danger.

In the twentieth century, two charismatic leaders—Adolf Hitler and Franklin D. Roosevelt—rose to power during devastating economic crises. Cambridge University professor Piers Brendon contrasts these two towering figures:

> Each man played the hero in a drama of deliverance, a shining knight slaying the dragon Depression. . . . However, the differences between President and Führer were fundamental. Roosevelt aimed to breathe new life into the American economy so that it could stand

on its own feet, an independent entity generating peace and prosperity in a world of laissez-faire. Hitler intended to recreate the German economy as a kind of Frankenstein's monster, subordinate to his will and armoured for a war of racial supremacy.[14]

David Aberbach, a professor of Jewish studies at McGill University, has put forward an intriguing explanation for the appeal of charismatic leaders in periods of crisis.[15] Taking a psychoanalytic approach, Aberbach interprets charismatic leaders' capacity to convince followers of their unique ability to deal with a specific crisis in the following way:

Everyone has experienced various psychological traumas. For potential charismatic leaders, their struggle with those experiences "becomes a driving force."[16] When a similar crisis subsequently arises, the personal trauma of the charismatic leader and the collective trauma of the affected group coincide. Because the would-be leader has been deeply "schooled" in that trauma through his or her personal struggle, the "psychological components" of the trauma, in all their complexity and subtlety, are intensely familiar to the leader. Incidentally, this explanation is consonant with Warren Bennis's and Robert J. Thomas's finding that the effective leaders they interviewed had been fired in their own traumatic crucibles.[17]

Consequently, the leader's pronouncement that he or she can cope with a particular crisis rings with authenticity, handily convincing followers. The situation ripens for the leader to become a "vehicle for the followers' projections and transferences."[18]

Given their awesome magnetism, charismatic leaders seem omnipotent. Their entourages work assiduously to promote that illusion.[19] Illusions inflating the leader's power, however, often undermine faith in our own strength.

Charybdis of Crisis: The Dangers Nontoxic Leaders Confront

Even without crises, toxic leaders have arisen in every era and society. Still, crisis creates an ideal climate in which normally reasonable, nontoxic leaders, fed by the neediness of their followers, can quickly grow to toxic heft.

In the wake of September 11, Mayor Giuliani, whose courage and compassion had sustained a grieving, frightened city, nearly broke through the fragile barrier into toxicity. Despite the fact that Giuliani's two-term administration was approaching its legal limit, the Giuliani camp began maneuvering to extend it.[20]

The City Council and several mayoralty candidates rebuffed the overtures. Giuliani quickly hoisted himself back onto the high road, barely escaping a descent from the heights of heroism into the quagmire of toxic leadership.

Crises frequently create the treacherous Charybdis in which currently nontoxic leaders can founder and drown because threats to the group's survival transcend the leaders' ordinary coping mechanisms and resources. Though we are all at risk in crises, leaders perhaps are even more endangered than the rest of us. In such times, leaders find themselves with special needs. Like everyone else, they must confront difficult and completely novel situations.

- They need sound advice from those with greater relevant knowledge and experience than they have.

- They need to cut through the information overload—frequently irrelevant, incorrect, or in an unusable form—that engulfs leaders during such turbulent periods.[21]

- Leaders need to structure their advising relationships to avoid the quick consensus trap of groupthink, as well as other bureaucratic and political riptides.[22]

- These leaders need to think seriously about the possible second- and third-order consequences of all available options.

The Anthrax Scare

The anthrax scare following 9/11 demonstrates how leaders can make poor crisis decisions based on several common strategies. First, they may act on inadequate advice from "experts" eager to satisfy the decision makers' needs. Second, leaders may act too quickly in response to their perception that desperate followers want immediate answers, even before the leaders have fully grasped the problem. Third, a sense of urgency may push them to act without sufficient consideration of potential second- and third-order consequences. When these factors come into play, leaders can easily find themselves over their heads in the whitewater of crisis.

Even the best-intentioned leaders can find themselves buffeted by two opposing currents: the urgent need to craft a solution before the full extent of the crisis unveils itself, and the temptation to display more confidence than the situation warrants. These two themes sound prominently in the God symphony. In both circumstances, followers' needs for safety too often tempt leaders to accept uncritically their advisors' hastily assembled proposals.

The need to provide unwavering leadership to calm followers' fears can mislead even the best-meaning leaders, as well as their advisors, into stifling their own inner doubts. Far better to heed the ancient dictum *festina lente*—make haste slowly—coupled with University of Southern California president Steven Sample's succinct recommendation to "think gray, see double, never completely trust an expert."[23]

Pressed to allay citizens' fears after 9/11, the Centers for Disease Control (CDC) prematurely offered assurances to the privately run U.S. Postal Service that proved both flawed and, in some cases, fatal. They quickly and confidently dismissed postal officials' fears that anthrax spores might leak from sealed envelopes handled by postal personnel. Convinced, the Postal Service took no special precautions. Consequently, several mail handlers succumbed to the disease. Between October 2001 and February 2002, the FBI reported more than eight thousand cases of "use or threatened use of anthrax or other hazardous materials."[24]

Leaders need to ensure that their definition of the problem is reasonably close to the mark. Sometimes the magnitude of the situation seems immediately apparent, as the September 11 attack did at first. Yet each hour of that fateful day expanded the horror beyond anyone's expectations. Even when the full extent of a problem initially seems abundantly clear, leaders must take care that their short-term solutions not only are relevant but will not preclude longer-range strategies for which the need may become apparent only later.

One Crisis Leads to Another: Misreading the Warning Signals

Crises have a curious way of generating multiple offspring. It is no mean task to flush out those secondary and tertiary crises hidden in the crevices of solutions to the initial one. Sometimes, as we've just seen, the first solutions that decision makers put in place seem appropriate and effective. Still, if decision makers have not considered the many future twists and turns that the crisis can take, they may find that their initial remedy has turned sour or makes other subsequently needed solutions impossible.

Opportunities Knock

Crises can also have their positive side. They provide opportunities, as well as dangers, for both leaders and followers. The *Wall Street Journal* reported the ebb and flow of corporate leadership in the wake of the World Trade Center attack. For example, at

Merrill Lynch, whose headquarters were located across the street from the ill-fated towers,

> President E. Stanley O'Neal has taken over more and more of the day-to-day responsibilities of running the securities firm. Mr. O'Neal . . . was named to the No. 2 spot in July, and isn't expected to take over duties from the chief executive, 62-year-old David Komansky, for several years. But since the terrorist hijackers struck . . . , Mr. O'Neal has asserted more control at the firm. As he and two other top executives dashed to the street . . . he told his colleagues to split up. "We shouldn't be together, just in case," he said. In subsequent days, he oversaw the company's efforts to relocate 9,000 brokers, traders and other employees. . . . In the past two weeks, he has jettisoned several top executives close to Komansky, including his rival for the president's post whom Mr. Komansky had favored.[25]

If some seated leaders seem to thrive in crises, while others crash in flames, still others who have lost their way rise to the challenge. By debriding irrelevant and trivial goals, crises swiftly reorder the priorities of leaders and followers, alike. They highlight the basic steps to survival, making previously uncertain leaders seem more surefooted and focused.

Some directionless leaders seize a crisis as an opportunity to set a new, more meaningful course. For others, the new direction is thrust upon them. President George W. Bush's first eight months in office meandered aimlessly, tentatively seeking first one objective and then another. Not until the attack on the World Trade Center was Bush able to identify his "mission": the eradication of terrorism and the promotion of freedom around the world. He eloquently articulated this goal in an address to a joint session of the U.S. Congress:

> Great harm has been done to us. We have suffered great loss. And in our grief and anger, we have found our mission and our moment. . . . The advance of human freedom, the achievement of our time and the great hope of every time, now depends on us.[26]

In the immediate aftermath of Bush's speech, even his detractors viewed the vivified president through new, more receptive eyes.

Still, while crises may help directionless leaders find their path, if they cannot resolve the crisis expeditiously, their followers soon may become restive and dissatisfied. Thus, the war on terror metamorphosed first into the war in Afghanistan and then into the war on Iraq. As the vows to find Osama bin Laden and Iraq's weapons of mass destruction remained unfulfilled and more troops died in the postwar period, even Bush's strongest supporters began to raise questions.

Making Up for Previous Mistakes

For leaders struggling to compensate for earlier mistakes, a crisis may provide a fresh start. Only four months into his new role as CEO of American Express, Kenneth I. Chenault wrote off $182 million in high-yield junk bonds, leaving Wall Street in profound disbelief. That, he assured the Street, was a one-time event. Then only three months later, in July, Chenault stunned investors by announcing a further $826 million write-off on the same Minneapolis money-management operation. That pushed AmEx's second-quarter income into a 76-percent slide. Chenault's halo was rapidly dimming.

Then came September 11, leaving eleven AmEx employees dead and the offices in ruins. This time Chenault acted deftly to ensure that AmEx's operations would not miss a beat. He swiftly moved the firm from its damaged, spacious offices across from ground zero to new, unprepossessing quarters in Jersey City, where he guided his shell-shocked company through uncharted waters. *Business Week* reported,

> In Salt Lake City on a business trip when the terrorists struck, Chenault took command long distance. When the first plane crashed, Chenault was on the phone with a New York colleague from his hotel room. He . . . instructed security to evacuate the building immediately. . . . The hundreds of ad hoc decisions made by Chenault and his team were guided by two overriding concerns: employee safety and customer service. AmEx helped 560,000 stranded cardholders get home, in some cases chartering airplanes and buses to ferry them across the country. It waived millions of dollars in delinquent fees on late-paying cardholders and increased credit limits to cash-starved clients.
>
> Most telling, Chenault gathered 5,000 American Express employees at the Paramount Theater in New York on Sept. 20 for a highly emotional "town hall meeting." During the session, Chenault demonstrated the poise, compassion, and decisiveness that vaulted him to the top. . . . Twice, he rushed to . . . embrace grief-stricken employees. Chenault said he would donate $1 million of the company's profits to the families of the AmEx victims. "I represent the best company and the best people in the world," he concluded. "In fact, you are my strength, and I love you." It was a poignant and unscripted moment.[27]

Business Week concluded that Chenault had "shown the right . . . stuff." In less than three short months, the AmEx CEO had revived his credibility as a leader.

After that, Chenault's leadership quotient skyrocketed. The media couldn't get enough of Chenault, photographing him accompanying President Bush at ground zero and later helping Mayor Giuliani and Governor Pataki make the case for an increased federal rebuilding package. Somehow, like Giuliani, in the trials of crisis, Chenault found his stride.

In Sync with the Moment

Conventional wisdom argues that great times evoke great leadership. We tend to focus on the fit between the leader's strengths and the needs of the historical moment.[28] Ironically, the very same behavior previously reviled by followers may seem like the perfect prescription when crisis strikes. A good match between the leader's action and the needs of the crisis can turn a previously hopeless failure into a hero.

The career of Steve Jobs, cofounder of Apple Computer, presents an example of how the context of crisis can change followers' perceptions of a leader's style and strategy. During Apple's start-up years, Jobs's charismatic, driving, upbeat style put the upstart company on the map. As Apple grew into corporate adolescence, the board of directors and CEO John Sculley ousted Jobs, citing a misalignment between Jobs's style and the company's needs. Only later, when Apple found itself in a nearly fatal tailspin, did the company recall Jobs, now hailing those same behaviors as valuable strengths. Since then, Jobs's ongoing rescue of the struggling computer company has won plaudits from insiders and industry analysts alike.

Renewal in Crisis

There is still more to the relationship between crisis and leadership. Crisis prompts some leaders to renew themselves, to tap previously untapped and, up until then, irrelevant or unrequired talents. These strengths help some leaders exceed their previous performance levels. Sometimes dire circumstances can evoke talents that the leaders themselves didn't know they had. For example, leaders who have prided themselves on their detached, analytic decision-making style during a crisis may discover an amazing capacity to connect emotionally to their followers' needs. AmEx's

Kenneth Chenault's action in the days following 9/11, described earlier, is a clear example.

Perhaps the most spectacular recent renewal of a floundering leader is former New York mayor Rudy Giuliani, with whose case I began this chapter. Few now even wish to recall that on September 4, 2001, Giuliani, a lame-duck leader with a bleak political future, hurried down the Labor Day West Indian American Parade route in Crown Heights, bombarded by the catcalls of parade watchers.[29] Only one week later, Giuliani's effective leadership in crisis became textbook material. Giuliani's postcrisis approval ratings soared 30 percent and, as of this writing, remain at atmospheric levels in his new corporate role as crisis consultant, much sought after by business firms and governments alike.

Rising Authoritarianism

Strong leadership, of course, need not be toxic. Crises often cry out for tough measures. Faced with falling profits, corporate bosses mandate curtailed travel, as well as hiring, promotion, and salary freezes. In severe crises, such as wartime, a leader's call for curfews and rationing may be both necessary and appropriate.

Yet crises can create circumstances that prompt some leaders, even in democratic societies, to move beyond merely strong leadership to unwarranted authoritarianism. In such times, leaders may impose constraints on traditional civil liberties and violate other democratic norms.

When an extraordinary event, such as 9/11, stresses the culture's usual coping mechanisms, leaders may respond by creating a brand-new, sometimes massive institution, such as the Department of Homeland Security. Leaders move to reinstate a sense of security. New rules restricting certain behaviors quickly appear. To wit, after 9/11, passengers may no longer carry penknives or tweezers aboard airliners. New legislation affecting the comings and goings of noncitizens receives swift approval while an anxious, terrorized population sighs in relief. In this and other ways, the culture acts to quiet our anxieties provoked by the discombobulation of the ordinary routines of daily life.

Authoritarianism, a hallmark of toxic leaders, seeps in through the fissures created by crises. In tumultuous times, toxic leaders' predilection for authoritarianism fits neatly with their anxious followers' heightened insecurity. Besides the very specific fears evoked by the here-and-now crisis, the more generalized threat presented by the crisis stirs the same existential anxieties that once sent us scurrying into secure maternal arms. As adults in crisis, we desperately wish for the next best thing: decisive leaders. It is not surprising, then, that we actively seek the embrace of strong, even dictatorial leaders. Set adrift in threatening and unfamiliar seas, most of us willingly surrender our freedom to any authoritarian captain.

Authoritarianism and Scapegoats

Authoritarian leaders often impress their followers by exercising power against groups whom the followers dislike, fear, or envy. And since crises palpably stoke our paranoia, we easily believe that our leaders have "good reasons" for their actions, even if they refuse to disclose them. Consequently, the spared followers raise few objections when toxic leaders castigate a scapegoat.

Such was the case during World War II, when the Nazis barricaded Polish Jews behind ghetto walls while their relieved neighbors looked away. In France as well, when the Nazis rounded up Jewish citizens for deportation, few of their compatriots raised objections. In the United States, Japanese-American citizens found nary a champion when they were forced to sell their homes, businesses, and lucrative farmland before being hustled off to internment camps. The Rev. Martin Niemöller's famous lament poetically articulates the failure to resist injustice:

> When Hitler attacked the Jews I was not a Jew, therefore I was not concerned. And when Hitler attacked the Catholics, I was not a Catholic, and therefore, I was not concerned. And when Hitler attacked the unions and the industrialists, I was not a member of the unions and I was not concerned. Then Hitler attacked me and the Protestant church—and there was nobody left to be concerned.[30]

There are serious lessons to be taken from such history: When toxic leaders initially attack a low-value group, they rarely encounter significant resistance. More important, they rarely stop there. Eventually, toxic leaders target whomever they choose, whenever and wherever it suits their purposes. By that time, however, the new prey has been tranquilized into a false sense of security, leaving it quite defenseless.

Trading Security for Freedom

In crises, authoritarian leaders tend to come forward with stringent measures designed to "protect" us from the immediate dangers we face. Such policies, frequently encased in binding legislation, lock us into long-term restrictions. We allow, in fact welcome, these "safeguards," without noticing we are manacling ourselves to un-freedom in a dangerous trade-off for security. We barely consider how arduous—if not impossible—it will be to unlock these shack-les when the political heat cools down.

In our distress, we tend to accept tyranny and anarchy as the only two possible choices. Leaders who aspire to power by insisting on security over freedom are reluctant to promote other options. Blinded by this false dichotomy, we may not perceive the wider range of possibilities for action that lie between these extremes.

When God Knows Best: Acquiescence to Authoritarianism

When leaders agree to play God, followers begin to lose their in-dependence. And, as Benjamin Franklin noted scornfully, "They that can give up essential liberty to obtain a little temporary safety deserve neither liberty nor safety."[31] Nor can we rely completely on a democracy to protect our independence when this occurs. For when leaders step into God's sandals in uncertain times, even the most freedom-loving followers may acquiesce to authoritarianism.

Having a structure and an ideology that they *must* accept bol-sters the followers' sense of security. Anxiety seeds a frantic will-ingness among most—but fortunately not all—followers to ignore the pincers quietly closing in around their freedom. As followers, many of us all too easily ignore the constraints on dissent, includ-ing those that exceed any rational limits. Nonetheless, as we see with whistle-blowers, a few stalwart individuals speak up, despite serious costs to themselves.

A recent example of how the bounds of rationality can snap in times of anxiety: Alliance Atlantis fired Ed Gernon, executive pro-ducer of a two-part television miniseries entitled *Hitler: The Rise of Evil* for CBS, after the filmmaker warned of similarities between the tightening American political climate prior to the Iraq war and that of Germany in the predawn of the Third Reich. The *TV Guide* article suggested that Gernon saw the CBS special portraying the political context in Germany in the post–World War I era as a "cautionary tale for contemporary America."

Here is an excerpt from the article that led to Gernon's ouster:

> "It basically boils down to an entire nation [Germany] gripped by fear, who ultimately chose to give up their civil rights and plunged the whole world into war. I can't think of a better time to examine

this history than now." . . . Gernon stated his belief that fear fueled both the Bush administration's adoption of a preemptive-strike policy and the public's acceptance of it: "They will stand by and let it happen because of the fear of what will happen if they don't." Gernon says a similar fearfulness in a devastated post–World War I Germany was "absolutely" behind that nation's acceptance of Hitler's extremism. "When an entire country becomes afraid for their sovereignty, for their safety," he says, "they will embrace ideas and strategies and positions that they might not embrace otherwise."[32]

Whether or not we agree with Gernon, the irony of his sacking in a country that sanctifies free speech is clear: An individual in a democratic society, whose own work demonstrates how fear can lead to dictatorship, is shown the door for calling attention to that very danger at home. In a jointly issued statement, Canadian production company Alliance Atlantis and CBS described Gernon's comments in *TV Guide* about the Hitler miniseries as "insensitive and outright wrong."[33] Strong words but even stronger action for a democratic society.

The Dangers of Silencing Dissent

The political arena has no monopoly on quashing dissent in times of crisis. In the twin shuttle disasters, those of the *Challenger* and the *Columbia*, engineers who disagreed with management decisions found themselves stonewalled. Investigations of the most recent disaster, the *Columbia* explosion, reveal that a cadre of engineers associated with the project worried about the impact of the foam that had struck the left wing of the shuttle at liftoff. According to the *New York Times*, five days after launch "virtually every one" of approximately thirty engineers from NASA and its aerospace contractors who met in conference, augmented by teleconferencing, agreed that the space agency should attempt to acquire images of the impact zone, through satellites or ground telescopes.[34] The group selected NASA engineer Rodney Rocha to report their recommendation to the shuttle mission managers.

Rocha had already e-mailed the shuttle engineering office requesting to have the astronauts "visually inspect the impact area through a small window on the side of the craft." The manager of the shuttle engineering office never replied. Rocha sent a second e-mail request, now asking in boldface, **"Can we petition (beg) for outside agency assistance?"** This time, the chair of the mission management team "canceled Mr. Rocha's request and two similar requests from other engineers associated with the mission."[35]

The manager of the shuttle engineering office informed Mr. Rocha of the decision. Thus, despite at least half a dozen unambiguous attempts by Rocha and other engineers, these efforts to object to and possibly offset a bad management decision met a dead end. "Launch fever"—some might call it "crisis clampdown"—had taken over. And we all know the sad result.

Demands for Constraints; Submission to Constraints

Hindsight allows us to see clearly the costs of squelching objections to leadership decisions made during crisis. It is considerably more difficult to weigh the consequences while we are in the throes of crisis. How, for example, has the general public responded to the injection of various controls over their daily lives, both before and particularly after 9/11?

In recent decades, following a rash of airplane hijackings, airline travelers routinely accepted the prohibitions against joking about terrorism in any form. After 9/11, the airlines, at the government's behest, turned up the heat. Travelers willingly bowed to elaborate physical searches. These search procedures created long, snaking lines of passengers in various stages of undress that previously might have warranted charges of indecent exposure. Travelers unquestioningly removed their jackets and shoes at the bidding of security guards equipped with electronic wands, which they waved over every inch of passengers' spread-eagled anatomy. This grandmother on her way to visit a sick grandchild was obliged to reach into her camisole to prove that the "mad money" she had pinned to her undergarment really was no Uzi. Needless to say, it is hard to know just where to draw the line.

Good Intentions and Overreaction in Crisis

In times of crisis, when followers demand more security, those in leadership positions, presumably with good intentions, may overreact. Yet, as Senator Daniel Webster remarked more than a century ago,

> Good intentions will always be pleaded for every assumption of authority. It is hardly too strong to say that the Constitution was made to guard the people against the dangers of good intentions. There are men in all ages who mean to govern well, but they mean to govern. They promise to be good masters, but they mean to be masters.[36]

Attorney General John Ashcroft's actions in the turmoil immediately after September 11 provide a clear example of authoritarianism following swiftly on the heels of crisis. In the postattack
furor, the Justice Department swept into detention hundreds of
immigrants, mostly from the Middle East. Some had alleged terrorist connections, but others were detained for minor traffic vio-
lations, some for expired visas, some for petty criminal offenses,
and still others for no stated reason at all.

At first, the attorney general refused to identify the detainees or
specify their exact number, asserting that such action would constitute an invasion of their privacy. The strength of a democratic
tradition, however, eventually led to bipartisan protests from congressional leaders, the media, and the public. Only then did Ashcroft reluctantly agree to reveal some numbers and the names of
those individuals who had actually been charged. Months later,
however, and despite a brief congressional hearing, many noncitizens remained in custody, absent charges, their identities held secret, and without legal assistance or contact with their families.

Postcrisis Legislation: Easy to Enact, Hard to Repeal

In the wake of the September attack, the Justice Department
recommended legislative proposals to strengthen national security.
The *New York Times* reported that the original legislation proposed
by the administration would have authorized expanded surveillance
of telephone conversations and e-mail, as well as government in-
spection of logs of Internet use, including address and subject fields
of e-mail messages. The legislation also asked for increased search
authority, enlarged powers to seize suspected terrorists' assets, and
indeterminate detention of illegal immigrants without the filing of
formal charges. Similar acts, in other historical contexts, have been
clear precursors of impending toxic leadership.

Fortunately, amid voluble media criticism, cooler legislative
heads in both political parties trimmed several of the more excessive measures. A sunset clause requiring Congress to revisit the
legislation after four years provided the gangplank that brought
most of the more cautious congressional leaders aboard. More
troubling, however, was the strong public support for these
constraints.

Nonetheless, two years after 9/11, the *International Herald Tribune* and the *New York Times* reported that the Patriot Act, designed
to gain greater control over terrorism, was being used "against
drug traffickers, white-collar criminals and child pornographers."

A report from the Justice Department, prepared for the Congress, indicates that "the ability to secure nationwide warrants to obtain e-mail and electronic evidence 'has proved invaluable in several sensitive nonterrorism investigations,' including the tracking of an unidentified fugitive and an investigation into a computer hacker who stole trade secrets."[37] And "Justice Department officials say they are simply using all the tools now available to them to pursue criminals—terrorists or otherwise."[38]

Shortly after the terrorist attack, on November 13, 2001, President George W. Bush signed a presidential order authorizing military tribunals to try suspected terrorists. The military tribunal would bypass the civilian U.S. justice system. The presidential order calls for military tribunals that can mete out the death sentence on a two-thirds decision, a sentence subject neither to review nor reversal. As of this writing, President Bush has defied objections from media, congressional leaders, and a vocal minority of the American public. He has remained firm, citing as his precedent President Franklin D. Roosevelt's use of such powers with the Nazi infiltrators during World War II. With cooler-headed hindsight, most historians treat Roosevelt's action as a shameful chapter in U.S. history.

Shifting Attitudes: During and After Crisis

In the immediate aftermath of crises, followers tend to accept, even to insist upon, stringent constraints that they had rejected in more tranquil days. During the 2000 presidential campaign, pollsters reported that voters were expressing increased discomfort about invasion of their personal privacy by businesses and government. Yet in the two days following the 2001 World Trade Center attack, the *New York Times* and CBS News polls indicated that 74 percent of those questioned said they "believed that Americans would have to 'give up some personal freedoms in order to make the country safe from terrorist attacks.' "[39] Within a week, that number rose to 79 percent. Two days after the attack, the same poll revealed that 39 percent of the respondents expressed a willingness to allow regular governmental monitoring of ordinary citizens' e-mail and telephone conversations. A week later, the ranks of the willing swelled to 45 percent. A hefty 56 percent supported the introduction of national electronic ID cards.

That, however, is not the whole story. When calm returns, citizens in a democracy begin to chafe under the limitations on their civil rights. Nonetheless, civil liberties curtailed in the heat of a crisis are difficult to reclaim from legislative entombment. For example, two years after the Oklahoma City attack, a Pew Research Center poll revealed that the percentage of respondents who saw the necessity for limiting their civil liberties had fallen from 49 percent to 29 percent.[40] The same pattern occurred in the post-McCarthy period.

Freedom of Speech: An Endangered Species?

Even freedom of speech, so pivotal to democracy, can rather quickly become an endangered species during a crisis. Groupthink, the premature rush to consensus, tends to germinate in a crisis milieu, as many leaders belatedly discover.[41]

Those who speak out against a leader's decisions during anxiety-ridden times often bear the wrath of self-appointed watchdogs of conformity. One such group, the American Council of Trustees and Alumni (ACTA), issued a report two months after the World Trade Center attack. In that report, ACTA cited university administrators, faculty, students, and even visiting speakers for expressing their dissent about the war in Afghanistan. Not only did the report name and blame individuals for criticizing current American policy, but it censured opinions ranging from "[We should] build bridges and relationships, not simply bombs and walls" to "[B]reak the cycle of violence" and "[I]gnorance breeds hate." The report, entitled "Defending Civilization: How Our Universities Are Failing America and What Can Be Done About It," criticized a campus sign stating, "Hate breeds hate," as well as one quoting part of Mohandas K. Gandhi's well-known observation "An eye for an eye soon makes the whole world blind." In an ironic twist, the authors reproached the minions of academia for allegedly criticizing our political leaders, but then, in the only sentence in the report underlined for emphasis, they insisted that "academic freedom does not mean freedom from criticism."

This crisis-stimulated willingness, even furor, to curtail personal liberties nourishes the toxic inclinations of some leaders. We often leave important decisions completely to strong leaders because we succumb to the illusions that they "know better than we do" and they "can keep us safe." Although this strategy may temporarily temper our anxieties, it also flirts dangerously with toxicity. Clearly, we need to ponder deeply how to establish effective security in times of crisis without allowing our leaders, well-meaning or deliberately toxic, to overstep the bounds that characterize a democratic, free society.

Nontoxic Leaders Can Play a Positive Role

Within the context of crisis, leaders have a special function: to interpret the changing, often painful reality. That reality frequently threatens to drown us in ambiguity and situational fears. Good leaders interpret the world as factually as possible, without feeding our illusions, but also without undermining our motivation to persist. In the days immediately following the attack on the World Trade Center, Mayor Giuliani did precisely that. He realistically described the unthinkable destruction while still holding out determined hope.

Such leaders can reinforce or, in unusual circumstances, even change the culture. They do not use our thirst for illusions to mislead us into a false sense of security. Good leaders articulate the dangers, but they also suggest constructive ways in which we, not just they, can address them.

Foresighted and courageous leaders may take some steps to limit the damage from inevitable future natural disasters, as Mayor Dianne Feinstein did with a pre–Loma Prieta earthquake retrofit of Candlestick Park. Still, because such events resist exact prediction, leaders cannot totally immunize their followers against these devastating events. Nonetheless, despite the leader's human limitations, followers continue to want leaders to protect them from forces beyond anyone's control.

Symbolic Acts

While they rarely can prevent such disasters, leaders' symbolic acts in times of disaster can spread a healing balm. Those leaders who fail to visit the scene of a catastrophe create a lasting impression of callous indifference and impotence. Some political analysts suggest that former President Clinton's words of comfort to the survivors of natural and human-generated disasters—such as the November 1999 earthquake in Turkey and the April 1995 bombing of the Oklahoma City federal building—were among his most significant acts. In the postquake days, Clinton comforted nine thousand Turks in a muddy tent camp huddling in the rain: "Keep your spirits up, keep the smiles on your children's faces, keep helping the people who lost their loved ones in the earthquake . . . And know that together we will get through this to better days."[42] Leaders who empathically "feel our pain" *do* help to relieve our anxiety during crisis, despite the media's skepticism.

In the aftermath of the 1984 chemical disaster in Bhopal, India,

Warren Anderson, CEO of Union Carbide, flew to the scene to console traumatized employees and their families. Although the Indian government arrested him and his entourage, Anderson earned high marks from his employees, if not from less personally involved academic and media critics.[43]

Yet a note of caution: Toxic leaders are always nearby, just waiting for their chance to take control. Their magical solutions and illusions of omnipotence can be particularly seductive in uncertain times. When they offer us the chance for ennoblement, they may be irresistible.

Crisis, as the Chinese ideogram indicates, entails both risk and opportunity. For current leaders who cannot cope, crisis may undo them. For other sitting leaders, particularly those who are foundering, crisis can help them establish a new agenda, find their direction, and renew their credibility. Crisis also sets the stage for the emergence of new leaders, charismatic and other would-be heroic leaders, posing radical solutions. Crisis also makes us vulnerable to toxic leaders, who use such occasions to introduce authoritarianism.

In the next chapter, let's examine how, in an incomplete world, our need for self-esteem, driven by society's achievement ethic, saps our resistance to toxic leaders.

6

An Unfinished and Unfinishable World: Self-Esteem, the Achievement Ethic, and the Call to Heroism

Man is perishable. That may be, but let us perish resisting, and, if nothing is what awaits us, let us not act in such a way that it would be a just fate.
—Étienne Pivert de Sénancour

Within our contradiction-riddled world, we confront an acute dilemma, a dilemma stemming from the frustrations of our human condition. We exist in a physical body destined for the ash heap, while our spirit craves a different destiny, that is, eternal life.

Rationally, we recognize there is no hope that our bodies can live forever, so we reach instead for symbolic immortality: living on in the minds of future generations. To be worthy of such symbolic immortality, we know, we must do or be something that exceeds the limits of ordinary human achievement, something truly heroic. An Albert Einstein, a Marie Curie, a William Shakespeare, an Abraham Lincoln, a Martin Luther King Jr., a Susan B. Anthony, a Mohandas K. Gandhi—all continue to have a powerful presence for generations unborn during their lifetimes.

To gauge how closely we approach such heroic proportions, we measure our unique strengths and talents against the standards our society sets for outstanding achievement in various fields. Our self-esteem, that sense of ourselves as worthy beings, grows or diminishes at every encounter with society's exacting achievement standards. Yet the world in which we keep trying to achieve poses monumental challenges that confound our quest.

An Unfinished and Unfinishable World

As if the daily tension between certainty and uncertainty, physical existence and immortality were not enough to complicate our lives, still another feature of the world adds to our challenge. We live in an *unfinished* world, with so much still to be done—diseases to be conquered, poverty overcome, peace secured, if only somewhere, for some time. Within this incomplete arena, we are called to action. The unfinished world incites us to take it one or two steps closer to completion, to enhance it through our own heroic efforts. In this amphitheater of life, we draw upon our talents and yearning for self-esteem to help meet that challenge. In so doing, perchance we can achieve immortality.

The challenge to complete this unfinished world can never be totally met for several reasons. First, it is unfulfillable because every step toward completion punctures another illusion about our previous knowledge or limits of achievement. Each new planet that we discover tells us there might be more somewhere out there in the vast universe. Every shattered Olympic record teaches us that what we previously thought was the absolute limit of human physical endurance or skill was not. Thus, each new fragment undoes a piece that we thought was finished.

As we put this new knowledge or accomplishment in place, we realize that there are other parts yet to be discovered or achieved to solve even that small section of the puzzle. Consequently, to complete such a world requires unceasing labor at a monumental, undoable task. We are Sisyphus redux, forever pushing an immense rock up the side of a mountain, only to have it roll down again.

Second, the unfinished world cannot be completed because some things may simply be unknowable or undoable. There are moments when even the most sophisticated among us mistakenly think we have reached the ultimate point of completion in a particular field. Thus, for example, Thomas Watson Jr., CEO of IBM, reportedly stated in 1941, "I think there is a world market for about five computers." Several decades later, in 1977, Ken Olsen, founder of Digital Equipment Corporation, insisted, "There is no reason anyone would want a computer in their home." And as late as 1981, none other than Bill Gates of Microsoft declared, "640K ought to be enough for anybody."[1]

An intriguing article by Sharon Begley in the "Science Journal" section of the *Wall Street Journal* discusses the work of several renowned mathematicians—Kurt Gödel, Alan Turing, and Gregory Chaitin. Their research suggests that some aspects of the world may actually be unknowable.[2] Thus, in a second, scientific sense, the world is unfinishable.

Despite earlier optimism that we could measure nature with increasing accuracy, Czech-born mathematician and logician Kurt Gödel stunned the mathematical world in 1931 by proving that "within a formal system questions exist that are neither provable nor disprovable on the basis of the axioms that define the system."[3] Mathematicians recognize this as Gödel's undecidability theorem. Gödel also stated his incompleteness theorem, which says that in some complex systems in which decidability of *all* questions is required, there will be contradictory statements. Taken together, Gödel's theorems suggest a startling conclusion: Some problems simply *can't* be solved by existing rules. Such problems require a more complex set of axioms. "Some statements in mathematics can be neither proved nor disproved."[4]

Later, British mathematician Alan Turing took another important step, proving that some numbers and functions can't be computed by any logical machine. And still more recently, IBM mathematician Gregory Chaitin has shown that Gödel's and Turing's work make it clear that there are fundamental limits in mathematics. In other words:

> You might be able to prove every conceivable statement about numbers within a system by going outside the system in order to come up with new rules and axioms, but by doing so you'll only create a larger system with its own unprovable statements. The implication is that all logical systems of any complexity are, by definition, incomplete.[5]

So there may be some things about the world that are simply unknowable and therefore unfinishable.

Third, the world is endlessly unfinishable in still another sense: Each age brings its own, unprecedented challenges. In our great-grandparents' era, for example, our limited knowledge of kidney disease meant that nephritis carried a death sentence. End of discussion. No bioethicists were needed to deal with this issue. In fact, the field of bioethics didn't exist until the early 1970s.[6] When technological advances eventually led to kidney transplants and dialysis treatment, new pieces of the kidney disease minipuzzle fell into place. In the wake of these breakthroughs, the bioethical challenge emerged: how to allocate the scarce resources of kidney dialysis treatments and organ donations. So those new "solutions" merely point to new, unfinished problems for our generation, or perhaps our children's or our grandchildren's, to resolve.

An Unfinishable World and the Call to Heroic Action

All the questions left unanswered by the incompleteness and the unknowability of our world exacerbate our existential angst and goad us to seek answers to what all this means. What is the meaning of life? What is the meaning of our specific lives? What is the meaning of the unfathomable gaps and inconsistencies we see around us? We witness immense wealth alongside immense poverty, and we see that great happiness is neighbor to great despair. Nor is it particularly obvious why the harvest of the world goes to some and the husks to others. Real estate magnate Donald Trump reportedly counts his net worth at over $3 billion.[7] Mary Smith and José Espinosa, the local math teachers, estimate theirs as not worth estimating.

Leaders call us to address the unfinished pieces of the world. To complete one minute fragment, to remove just one imperfection, big or small, be it cancer or a run-down neighborhood park, would be a worthy achievement. And these grand accomplishments open a symbolic way to transcend our inevitable physical death and earn immortality. That is where our nagging self-esteem comes into play. For it is self-esteem that provides the engine of our response.

Yet the challenges leaders identify in an uncertain and unfinished world don't yield to easy solutions. In fact, the conditions we have been considering—uncertainty, chaos, crises, contradictions, and an incomplete world—can lead to great glory or desperate disgrace. When our own efforts to rise to these critical challenges fall short, we look to others who convince us that they are up to the task and that they can show us how. By joining their team, we can share in their glory. Thus the stage is set for our submission to toxic leaders, leaders who call us to tasks they hold out as noble, but only later reveal their poisonous underbellies.

The Achievement Ethic

Each society sets its own achievement ethic by which we measure our self-worth and assess the meaning of our lives. When we exceed that standard, we rise above the crowd. Others look to us for guidance. Having vaulted over the high bar of achievement, we believe in ourselves. We feel less dependent on leaders who promise us fulfillment and safety.

Yet the bar can be set so high that it is impossible to reach. Then we are in danger of looking to others who say they can do it, who seem larger than life, and who promise us greatness we cannot achieve on our own.

Social and behavioral scientists have long studied the need for achievement in individuals and families, as well as in cross-cultural perspective.[8] In general, they have focused on achievement as a positive value, the more the better. This fascination with achievement can be read as a reflection of how pervasively the culture values it and, by association, also values leadership that embodies and endorses achievement.

Our internalized achievement ethic is one of many *psychosocial* forces that influence our susceptibility to leaders. I label such forces "psychosocial" because they result from the interplay between our own internal needs and the external world.

Each society, as we have seen, fashions its own achievement ethic, defining which accomplishments and how much of those deeds shall be treated as real achievements. In one society, amassing a collection of cowrie shells represents the acme of achievement; in another, physical prowess or spiritual serenity is the top rung. In still other groups, leadership of a corporate giant and a jet-set life style connote success. Whatever the exact nature of our society's achievement ethic, when we internalize it and make it our own, it becomes the standard against which we measure our personal performance.

Taken to a reasonable level, a society's achievement ethic motivates its members to reach for the pinnacle. Unfortunately, it is often pushed obsessively by well-meaning caretakers and others, who urge us to perform far beyond that level. Then our lives become driven and distorted into an endless pursuit of unattainable achievements. In an effort to have her youngster, Justin, declared "the smartest little boy in the world," Elizabeth Chapman, a twenty-nine-year-old single mom, created a bogus intelligence record for him, including the highest IQ score ever achieved (298-plus).[9] She also enticed the hapless youngster into cheating. The hoax was uncovered only when the eight-year-old, by then a minor celebrity, was admitted to a psychiatric hospital with signs of severe emotional distress.

Our self-esteem, lashed to an obsession with achievement, leads us to another paradox with which we humans must wrestle: how to be truly human, that is, how to be genuinely unique, while still living comfortably, even heroically, within the approving gaze of society that sets a common standard. Satisfying that paradox entails a difficult balancing act. Later, we shall explore how we attempt this feat: either by reaching for leadership through our own actions, that is, by becoming a leader or joining forces with one, or by performing in some other heroic fashion.

The achievement ethic acts as a psychosocial force that increases our vulnerability to leaders, good, bad, and in between. Generally, if our own accomplishments meet or exceed the standard set by our society, we feel rather good about ourselves. We may even believe we are worthy of a leading role in our part of the universe, be that the local high school or the world stage. If we are not up to the challenge or if others perform far better than we can, we tend to regard those high achievers as superior to us.

Apparently, even established scholars, such as historians Stephen E. Ambrose and Doris Kearns Goodwin, have succumbed to the siren call of the achievement ethic.[10] First Ambrose and then Goodwin admitted that large portions of their highly acclaimed works were plagiarized—unwittingly, they both avow—from other authors.

Vicarious Heroes

Because high achievers astound us by surpassing the previously set standards, we bestow on them the accolade of "hero" or "genius." We pin gold medals on their chests. We honor them with ticker-tape parades. We confer Nobel prizes on them. We accept their right to lead. Recognizing the superiority of these outstanding achievers, we seek vicarious heroism by identifying with them. If we can somehow become part of their spectacular accomplishment, by joining their entourage, their organization, their fan club, or their mass following, then some of their heroism rubs off on us.

Even when these heroic leaders move beyond acceptable behavior, we often tolerate it, either as their entitlement or as evidence of our inability to stop them. If we decide they are geniuses, despite the lack of any confirmatory metric, we endow them with the right to eccentricities from simple bad manners to uncontrollable rage or authoritarian hauteur.[11] Then, in a curious tautological dynamic, we use their eccentricities as evidence of their genius. We also frequently pay the price for simply being in their presence. At least until we decide the price is too high.

We bestow the title "genius" on individuals in all manner of fields, from football coaches such as the Rams' Mike Martz and the Patriots' Bill Belichek to corporate leaders such as DBL's Michael Milken, composers such as Wolfgang Amadeus Mozart, artists such as Pablo Picasso, and symphony conductors such as

Charles Dutoit. Belichek's father, a former football coach, responded to a *New York Times* headline heralding his son as a "defensive genius" by saying that "genius" was a strange label for "somebody who walks up and down a football field."[12]

Some "geniuses," however, blend toxicity with genius. During twenty-five years as music director of the Montreal Symphony Orchestra, Dutoit brought the orchestra to international prominence, while his autocratic demeanor "earned the fear and respect of audiences, musicians, politicians, and journalists."[13] Only after several musicians felt they had been publicly humiliated once too often did they join forces to revolt against the maestro.

The Downside of the Achievement Ethic

This worship of achievement is a widespread phenomenon, coloring many seemingly different societies. Parents and teachers, as well as religious and political leaders, endorse it. This dedication to achievement persists despite the recognition that in some achievement-driven societies, the failure to accomplish can bring about dire consequences. In Japan, for example, denial of admission to top-level universities has led many adolescent students to suicide. In such group-oriented societies, inability to achieve is viewed as far more than an individual matter. Failure to excel reflects upon the entire family. Competition, of course, remains a favored path to outstanding achievement. It is the sine qua non for proving superior worth to oneself and others.[14]

The Religious Symbolism of Money

Ernest Becker's recognition of the downside to achievement striving provides a much-needed antidote to our addictive quest for success.[15] According to Becker, societies create ideologies that allow us to devote ourselves to our own immortality. Money, a convenient metric for comparing our accomplishments to others', can become the "universal immortality ideology."[16] Money, the ultimate measure of achievement for many, in turn, translates into power.

> All power is in essence power to deny mortality. . . . Power means power to increase oneself, to change one's natural situation from one of smallness, helplessness, finitude, to one of bigness, control, durability, importance. In its power to manipulate physical and social reality, money in some ways secures one against contingency and accident; it buys body-guards, bullet-proof glass, and better medical care. Most of all, it can be accumulated and passed on, and

so radiates its powers even after one's death, giving one a semblance of immortality as he lives.[17]

Both Max Weber and Becker understood that the pursuit of achievement, measured in money, can be a religiously endorsed method for achieving immortality.[18] The accumulation of money, concrete evidence of achievement and worthiness of immortality, then becomes an endless goal. And money per se provides a clear source of self-esteem. Consequently, to paraphrase the well-known aphorism about being too thin and too rich, one can never have too much money nor too much immortality. And perhaps one reason we do not use our bountiful global resources to eradicate poverty is that we would simultaneously erase our measure of who deserves immortality and who does not.

Need for Self-Esteem

Self-esteem—a sense of our self-worth—is the second psychosocial force, along with the achievement drive, that figures in our vulnerability to toxic leaders. For it is on their glory that we can feed when our self-esteem takes a serious hit in the life-or-death game created by the achievement ethic.

Because we cannot see ourselves directly, we often look to others for their assessment of us. George Cooley called this "the looking-glass self."[19] In part, our self-esteem grows or diminishes in response to our perception of how others evaluate us against society's yardstick.

Self-esteem provides the armature to which we attach the clay of our personalities. Without it, we lack the capacity to know who we are, what we want, and how to go about achieving our goals, be they noble or mundane. Psychologist Abraham Maslow proposed that the need for a "stable, firmly based, usually high evaluation of themselves, for self-respect or self-esteem, and the esteem of others" is an important component in human beings' "hierarchy of needs."[20]

Parents as well as alternative early caretakers and, later, teachers and other mentors play an important role in shaping our sense of self-worth. True, loving parents and supportive teachers who applaud our efforts nurture the germ of our self-esteem. Yet there is more to the self-esteem story.

We build our self-esteem gradually through our interactions, positive and negative, with those around us, from the sandbox to the corner office suite. Our encounters, both good and bad, with our external environment force us to revise and clarify our sense of ourselves. As we move through the world, we bring our talents, skills, and abilities to bear in different situations. The outcome of each encounter leaves its mark, some more intense and longer-lasting than others, on our self-esteem.

Self-esteem, then, develops in response not only to the mélange of messages we receive from early caretakers and the larger society, but also to our own experiences of success and failure.

Each of us probably can remember, in sharp detail, situations long past in which we felt humiliated by a failure or elated by a success. As the research on "bad is stronger than good" suggests, however, we probably still feel the sting of our past defeats far more acutely than the ecstasy that followed a job well done. The memory of a bad grade on a math test or a missed field goal can still bring a heavy thud to our stomachs.

We enhance our self-esteem by personal accomplishments in athletics, academia, the professions, the arts, politics, the military, community activities, and many other fields. Each time we succeed, measured against the cultural norms by which we evaluate ourselves, our self-esteem increases. When we fail, our self-esteem suffers a blow, sometimes temporary, at other times long-lasting.

We look to the culture, that symbolic theater of action, for the standards against which to measure our accomplishments.[21] When we meet or exceed those ideals, we temporarily satisfy our insatiable desire to be significant individuals in a meaningful world. Extraordinary success puts us in line for immortality. Still, Becker reminds us that culture promotes the lie that we can transcend death by great acts of achievement, with leadership serving as a prime vehicle. And it is leaders, often toxic leaders, who purvey that elixir of immortality to their followers.

When We Don't Measure Up

In very complex ways, self-esteem propels us, as adults, to seek the leader within us. When we fail or when we doubt our capacity to succeed, we look to others who we think are more up to the challenge. Often, from our front-row seat within a leader's entourage, we learn from observing the leader. We perceive how to behave in ways that enhance our self-esteem.

Leaders customarily challenge us to reach goals that seem beyond our grasp. If we succeed, we may expect notable rewards. Sometimes, when we cannot meet the cultural standards of our leader or group, we may opt to define ourselves in direct opposition to them. Then we assume the role of social outcast, an isolate who purposely rejects what society asks of us. At other times, when we perceive the group's behavior and values as cynical or corrupt, we may choose to reach for a higher personal standard. Then we become the "outsider within" and perhaps eventually a whistle-blower or maybe the leader of a revolution intended to set things right.

When we cannot reach the standard the culture sets for us, we may alternatively turn to a leader who reassures us that those demands are irrelevant, bogus, or oppressive. Because our self-esteem has suffered a blow, we are particularly vulnerable to leaders who claim that the norms of their group are far more meaningful and, indeed, justified by the vacuous or belittling standards of the group by whom we feel rejected. In this new context, our self-esteem experiences a growth spurt. The leader promotes alternative standards, justifying behavior that is countercultural, anticultural, sometimes even criminal. In this way, the David Koreshes and the Charles Mansons of the world attract devotees to the Branch Davidians or the "family."

When we become convinced that we ourselves cannot be heroic, we begin to look for others who can. Perhaps by attaching ourselves to them, by pledging allegiance to their cause, we can satisfy our unfulfilled yearnings for ever more self-esteem and our insatiable need for achievement. This reverence for their superiority, along with our loss of faith in our own abilities, contributes to our reluctance to overthrow leaders, even when we recognize they are or have become toxic.

The Extremes of Self-Esteem: Where Do They Come From?

We tend to think that high self-esteem comes from supportive caretakers and success experiences. In some cases, however, extremes of self-esteem develop as a defense against an *un*supportive or even an abusive environment. Oprah Winfrey, for example, survived an early childhood stalked by poverty and a molesting male relative. Despite those difficulties, Winfrey told an interviewer, "All my life I have always known I was born to greatness."[22]

Extremes of self-esteem—at the high or the low end—can lead us into the wilderness of leadership. Our self-esteem may be so inflated that we believe, from early on, that we are "destined" to be leaders. Anecdotes abound describing Winston Churchill's long-held belief that his destiny was to become Great Britain's prime minister—this despite a childhood burdened by a denigrating father, an inattentive mother, and unimpressed teachers. Piers Brendon describes Churchill's behavior at country weekend parties, where he routinely bored party guests with long tirades about his expectations for greatness.[23]

At the other extreme—low self-esteem—we may feel unable to rely on ourselves for anything constructive. This searing lack can drive us in two related directions. On one hand, some individuals who early on suffer damage to their self-esteem may devote their lives to evoking the approval of others, engaging, if necessary, in exceptional heroics. Woodrow Wilson, another youngster who felt the pangs of paternal disapproval, offers us a clear example of such a scenario. Wilson wove his need to prove his worth into an adolescent obsession to become a great political leader. Alexander and Juliette George describe Wilson's early feelings of inadequacy and the spur they created for his later relentless pursuit of a heroic dream: "Had he as a boy felt unimportant? Then anything he or anyone else could do to convince him that he was uniquely qualified to accomplish great things—perhaps even something immortal—would be a balm."[24]

On the other hand, as we have seen, the lack of self-esteem prompts many other individuals to seek a strong leader, no matter how toxic, to provide substance and guidance in their lives. One terrifying example: the Manson family. Some members of the Manson family, including Linda Kasabian, reported they believed its leader, Charles Manson, to be Jesus Christ.[25] Identifying with a powerful leader takes up the slack by helping the follower develop a derived sense of heroic worth.

The Incomplete World and the Call to Heroism

The incompleteness of the world presents ample opportunities for us to make important, sometimes heroic contributions, often at the urging of visionary leaders. And since we, along with the world in which we live, are incomplete, we may seize the chance to complete ourselves by heroic action. In the process, we take some small step toward finishing a piece of the world. Or so we think.

At times, the yearning for heroism can result in misbegotten or even disastrous acts. Senator Bob Kerrey earned the Medal of Honor for his service in Vietnam. Yet Kerrey and his small squad of Navy Seals remain haunted by the nightmare of their 1969 commando massacre in an isolated rural village in the eastern Mekong Delta. They cannot forget that on one harrowing night more than three decades ago, they violently murdered a hamlet of civilians, including children and grown women—one reportedly pregnant. Nor have their victims' families escaped their own lingering anguish, imposed on them by "heroes."

Yet, heroic achievements and self-esteem have a positive side as well. They hold a piece of the puzzle that can untether us from toxic leaders. They are the core ingredients in the mix that enables us to stand up to and even unseat toxic leaders. So there is far more to the story.

In sum, the interplay of these internal, external, and psychosocial forces leaves us exquisitely susceptible to toxic leaders. We accept our "Velcro" relationship to these leaders because it feeds multiple needs—some apparent, others less obvious—that I shall explore more deeply in the chapters to follow. These needs, however, often obscure their inevitable hidden costs.

The Choices We Make

In *The Connective Edge*, I wrote about the choices we make whenever we act.[26] Such choices reflect different desires and calculations that may oscillate, over the course of our development, between our personal interests and those of others. We make such choices either in terms of what Stanford professor James March calls a "logic of consequences," that is, the outcomes we may calculate or expect to produce the greatest value, or what he terms a "logic of appropriateness," that is, the outcomes appropriate to our truest personal identity.[27]

To complete ourselves in ways that tell us what kind of a person we are and what that kind of a person does in any particular situation, our actions must match our conception of the best self we can be. And that is where self-esteem becomes pivotal, for to act in any way less than our best self would act is to limit or damage our self-esteem. Reaching for that optimum expression of self is one path to heroism. According to March, "In the end, perhaps, humans establish their claims to uniqueness not so much by responding to the demands of consequences as by responding to the demands of identity."[28]

The visions of toxic leaders usually stop shy of calling forth our best self. Although they might have the ring of heroism or the grandeur of a Wagnerian opera, they focus primarily on the collective self or our chosen group. The toxic leader's vision rings of exclusivity and narrowness. It may demand "purity," but that faultlessness is not derived from self-improvement. Rather, this purity usually calls for removing the stain of the Other. In its grandiosity, the toxic leader's vision may appeal to our sense of the heroic. Look more closely, and we see an empty heroism that makes us seem great at the expense of making others seem small. Another illusion, at best.

~

In an unfinished and seemingly unfinishable world, much remains to be done. So it is perfectly natural for us to help complete that world by taking on the challenges our culture poses.

Besides articulating these challenges, the culture also espouses an achievement ethic, urging us on to great accomplishments. When we don't measure up to society's standards, we look to others whose demonstrated superiority moves us to regard them as leaders and heroes. When these outstanding individuals engage in toxic behavior, our uncritical awe, coupled with the awareness of our own inability to challenge them, leads us to accept, even admire, them.

While self-esteem and the achievement ethic add important pieces to the puzzle of why we tolerate toxic leaders, they do not complete it. We need to seek other pieces in the rationalizations and control myths by which followers persuade themselves they cannot topple a toxic leader. Let's start that search in Chapter 7.

III

HOW WE CREATE WILLING FOLLOWERS AND TOXIC LEADERS

7

Rationalizations and Control Myths: Keeping Toxic Leaders in Power

Leaders serve many purposes for their followers. If they didn't, we wouldn't yearn for them, seek them out, or even create them when they don't exist. So it is quite understandable that followers are loath to give them up, even when they are less—often far less—than perfect. In fact, this chapter is devoted to exploring how we work on our own minds and hearts to keep toxic leaders in power.

In contrast to constructive leaders who toil relentlessly to steer the vessel on a straight course, toxic leaders may or may not keep the ship afloat. Yet we keep selecting them despite their poor performance. Al Dunlap's record serves as a case in point: "[T]hroughout his career, the companies he worked for tended to disappear after he left. In almost every case in which Dunlap occupied a leadership position, the companies were sold or liquidated."[1]

Toxic leaders, such as Dunlap, often push us in negative directions, diminish us, and leave us worse off than when they found us. We may complain about them, but we rarely unseat them, regardless of how toxic they are.

Even when Enron employees found their retirement accounts in shambles as the company's stock plummeted, they continued to support their leaders. Many kept purchasing stock on the advice of chairman Kenneth Lay, who urged them to buy (and to recommend the stock to their friends and relatives) at the once-in-a-lifetime bargain price, which, Lay insisted, was bound to go up. Only on the day that Jeff Skilling resigned did Enron vice president Sherron Watkins send an anonymous memo to Lay about improper accounting practices that concealed over $1 billion in company debt. In that memo and subsequent nonanonymous ones, Watkins's major concern was the risk to Enron that public discovery would bring. She now regrets "naively [thinking] that I would be handing Ken Lay his leadership moment."[2] Even when Watkins testified before the House Energy and Commerce Subcommittee on Oversight and Investigations, she still portrayed former Enron CEO Kenneth Lay simply as a blameless dupe of Jeffrey Skilling, former COO, and former CFO Andrew Fastow, as if such gross incompetence, without deliberate duplicity, were not sufficient to label a leader "toxic."

Dennis Kozlowski pilfered Tyco's coffers for close to a decade, but no one stopped him, either, until he hit the $600 million mark. And, remarkably, two years after Drexel Burnham Lambert lay in ruins, Michael Milken's employees, many still jobless, vigorously defended their former leader on Phil Donahue's TV talk show.

In the nonprofit and political arenas, too, we have similar evidence. It took decades—in fact, almost half a century—for lay members of the Catholic Church in Boston to call for the ouster of toxic religious leaders involved in the sexual molestation of hundreds of young parishioners.

Since we see similar behavior among followers in different contexts, we have to believe it is *not* something special about the corporate world, the political process, or the church hierarchy that keeps their toxic leaders in power. If we were just considering political leaders, we might argue that they have the power of the military, an intelligence agency, a police force, or all three behind them. But a 3 a.m. phone call from Harold Geneen, CEO of ITT for eighteen years, inquiring about some number on a senior executive's quarterly report, allegedly made the hapless individual on the other end of the line break out in a cold sweat.[3] Despite the lack of an FBI or a military force, let's not underestimate the power that control over formal and informal corporate resources, as well as the authority to demote, promote, and fire, brings to a business leader. Nor are religious institutions without their own means of intimidation. Still, there is far more to the story than toxic leaders simply using the resources at their command to intimidate followers, although toxic leaders do not shy away from such action.

To discover why followers allow toxic leaders to remain in power, we need to consider the followers' reactions. In Part II, we examined how leaders come to power by addressing their followers' needs, from their existential angst to various strands of their psychological motives and the cultural expectations that shape their behavior. Here, I want to move into new territory, to explore those rationalizations and what I shall call "control myths," which convince followers that they can't or shouldn't even try to topple a toxic leader once in power.

Most important, we shall see how these rationalizations and particularly the control myths are inextricably linked to our existential fears as well as to our psychological needs. They are also intertwined with our self-esteem and the achievement ethic of our particular culture, two critical factors that grow from the interplay of our unique internal needs and the demands of the world in which we live. And, as we might have guessed, they connect to the hierarchy of needs described by psychologist Abraham Maslow. This complex set of needs, cultural norms, rationalizations, and control myths imprisons us in an invisible suit of armor from which it is virtually impossible to break free.

The Major Rationalizations

Those of us who have experienced life under a toxic leader, be it a boss, a spouse, or a political ruler, know how difficult it is to escape.[4] There are many reasons that we give ourselves and others for why we put up with bad leaders. Since at the outset of this journey we agreed to delve into discomforting topics in a straightforward way, let's be up front with ourselves and recognize these reasons for what they are: *rationalizations*, those explanations we give ourselves for why we *can* or *cannot* act.

In the research for this book, I repeatedly asked the people I interviewed why they stayed in organizations where they were subjected to a toxic leader. The same rationalizations recurred with the regularity of the tides. The rationalizations that we followers give ourselves eventually harden into *control myths*: those beliefs we solemnly hold about why we *should* or *should not* act. These beliefs then rigidify within our superegos, where they set up shop to control our behavior.

The rationalizations are on the tip of every oppressed person's tongue. They are the spontaneous answers we hear when we ask, "Why did you put up with such a leader?" To set these rationalizations and the other needs we discussed earlier within the larger framework of human needs, let's take a short side trip into some well-known work on human motivation: Abraham Maslow's hierarchy of needs.

Maslow's Hierarchy of Needs: A Lens for Viewing Control Myths

Abraham Maslow's hierarchy of needs provides a lens through which we can sharpen our view of these rationalizations that ultimately crystallize into control myths.[5] Although most readers may be familiar with Maslow's thinking, it might be worth an abbreviated reminder here, since the various levels in the hierarchy are relevant to the psychological, existential, and psychosocial needs we described in earlier chapters. Those with fresher memories of Maslow's work can just skip ahead.

Maslow distinguished between two gross categories of human motivation: deficiency needs and growth needs. The deficiency needs begin with physiological needs, such as hunger, thirst, and other bodily requirements. Maslow saw safety or security needs as the next level of deficiencies calling for satisfaction. Belonging and love needs, that is, the need to be part of a group, to be accepted and to associate with others, are the next step up the hierarchy. After that come the esteem needs, the needs for approval and recognition.

According to Maslow's epigenetic framework, we must meet our deficiency needs before we can begin to address our higher-level growth needs. That is to say, each stage or level of need must reach a reasonable degree of satisfaction before we can proceed to the next stage, except in unusual circumstances. For example, followers who are hungry, endangered, isolated, or imbued with a sense of self-disdain can hardly be expected to worry about reading Shakespeare, much less developing the ego strength and maturity necessary to cast off the oppression of a toxic leader. And let's also remember that the hierarchical sequence is not set in stone. In fact, Maslow describes various conditions under which the degree of satisfaction or the ordering of the needs may not be exactly as he delineated them.[6]

The need for self-actualization sat at the top of the pyramid in Maslow's original hierarchy. Maslow understood self-actualization as a continuing appreciation of life, a problem orientation (versus an ego orientation), and a focus on personal growth, as well as the ability to enjoy peak experiences.[7] Most of us probably recall Maslow's appealing description of self-actualizers as individuals who not only accept themselves with all their warts but also seek to realize their full potential. They act spontaneously and creatively, gustily pursuing their own interests. These attractive qualities of the self-actualizer often are associated with the need for privacy and an untroubled detachment from the opinions of other people.

In 1971, however, Maslow revised his concept of the growth needs in two important ways.[8] First, he identified two lower levels of needs *below* self-actualization—cognitive and aesthetic needs.[9] Second, he differentiated a level *beyond* self-actualization, one that is particularly relevant here: transcendence.

In this significant reconceptualization of the hierarchy of needs, Maslow introduced transcendence as the ultimate level of growth beyond self-actualization. Transcendence, for Maslow, encompasses the need to rise above the interests of the self, to find fulfillment in helping others reach *their* potential. Transcendence, according to Maslow, involves at least thirty-five dimensions, ranging from self-forgetfulness to "transcendence of ego, self, selfishness, ego-centering, etc., when we respond to the demand character of external tasks, causes, duties, responsibilities to others and to the world of reality."[10]

In terms of the issues raised in this book, we recognize transcendence as the stage at which people are ready to move beyond the narrow, albeit compelling, concerns and aspirations they have for themselves and their loved ones. At that point, they are prepared to respond to the call of something greater: a truly noble vision. Such lofty visions often define a larger enterprise that aims at some unfinished aspect of the world.

People who manage to reach this level of transcendence are able to forgo their own personal interests and self-concerns. They behave in a state that Maslow called "self-forgetfulness."[11] Instead of focusing on their own needs, even on self-actualization, they strive to help rectify the deficiencies of other individuals and groups. They have no need to differentiate between "us and them."[12] In our terms, they are ready and eager to complete some unfinished segment of the world.

Back to the Rationalizations

Bearing Maslow's revised hierarchy in mind, let's return to the rationalizations followers use to let toxic leaders continue to do as they please. Since rationalizations propagate more quickly than we can count them, let's simply pick a handful of the most common ones to inspect more closely.

I have grouped these rationalizations roughly according to Maslow's hierarchy of needs. Let's examine each one first as it is commonly or colloquially labeled, and then as we might translate it into a toxic leadership perspective.

Physiological needs (hunger, thirst, bodily comforts, and so on)

- "This job puts a roof over my kids' heads and pays the bills." (Translation: *Submitting to the toxic leader provides critical resources.*)

- "Other jobs are scarce right now." (Translation: *Alternative resources are difficult to find.*)

Safety needs (security from danger)

- "The last person who tried to confront the leader got fired." (Translation: *Attempting to oppose or unseat the leader is too risky, because, if I don't succeed, I may be undone in the process.*)

- "We're in a difficult period right now, so I guess I'll have to hang in for the moment." (Translation: *There are serious issues, even crises, to be addressed that loom larger than toppling the leader. This is too dangerous a time to confront the leader.*)

- "In fact, the current leader isn't so bad after all. We could easily get someone much worse." (Translation: *The devil I know is better than the one I don't.*)

Need for belonging and love; need for self-esteem (need to affiliate with others and be accepted; need to be competent, to be approved and recognized)

- "Everyone else seems to think the leader is great." (Translation: *There isn't enough support from like-minded people, and if I go against what the group seems to want, I'll be ostracized.*)

- "I can't do it all by myself." (Translation: *Unseating the leader is too difficult and requires more effort than I can muster.*)

Cognitive needs (need to know and understand; need to explore and find meaning)

- "Who would replace him/her?" (Translation: *There isn't any-one more competent to replace the leader.*)

- "The situation is so complex." (Translation: *The leader will explain and help me to understand; I'd better not change horses in midstream when I don't understand the whole situation.*)

Aesthetic needs (need for symmetry, beauty, and order)

- "Things are out of control. We need the leader to put things in order." (Translation: *The abundance of change, chaos, and ambiguity in the world overwhelms us with situational fears that a parental surrogate, such as the leader, can calm.*)

Need for self-actualization (need for self-fulfillment)

- "I have so much on my own plate. I don't have time to try to unseat the leader or take over the leader's work." (Translation: *If I unseat the leader, I'll have to forgo my own interests and assume the onerous responsibilities the leader ordinarily carries for the rest of us.*)

Need for transcendence (need to rise above narrow personal considerations, need to transcend time, culture, death)

- "I have everything, but something is missing." (Translation: *I want to find meaning by participating in something greater than myself, in some really important cause, like helping others.*)

Control Myths

The rationalizations that we use to explain to ourselves why we can or can't act are fired in the kiln of our own existential, psychological, and psychosocial needs. They emerge hardened into control myths, deeply held beliefs about what we should or shouldn't do, that freeze us into inaction.

Because we submerge control myths below the surface of consciousness, we rarely notice them at work. They are hard at work nonetheless, nestled in our superegos, keeping us from doing what we have come to believe is wrong or dangerous. We might think of control myths as akin to the code that runs the various computer programs we use: unseen, operating in the background, but directing things regardless. In fact, it might be even more appropriate to think of them as virus-infected programs that gradually degrade what we are trying to do.

We are generally unaware that these control myths are influencing our behavior (although we would recognize them immediately if they bubbled to the surface, as they do in times of stress). Both because of and despite the fact that they travel incognito, these powerful control myths prevent us from even attempting to overthrow toxic leaders.

Just as there are dozens of rationalizations, there are also many control myths. And these control myths, like their more pliable relatives, rationalizations, in most cases can be linked to Maslow's hierarchy. In fact, some control myths reflect more than one level of the hierarchy.

Control myths are so plentiful that we hardly need an exhaustive review to understand how they operate. Instead, let's simply consider six major categories of control myths, each with a few examples, that propagate in the dark waters beneath our awareness: (1) control myths that make us feel both inferior and safe; (2) control myths that instill the fear of repercussions; (3) control myths that would reduce our benefits; (4) control myths that protect the general status quo; (5) control myths that enable us to avoid our own responsibilities as leaders; and (6) control myths that promise ennoblement and immortality.

Control Myths That Make Us Feel Both Inferior and Safe

These control myths are grouped together because they reflect the follower's need for safety, sense of dependency ("love" in Maslow's terminology), and awareness of inferiority to others, particularly someone we consider a leader. These myths also express feelings of incompetence to take on challenging problems or more powerful individuals. For Maslow, such feelings of inadequacy represent an unfulfilled need for self-esteem.[13]

This set of control myths inflates the leader to super-human proportions, indirectly expressing our fears of our own incompetence.

- "The leader is stronger than we are and has more resources." (Safety and self-esteem)

- "The leader knows more than we do." (Safety)

- "The leader has our best interests at heart and can handle tough issues—from budgets to death—that are beyond our ken." (Safety, belonging, and love)

Control Myths That Instill the Fear of Repercussions

These control myths speak about the repercussions that may flow from challenging the leader. They express the fear that any individual who stands up to the leader and fails will suffer reprisals.

Reprisals span a broad spectrum, beginning with the more religious or spiritual fear of being punished by an even higher power and/or being recognized as morally lacking. In addition, there is the fear that a challenger would be exiled from the center of action for trying to overthrow or stymie the leader. If followers join forces with lower-status collaborators, the higher-level followers risk contamination from that association. Or worse yet, they may be ostracized and sentenced to social death.

- "The gods favor the leader, so we risk the gods' anger if we challenge the leader." (Safety, belonging, and love)

- "It is morally wrong to challenge the leader." (Belonging, esteem)

- "An unsuccessful challenge to the leader will result in punishment for the challengers, as well as those they represent." (Safety)

- "If bad things happen from our following the leader, we can't be held to blame." (Safety, belonging, love, and esteem)

- "Those of us closer to the leader should not join forces with other less powerful groups, lest we become contaminated." (Belonging)

Control Myths That Worry About the Followers' Benefits

This set of control myths speaks to the more pragmatic fears of being deprived of the resources that leaders might otherwise make available to their loyalists. These myths focus upon the reduction of current and future benefits that the followers enjoy as steadfast members of the leader's constituency.

- "The leader controls important, scarce resources that we may use only if we remain loyal." (Physiological needs, safety, and belonging)

Control Myths That Protect the General Status Quo

These control myths are based on reverence for the general status quo. They encourage followers to protect the existing social arrangements. They lend legitimacy to the current social stratification system that assigns people and groups to their relative positions in the organization or the larger society. These control myths are linked to Maslow's aesthetic needs for order, symmetry, and beauty.

Because these control myths are in tune with the general cultural ethos of the larger group, be it the company we work for or the larger society to which we belong, they are very hard to oppose. The weight of tradition only adds to their imposing strength.

- "The power relationship with the leader is an unchangeable part of the power structure that we take for granted. That's just the way it is and always has been." The weight of tradition predisposes us, as followers, to see the social structure as a given, with the leaders possessing more power than the followers. (Safety and belonging)

Control Myths That Enable Us to Avoid Our Own Responsibilities as Leaders

These control myths are very useful for convincing us that we don't have to shoulder the difficult tasks of leadership. They allow us to go about our business, to self-actualize to our hearts' content, or at least to the extent allowed by the toxic leader.

- "It's a relief to have the leader take charge so we can 'do our own thing,' without having to take on those odious tasks that inevitably come with power (like developing budgets and attending boring social events). Just let the leader provide the resources for us to do our thing properly, and we'll look the other way when the leader acts inappropriately." (Safety and self-actualization)

Control Myths That Promise Ennoblement and Immortality

These control myths are particularly compelling because they address the most positive aspects of human aspirations: heroism, courage, achievements, and other contributions to humanity. (The earlier ones focused on negative issues, primarily our weaknesses.) The control myths that promise ennoblement and immortality speak to the needs that Maslow describes as self-esteem, self-actualization, and transcendence.[14]

These myths instill us with both courage and encouragement to select some piece of the unfinished world and complete it. They remind us the culture applauds those who respond to the achievement ethic. They promise that our acts of heroism will fill our needs for self-esteem as well as our lower needs, such as those for safety, belonging, and love.

The control myths concerned with ennoblement and immortality are perhaps the most dangerous of all. They make us vulnerable to leaders, good and bad, who invite us to help them realize their "noble visions," but they don't show us how to differentiate between constructive and toxic leaders.

There is a related danger hidden in the myths that promise ennoblement and immortality: At the outset, it is not always obvious that a leader's vision is toxic. An even more subtle peril is embedded in a noble vision that starts out constructively but transmogrifies into a dysfunctional and perhaps even evil undertaking.

Let's consider a medley of control myths that speaks primarily to ennoblement and immortality:

- "This leader is a unique being. Participating in his/her vision will make me unique, too." (Self-esteem and belonging; self-actualization and transcendence)

- "Whatever promises the leader makes will come true." (Safety)

- "This leader's vision is so ennobling, I would follow her to the ends of the earth." (Self-actualization and transcendence)

- "When I am part of the leader's group, I can do no wrong." (Aesthetic [order, symmetry, and beauty]; self-actualization and transcendence)

- "Being part of the leader's group fills me with a sense of doing something truly important." (Cognition and transcendence)

- "The vision is worth any sacrifice." (Transcendence)

- "Attaining the vision through my heroic efforts will earn me immortality." (Transcendence)

This set of control myths can easily addict followers to the drugs of illusion and self-delusion. Believing in the special, godlike qualities of the leader makes it difficult to evaluate his claims to mana. Because we believe so wholeheartedly in that individual, because we dedicate ourselves completely to helping the leader realize her vision, that vision—like any other self-fulfilling prophecy—is more likely to come true. Yet we attribute most of the success to the leader's vision, not necessarily to our own efforts or other contextual circumstances.

The promise of heroism and potential immortality is extremely appealing. It also helps us put sacrifice into perspective, as a necessary step in our existential longing to triumph over death.

The Incredible Potency of Control Myths: Controlling Ourselves, Controlling Others

Looked at in their totality, the control myths have enormous potency. Why are they so incredibly powerful? Because they operate below our conscious awareness, we don't examine them critically, nor question their validity. Because we act in accordance with their dictates, we transform the control myths into self-fulfilling prophecies. Then we believe in them all the more.

In short, we use the control myths, as the term itself suggests, to control our *own* behavior. Control myths soothe our anxiety and calm our fears. They tell us what to do and what not to do. They warn us of the consequences of ignoring their "wisdom." They also help us go about our lives, pursuing our own interests and leaving the complex issues to the leader. The control myths immobilize not only our minds and our hearts. They also disable our mouths, our brains, our brawn, and sometimes even our computers.

The control myths are particularly potent because they work not only for *our* needs but for the leader's as well. The control myths operate so effectively that the leader does not have to waste a moment's time imposing constraints on our behavior. We do it to ourselves.

By keeping ourselves in check, we give leaders free rein to act however they choose. Thus leaders rarely have to patrol the avenues of the discontented. Instead, they can focus unstintingly on the business of "running things" as they deem fit. Our lack of action and attention, our susceptibility to illusion, and our willingness to engage in self-delusion all open the way for the leader's excesses.

These deep-seated beliefs do much more than cause us to control ourselves and free up the leader from having to monitor our behavior. They help us police the behavior of other followers as well. Thus, anyone else who threatens to step out of line, who dares to violate these control myths, feels the group's scorn, combined with intense pressure to conform. We hear echoes of the Stanford prison experiment. And, as we saw in our earlier discussion of whistle-blowers, we routinely badger group members who speak their mind—or, worse yet, refuse to follow the crowd—with the familiar accusation "You're not a team player!"

Later, when we revisit whistle-blowers from a new angle, we'll describe the "whispering war," which undermines those who dare confront the leader.[15] That war, waged in hushed tones around the office coffee machine, in cyberspace by e-mails, and in private telephone conversations, is virtually impossible for the target of that invisible campaign to win.

Control myths coalesce into a complex power mythology that provides a framework for understanding why the "powerless" don't revolt. Cloke and Goldsmith argue that "hierarchy, bureaucracy, and autocracy depend on the maintenance of these myths; democracy requires that they be dismantled."[16] For the powerless exist only within the framework of a hierarchy that dictates the relative authority, prestige, and resources of different groups. That hierarchy is what former Oberlin College president Robert Fuller, writing about "somebodies" and "nobodies," has called "rankism."[17] And despite their conscious complaints about suffering at the hands of toxic leaders, followers help sustain them in power by internalizing the control myths and following their immobilizing dictates.

This chapter has focused on a set of rationalizations, excuses we give ourselves for not confronting a bad leader. These rationalizations, hardened in the flame of our existential, psychological, and psychosocial needs, eventually become control myths. These programmed instructions gain power from the human needs to which they respond. They compel us to keep ourselves and other potential resisters in check.

These powerful control myths swim, like a graceful school of fish, below the waters of our consciousness. There, undetected, they go about their work, eating away at our ability to evaluate properly leaders and their visions. Unnoticed, the control myths make it difficult for us to connect their powerful directives to our conscious behavior. The result: Toxic leaders are free to continue their own dance, their stunning leaps and twirls. In this heady atmosphere, even nontoxic leaders may begin to tiptoe gingerly across the toxic line.

What can followers really do to prevent such tragedies? For one, they can raise their rationalizations and control myths to the level of consciousness and confront them directly. Before exploring that issue, however, let's consider how followers might recognize when they, themselves, inadvertently are pushing an otherwise nontoxic leader over the line. That is the focus of Chapter 8.

8

Pushing Nontoxic Leaders
Over the Line

In this chapter, we'll meet three varieties of followers—benign followers, the leader's entourage, and malevolent followers—whose actions and needs can push nontoxic leaders over the line. These three types of followers can help to sustain established toxic leaders as well, but that is not our interest here.

To this point, we have concentrated on toxic leaders who, once in place, go from bad to worse. In this chapter, however, our focus shifts to leaders who start out wearing good-guy hats, but then, by responding to their followers' complex needs, end up with bad-guy hats pulled far down over their ears. Although the impact of followers' needs and actions will be our primary interest, indirectly we spotlight two types of leaders: those who go from good to bad and those essentially good leaders who are undone. In both cases, followers, with diverse motivations, have had a large hand in the leader's fate.

This is *not* an exercise in blaming the victim, that is, the hapless folks who suffer at the hands of toxic leaders. The purpose of looking through the opposite end of the telescope is this: to make followers more acutely aware of how they may unintentionally drive an otherwise nontoxic leader into toxicity.

In a sense, followers might read this chapter as a strategy for avoiding the creation of toxic leaders (although we readily acknowledge that many toxic leaders don't need any help). It is also a cautionary tale for nontoxic leaders, often neophytes, who fail to remain on alert as they negotiate the dark crannies of their complex organizations. For inexperienced leaders, it is a warning about dangerous followers, deliberate or unintending, who can undermine their loftiest goals.

Three Kinds of Followers

At least three major categories of followers can create a toxic leader or topple a nontoxic one:

- Benign followers, types A and P, whom I'll consider in a moment

- The leader's entourage

- Malevolent followers

In earlier chapters, I described how some benign followers, beset by existential anxiety, psychological needs, and situational fears, can fall victim to and suffer leaders who already operate under the toxic banner. In this chapter, we'll explore how these same followers (let's call this first subtype *benign type A* or *anxious benign followers*), for similar reasons, can force a good leader to don wolf's clothing. These followers want a leader to reassure them through grand illusions that they will find safety—better yet, heroism, fame, and perhaps immortality—by participating in the leader's "noble vision."

The second subtype, whom we'll label *benign type P* or *pragmatic benign followers*, are driven by practical concerns: their personal, economic, professional, or political well-being. These constituents press the leader to remove what they perceive to be pragmatic threats to their jobs, their retirement accounts, their reputations, their families, and other everyday aspects of their lives.

Sometimes greed and ambition prompt these P types to encourage the leader to engage in unethical or criminal practices or simply to turn a blind eye to signs of incipient toxicity. When avarice and ambition quicken the pulse of benign type P followers, they begin to shade into malevolent followers, as we'll see momentarily.

The second major group, the *leader's entourage*, plays a very special role. As the leader's alter egos, its members can lead the leader astray or keep an already toxic leader in play. Paradoxically, the leader often gradually changes places with the entourage and becomes *its* follower.

A third group of followers—*malevolent followers*, driven by avarice, ambition, envy, or competitiveness—deliberately seeks to undermine the leader. We haven't talked about this insidious group before, but in this chapter we shall see how its members can be the undoing of the unwary or novice leader who depends upon them. Although malevolent followers can also be an important constituency to full-blown toxic leaders, that is not this chapter's concern.

Benign Followers Seeking a Vision

For the moment, let's consider both benign types A and P—the anxious and the pragmatic types—as one large, general group. I think it is fair to do so because sometimes, as followers, we fall into both categories. Still, let's not forget the general distinction: that anxious benign types (benign type A) suffer from a combination of existential, psychological, and situational angst, aware of their fragility, mortality, and daily fears, whereas benign pragmatists (benign type P) worry about their practical personal, financial, or professional fortunes.

Sometimes, or course, type P's use pragmatic reasons to mask their type A concerns. Let's also bear in mind that the benign type A followers look for leaders who will create grand illusions. They want leaders who will promise to make the followers secure, even help them escape death—sometimes social, sometimes physical, sometimes both—while holding out to them a glittering chance for greatness and lasting renown.[1] Benign type P's are equally intrigued by the possibility of a great adventure, as the Enron case shows.

Occasionally, of course, the enterprise becomes so grand that it eclipses the leader. Then the followers focus more on the activity than the leader per se. For example, during the 2003 Iraq War, Corporal John Schaeffer, a twenty-two-year-old intelligence officer, told his father in a telephone conversation, "Isn't it nuts that they're paying me to do a job I would pay them to do? I'm a part of history."[2] Lest they die leaving no trace, these benign followers often push the leader to design a lofty blueprint that they then can help build. They prefer not to notice that the plan has major defects that eventually may topple both the followers and the leader.

Is a New Vision Really Necessary?

When new leaders are appointed or seek leadership positions, followers commonly look for the V-word—*vision*—as a litmus test for their leadership. In some cases, the leader initially may not possess a grand new scheme or even see the need for one. The leader may believe that his or her predecessor had gotten the strategic plan right but the implementation wrong, that better execution would make the existing vision work just fine. That approach, however, does not easily satisfy benign type A followers, who yearn to feel they are part of some grandiose plan.

Sometimes leaders have to learn that their followers need the stimulus of a grand vision. It took Lou Gerstner, former CEO of IBM, time to recognize this. At the outset of Gerstner's tenure, in 1993, the media eagerly urged the new CEO to reveal his vision for the ailing computer giant. His refreshing response: "The last thing IBM needs right now is a vision." For that candid assessment, Gerstner found himself at the center of a firestorm. Responding to the Sturm und Drang that his comment had produced, Gerstner cautiously began to sprinkle his speeches with the V-word.

Still, in May 1994, Gerstner's speech in Barcelona, Spain, was roundly criticized. It disappointed critics by failing to produce the visionary holy grail for which analysts and insiders were searching. By October of 1995, *Business Week* felt the need to reassure its uneasy readers that Gerstner did, after all, have something pretty close to a vision: network-centric computing.

> Louis V. Gerstner Jr. caused a stir two summers ago when he declared that the last thing IBM needed was to proclaim a grand vision. Gerstner proceeded to focus on cost-cutting and other management issues and proved the vision-hungry pundits wrong. But having studied IBM, the computer industry, and technology trends, the former McKinsey & Co. consultant has come up with, if not a vision, at least a plan for IBM.[3]

The next month, at a landmark speech at the COMDEX '95 conference in Las Vegas, Nevada, Gerstner uttered the word that journalists and financial analysts around the world were waiting to hear. Then, in a Valentine's Day speech in 1996, at the Uniforum meeting in San Francisco, Gerstner told his audience:

> Now, I didn't come here to be an ad man for IBM. I'm here to talk about a vision of a truly open, universally connected world. A vision that is shared, perhaps, you could argue was created, by the entire UNIX community: vendors, developers, users and resellers.[4]

In numerous subsequent appearances, Gerstner spoke the magic word, although it is not entirely clear that the IBM maestro ever gave much personal credence to it. For better or worse, he banked more on hard-knuckled managerial oversight and performance. In fact, in a radio interview after his retirement from IBM, Gerstner confided:

> The people inside IBM at the time said, "Give me a vision and I'll sit and talk to customers about it for three hours in a conference room." That was exactly wrong . . . people were talking exactly when they should have been listening.[5]

Nonetheless, for IBM insiders and outside analysts alike, the idea that the CEO possessed a vision seems to have been terribly important. Working hard and measuring their performance against a high standard of excellence weren't enough to inspire the restless followers. That straightforward algorithm left Wall Street cold as well. Gerstner, finally recognizing the power of language, began to frame his pragmatic approach in the symbolic images for which the followers were begging. Adopting the vision angle and other more pragmatic, occasionally authoritarian strategies (including, in Gerstner's words, "a few public hangings of people who didn't want to get on the new programs. That told everybody we were serious") breathed new life into Big Blue.[6]

We can hardly hope to pinpoint the exact contribution that Gerstner's reluctantly embraced vision made to IBM's impressive revival. Nonetheless, this example demonstrates that to make them come alive, some benign followers seem to need an impassioned belief that they are implementing a grand scheme. Apparently, Gerstner's exhortations excited enough IBM followers to help the corporate Lazarus rise from the virtual dead.

In the end, Big Blue's miraculous reincarnation dazzled the Street with 1998 revenues that reached a record $81.7 billion and a profit of $6.3 billion. If that weren't enough, IBM's market capitalization grew tenfold in the first six years of Gerstner's tenure. One moral to be taken from this tale of corporate resurrection: Never underestimate how much followers crave a lofty dream on which they can hang their commitment as well as their immortality.

As followers, we might ask ourselves, "What does it take for us to act on the basis of realistic, pragmatic directions and goals? How do we kick our addiction to visions? How do we learn to forgo illusions and all the traps that come attached to them?" A legitimate, exalted vision can be inspiring, but we also need to be able to move smartly without one.

The Impatient Followers

Oftentimes, impatient followers (including corporate boards, as we shall see in Chapter 9) are ready to jump ship for another leader who promises to satisfy their hunger for a glorious vision. When this happens, the followers' neediness can prompt the leader to develop a hastily concocted strategy. The result: The core ideas are not fully developed. Or they have an unnoticed flaw. Or the implementation plan is fragmentary or misguided. Or the long-term implications, which may spawn grievous negative consequences, remain unclear.

Here's one example of how the followers' need for a vision pushed one CEO into a true dead end:

A small dot.com company (we'll call it BBinC for Broadband in China) was off to a great start. The goal of the little upstart was to sell broadband to China, whose vast market was still untapped. If BBinC could pull this off, they would become a major player in the global broadband industry. BBinC's hefty capitalization came from a group of venture capitalists eager to gain a foothold in the Chinese market and make a killing in the new economy.

The young CEO (let's call him John Thornton) knew he had to develop an implementation strategy. He was working hard to do just that, but the plan needed more work and more time, and the main lender was growing restive. The other members of the BBinC staff were pushing Thornton to "go for it" with the rough-edged plan that he had already developed. They worried lest the impatient venture capitalists withdraw their support, in which case they'd all be down the tubes.

The harried CEO had severe doubts. While he felt certain that the plan was a real winner, it needed more fine-tuning. Thornton had not yet lined up any Chinese intermediaries who could contact potential customers in China. Without an elegant implementation plan and at least two Chinese associates in place, he didn't see how BBinC could go forward. Pressed by the venture capitalists' apparent edginess and his staff's impatience, the CEO hastily hired a Chinese associate, who didn't seem exactly right for the position. Thornton was counting on his first Chinese hire to identify another associate from mainland China to work in tandem to open up this vast market. Egged on by his worried stateside staff, Thornton submitted the plan to the venture capitalists and the rest of the board. They eagerly gave him the go-ahead.

The result was easy to predict: The Chinese associate never succeeded in bringing on another Chinese executive; worse yet, he never managed to land a single major contract for BBinC. The overhead for the Chinese associate proved to be a huge drain on the company. So did the well-trained stateside staff, who were treading water, waiting to move in with their technological know-how once a big contract had been signed. The money ran out before any major contracts could be secured, and the company folded.

Hastily Wrought Visions

Since hastily wrought visions tend to be defective in substance or planned implementation, they are often difficult to execute. This may propel the leader to push the pedal to the floor, assuming more and more power in a desperate effort to drive the vision into high gear.

Because so many leaders' power is built on the illusion that the leader is both omniscient and omnipotent, they have a hard time admitting failure. They become ensnared by the "human ego investment," described thirty-five years ago by Harvard professor James C. Thomson Jr. in a blistering critique of America's Vietnam disaster. In that tragic case, initially nontoxic leaders in search of a dream became the architects of the Vietnam War.

> Men who have participated in a decision develop a stake in that decision. As they participate in further, related decisions, their stake increases. It might have been possible to dissuade a man of strong self-confidence at an early stage of the ladder of decision; but it is infinitely harder at later stages since a change of mind there usually involves implicit or explicit repudiation of a chain of previous decisions.[7]

To shore up a flawed vision gone awry, an initially nontoxic leader may begin to exaggerate and then downright dissemble. In the process, the leader may become increasingly authoritarian and controlling.

When essentially nontoxic leaders pursue a much-vaunted plan without the initial hoped-for success, they commonly begin to build more and more infrastructure—special services, intelligence (spies), enforcers—to make it happen, to oblige compliance. Such leaders take increasingly strict measures to prevent anyone from criticizing or standing in the way. They tune up the PR department.

Caught in this frantic squeeze, the leader can become monomaniacal and suspicious, even paranoid, about anyone who tries to amend the dream. In this mode, it is difficult, if not impossible, for the leader to entertain important course corrections.

Consider a familiar case from the political realm: Chairman

Mao, with his infamous five-year plans, offers a vivid example of an initially positive leader who eventually turned toxic. When one grandiose scheme after another—the Great Leap Forward and the Cultural Revolution—failed to yield the results he sought, Mao's desperation escalated. Ultimately, he resorted to drastic totalitarian measures to achieve by force the positive results he so frantically desired.

For twenty-five years, Mao dictated the terms of life and death to nearly a billion people spread over nine million square kilometers. To establish his domain, Mao and his elite troops caused the deaths of more than thirty million of their own citizens, according to conservative estimates.[8] The 1950s Great Leap Forward, a movement that organized the Chinese peasants into communes and built backyard iron foundries, led to widespread starvation as well as extreme measures of repression. Later, the Cultural Revolution, an initiative to create an ideologically pure citizenry, resulted in the imprisonment and death of millions, including intellectuals and students. In his later years, Mao declined into paranoia, which frequently drove him to order the elimination of his closest associates.

Unevaluated Visions: When the Followers Won't Take a Hard Look

Sadly enough, followers' unrelenting thirst for a noble vision almost guarantees that the vision will eventually sour. The reason: Followers want the grand scheme so much that they don't evaluate it with a critical eye or metaphorically kick its tires to reveal its hidden weaknesses. When Mao eliminated the entire landowning class, the peasants rejoiced at their newly acquired land, not realizing their turn eventually would come. Remember Reverend Martin Niemöller's lament: "Then Hitler attacked me and the Protestant church—and there was nobody left to be concerned."[9]

From the corporate world, consider another example, this time of a leader whose extraordinary unchecked visions eventually destroyed him and his all-too-willing followers. In Howard Hughes's early career—before he became an eccentric iconoclast—the heir to the Hughes Tool Company demonstrated his brilliance as an entrepreneur, film producer, and aviator. In each arena, his exciting dreams drew followers as well as the media, who expected great things from him. Hughes's flamboyant plans so entranced his followers that they failed to hang on to their critical faculties. They gradually became yes-men, bedazzled by the "genius" of their leader.

To reach his highly publicized goals, Hughes became an overly meticulous manager, attempting to control every minute detail of every enterprise, from checking camera angles on film shots to test-piloting planes. He brooked no criticism from his associates. Enamored of his uncritiqued dreams, Hughes became suspicious of anyone who tried to influence or use any aspect of his "great works." Without followers strong enough to force him to question the soundness of his decisions, Hughes rushed headlong into one capricious enterprise after another. Without critical feedback, Hughes's projects often mushroomed into grand fiascoes.

Perhaps Hughes's signature failure was the development of the Spruce Goose, the common name for the H-4 Hercules, a cargo-type "flying boat" built by Hughes Aircraft during World War II. The Spruce Goose saga provides a good example of Hughes's intolerance for criticism. Originally conceived by Henry Kaiser, director of the Liberty ships program, the plane was designed in response to the need to transport materials and personnel to Great Britain over shipping lanes being savaged by German submarines. Kaiser soon quit the project, allegedly disgusted by continuous disagreements with Hughes.

When the war ended before the massive plane could be completed, the need for this "marvel" suddenly evaporated. Called before a congressional committee to explain the massive costs and delays of the government-funded project, Hughes took advantage of a break in the hearings to return to California, presumably to test the plane's engines. Instead, in a nose-thumbing gesture to Congress, Hughes personally piloted the Spruce Goose on its one and only flight. He managed to fly the immense birch plane just seventy feet above the Long Beach waters at eighty miles per hour for just under one mile. Congress thumbed its nose back, canceling the contract.[10]

Hughes nonetheless remained a visionary. For example, in what many perceived as a quixotic effort to improve the image of mob-ruled Las Vegas, Hughes began buying casinos and other real estate in Las Vegas in 1966, just ten years before his death. Some observers consider this venture latter-day evidence of Hughes's continuing but unreliable genius. Hughes's dazzling ability to pull the rabbit out of the hat played heavily in his inner circle's reluctance to challenge the decisions of the frequently out-of-control genius.[11]

It is not only benign type A followers who press leaders. Type

P pragmatic followers play their cards as well. They may simply close their eyes to the imperfections in the leader's vision because their very livelihoods depend upon realizing the dream. The more extravagant the vision, the more the pragmatic followers worry they might lose by not buying in or by pulling the plug. That was clearly the case at Arthur Andersen, Enron, and other recent corporate homes to toxic leaders.

To Criticize or Not to Criticize? That Is the Question

The more successful leaders become, the more reluctant followers become to challenge their decisions. In a story about Percy Barnevik, the former CEO of the Swiss conglomerate ABB, the *Wall Street Journal* describes how this much-respected corporate leader moved unchecked because each of his successes only further intimidated his followers: "Mr. Barnevik's charisma and clear vision for ABB helped turn the company into a world-wide power, but those same qualities left management reluctant to challenge him when they thought he was making a mistake."[12]

Barnevik kept acquiring companies, even when some proved to be money losers and others presented serious downside risks. For example, despite potential liability for asbestos damage, Barnevik purchased Combustion Engineering for $1.6 billion. Current estimates suggest that asbestos claims against Combustion Engineering could reach $4 billion unless the U.S. bankruptcy court intervenes. But few, if any, counseled Barnevik to be more cautious.

Even as dark shadows begin to transform the dream into a nightmare, followers frequently refrain from openly criticizing the leader's plan. Because followers are unwilling to confront the leader about a flawed decision, the leader becomes emboldened to continue on a misguided path. As Barnevik became more and more hooked on his acquisition strategies, he earned the inside nickname "Percyfal," a reference to Parsifal, the knight who sought the Holy Grail.

At ABB, employees privately grumbled about Barnevik's decentralized matrix structure but publicly applauded it. Despite widespread but tacit internal recognition that it generated "conflicts and communications problems between departments," there was virtually no public debate about the difficulties.[13] In Barnevik's case, even after he stepped down as CEO, "no one wanted to undo the Percy stuff."[14]

In those all-too-rare cases where a sole critic steps forward, the leader may not take the criticism seriously simply because no one else supports the dissenter. In fact, when only one intrepid messenger delivers the bad news, that individual, like the sentry who carried grim tidings to Creon in Sophocles's *Antigone*, may barely escape with his or her life. Nor is that initially brave soul likely to speak up again in the future. The sentry's comment, as he beats a disgruntled retreat from Creon's attack, echoes other threatened counselors' sentiments: "[O]ne thing's for sure: you won't catch me coming back again. It's a goddam miracle I got out of 'ere alive."[15] In fact, some contemporary would-be message bearers are not quite as fortunate as Creon's sentry.

Dissenters do better when they have a group standing with them. When multiple followers fail to protest the leader's questionable behavior, they are opening the door for the leader to step over the toxicity threshold.

The Corporate Chosen: The Culture of Success

Belonging to the trendiest, coolest organization, be it Enron in the 1990s or Drexel Burnham Lambert in the 1980s, is one way for followers to convince themselves that their lives have meaning. After all, they are the chosen, and when the leader insists that only the best can claim membership, then clearly you know you are important. It's like being accepted into heaven. What else could "chosen" possibly mean?

Somehow, status and meaning become one. Their merger is quite imperceptible. Self-esteem rises on the heady potion of symbols of success. If the followers can be seduced by status and the toys that come with it—corner offices, Porsches, first-class air travel, five-star hotels—then perhaps they won't notice that, despite the sweet icing, the underlying cake is simply tasteless cardboard.

Even Sherron Watkins, who later testified about Enron's accounting Tower of Babel, was so blinded by the trappings of success that she, too, bought into the culture.

> Even though she had been at Enron since 1993, she was still amazed by the high-end toys parked in the company garage, the dizzying array of BMW sedans, Porsche convertibles, Ferraris, Mercedes, Range Rovers, and customized SUVs. She loved Enron's oval-shaped tower of mirrored glass . . . the purposeful people from all over the world scurrying across the lobby's glossy granite floor to get to their desks faster . . . The company café featured spring rolls and gourmet wraps. The coffee bar featured custom lattes and mochas; mini-massages were available in the company gym. It was al-

most, but not quite, too much: If you deserved all this, you knew you were very, very important.[16]

Nor did CEO Ken Lay make any secret of the superior quality of Enron's employees. Lay described his strategy for selecting the elite to a *Washington Post* reporter:

"My goal when I came into this business was to try to get a superstar in every key position. You must have the very best talent, and then let them develop a good strategy." It was the gospel of Ken Lay: A company staffed with the best and the brightest, who were allowed to develop to their fullest potential, couldn't be beat.[17]

An addiction to the culture of success, that booster of self-esteem, can be a dangerous aphrodisiac for followers. And it spreads to the leaders as well.

Even nontoxic leaders can be seduced by the trappings of success, particularly when their followers' yawning need for self-esteem demands the same elixir. When followers succumb to the craving for success, they become desperate to remain a member of the chosen.

In the elite club of the successful, followers can easily lose their capacity to criticize or set limits on the leader, toxic and nontoxic alike. In fact, their own addiction to the achievement drug, which they mistake for meaning, can make followers urge their nontoxic leader to help them get their fix or at least look the other way when the toxic leader gets his. To complicate matters, even the leader's most trusted lieutenants can fall victim to this addiction.

The Leader's Entourage

The next key group of followers, the leader's entourage, has particular needs that can undo the leader. That relatively small retinue of folks who serves the leader on a daily, face-to-face basis constitutes a very special case.

These close-in followers function as the most trusted information gatherers and closest advisors to the leader. They carry out the leader's most critical tasks, above and distinct from the hierarchy.[18] They protect the leader from failure by maintaining their connections to reliable and helpful sources that give them a fix on realpolitik.

Members of the entourage also protect the leader by offering up their own heads on the chopping block when the leader is found wanting. They are the flak catchers, the ones who take the blame for what goes wrong—as things surely do in this complex world—and they also pass the credit on to the leader for what goes right.

The entourage is not composed of followers in the same sense that general employees are followers vis-à-vis the corporate leader. In the corporate world, they are the elite members of the royal court. They mostly have titles like "special assistant." Nor are they comparable to the public constituents that political leaders consider their followers. Rather, they are a close-in group of advisors and confidants, much like President John F. Kennedy's "Irish Mafia." That tightly knit group was composed of Jack Kennedy's brother Bobby along with his friends and trusted cronies Larry O'Brien and Kenny O'Donnell, each of whom played key roles in the young president's administration.

In many cases, the members of the entourage are leaders-in-training, who act in the leader's name. They are there to serve devotedly even when they do not feel a deep personal affinity for the leader, although they often do. In their defense, followers on the factory floor or in the voting booth, who view the leader from afar and thus rarely notice her clay feet, can more easily keep the flame of their devotion burning. The daily exigencies that the leader faces quickly expose her human frailties to the inner circle. That does not mean that nary a member of the entourage remains permanently in the leader's thrall. Some clearly do, like Kennedy's inner circle, President Franklin Roosevelt's kitchen cabinet, and President Ronald Reagan's retinue. All of these leaders, however, were remarkable for their personal charm, laced with self-deprecating humor.

Members of the entourage derive their status and raison d'être from their relationship to the leader. So they are always dedicated to keeping the leader in power. Consequently, despite their charge to guard the leader's flanks, their single-minded focus on gaining or maintaining power—the leader's and their own—may occasionally cloud their judgment.

The political campaign group is an entourage par excellence. They come together to ensure the candidate's election. If their candidate loses, their own status and power drastically ebb. So it is not particularly unusual, in a life-or-death struggle, for them to urge the leader to "do whatever it takes" to win. And sometimes, with or without the leader's go-ahead, the entourage may take the decision to engage in "dirty tricks" that subsequently bring down the leader. One tragic example, the Watergate break-in, presumably took shape largely at the hands of an overzealous Committee to Re-Elect the President.

Leaders draw upon their own inner circle because they understand how their fates are lashed together. Outsiders, even if they are part of the larger organization the leader heads, may not always be trustworthy. President Kennedy learned that sorry lesson during the Bay of Pigs fiasco, when he counted on advice from his military and intelligence advisors. After the Bay of Pigs,

> Kennedy was still angry, at least in private, where he did his shouting about his generals and admirals with tiers of service ribbons advertising their experience: "Those sons-of-bitches with all the fruit salad just sat there nodding saying it would work" . . . "I've got to do something about those CIA bastards" . . . "How could I have been so stupid?" . . . "I sat around that day and all these fellas all saying 'This is gonna work, and this won't go,' saying 'Sure, this whole thing will work out.' Now, in retrospect, I know damn well that they didn't have any intention of giving me the straight word on this thing." . . . He took the lesson that he could not trust other people's people.[19]

More often than not, the leader can identify the members of the entourage who can be counted on, even when such devotion means quietly engaging in skullduggery. Richard Reeves, in his intriguing book on John F. Kennedy, reflects JFK's awareness of the strength and willingness of certain members to "do whatever it took" to protect him.

> "You see Kenny there," he said once as O'Donnell slept on a plane. "If I woke him up and asked him to jump out of this plane for me, he'd do it. You don't find that kind of loyalty easily." Of Mrs. Lincoln, his secretary, the President said that if he called to inform her that he had just cut off Jackie's head and wanted to get rid of it, the devoted secretary would appear immediately with a hatbox of appropriate size.[20]

In many entourages, the individual members jockey for the leader's favor. In doing so, they may put forth an inadequately researched proposal for action that can endanger the leader. Sometimes they vie for position because the leader intentionally plays off individual members against one another—as FDR did with considerable charm and relish.[21] This internal competition within the entourage keeps the members off balance. In such circumstances, the members of the retinue are never quite sure about their individual standing. Hence, they are goaded into ever-greater demonstrations of devotion and daring, which occasionally lead to disaster for the leader.

Such internal competition can be a deliberate strategy by the leader to force the individual members to reveal their true positions on an issue as they joust for the leader's support. Nonetheless, setting these intimate supporters against one another can backfire catastrophically. Competitive colleagues in the entourage may feel driven to devise the "most daring," "most visionary" (but not necessarily most carefully thought through) strategy. Such ill-considered plans can entrap a nontoxic leader into extreme choices that explode into toxic consequences.

The leader, aware that not every member of the entourage is necessarily a genuinely devoted disciple, needs to be on guard against a palace coup. Specialists, whose deep but narrow knowledge gives them unique power, are not the most likely candidates to try to overthrow the leader. It is the generalists, the ones who more closely resemble the leader in talent and interests, whom leaders need fear most. Besides, not infrequently, the generalists seduce the specialists into joining their efforts to overthrow a leader. Thus the leader's deliberately engendered competition among the entourage can work to allay the leader's fears of being ousted by the entourage. At the same time, however, this competitive tension within the entourage can lead the members into serious lapses of judgment, which in turn can drive the leader beyond the limits of nontoxic behavior. Walking the tightrope of power is never easy.

Finally, the entourage has a special role that most other followers do not: Entourage members may be called upon to stand in for the leader, essentially to make decisions in the leader's place. As anthropologist F. G. Bailey suggests, by creating the entourage, the leader is trying to re-create himself.[22] When leaders believe they have whelped one or more alter egos within their entourage, they may unintentionally put themselves at their alter egos' mercy. These individuals become exceedingly powerful because the leader relies on their judgment and skill. Within the entourage, there may be specialists on whose expertise white papers are based and who, in essence, are calling the shots in those areas. The generalists are usually the members with astute political instincts, whose respected experience sometimes overrides the specialists' recommendations.

In this complex internal dynamic within the entourage, wherein the leader becomes the follower, the leader must rely on the judgment and integrity of both specialists and generalists. People in either role, particularly if their wisdom is impaired by the anxiety of competing with peers for the leader's favor, can inadvertently put the leader at great risk by poorly considered recommendations.

The Outer Circle of the Entourage: Retainers and the Culture of Power, Perks, Punishment, and Fear

There is an outer circle of the entourage, made up of retainers, or those employees who see to the personal needs of the leader. Unlike the inner circle of policy wonks and leader "wannabes," the retainers have no pretensions or expectations of becoming leaders or replacing the leader. The retainers' group includes such personal-service providers as drivers, bodyguards, photographers, barbers, butlers, chefs, mechanics, and others who meet the leader's personal needs.

Although the retainers are rarely in a position to push a constructive leader over the line into toxicity, only rarely do they leave the leader who becomes toxic. When retainers work for a toxic leader, they usually remain in their role for a mixed set of motivations. While they presumably resonate, like the rest of us, to their own existential and psychological needs, retainers frequently have several additional motivations as well. These include derivative power and possible privileges, including high salaries and access to special benefits such as travel and housing, as well as the fear of punishment or retaliation if they rebel or leave.

Retainers may also relish the fact that others fear them as part of the toxic leader's retinue. That fear by association may make them feel quite heroic. They may enjoy power because they can provide access to the leader. These retainers often recognize that without their link to the leader they would appear quite inconsequential and unintimidating. They also realize they are not indispensable.

Malevolent Followers: When the Leader Doesn't See It Coming

The next major set of followers—malevolent followers—are obviously the ones to watch. Astute organizational veterans can spot the malevolent followers. They are the Iagos of the world, who, like Shakespeare's dark presence, purport to be "honest men," worthy advisors, but who actually seek the downfall of the leader. Seeing potential benefits for themselves, ambitious, envious, and/or greedy followers can encourage a nontoxic leader to move into gray ethical territory. Inexperienced leaders, especially those unsure of their own ethical borders, are particularly vulnerable.

Iago's brethren spot the leader's special weaknesses, from vanity to insecurity. By manipulation and deceit, they play upon the leader's inevitable human frailties, like master violinists wielding their deadly bows.

In some cases, malevolent followers will work hard to topple a nontoxic leader to safeguard their own entrenched positions. In fact, desperate benign type P followers, worried that their jobs, their retirement accounts, perchance their livelihoods are at risk, can turn malevolent. Leaders new to an organization are particularly vulnerable, more so if they have not brought along their own entourage or have not yet built an internal cadre of strong supporters.

One former CEO of a manufacturing company, whom I interviewed, was still dazed from the deft knifework of senior executives worried that the new leader was threatening not only their turf, but their very jobs. Let's call this the John Franks case.

John Franks became the first nonfamily member to head a well-known automobile parts firm. The retiring fourth-generation scion had handpicked Franks, a younger man he had known over the years through various board memberships. Although Franks had not grown up in the firm, the board had enthusiastically endorsed the choice of the former CEO, Gibson Jones.

Franks greatly admired his predecessor and was exhilarated at the prospect of following Jones's estimable example. He had long admired the company and valued its traditions, including its well-known paternalistic stance toward employees.

This was Franks's first job as a CEO, although he had been a highly regarded general manager of a major division in an office supplies company. He felt he understood AutoExcel, since he and Jones had talked on many occasions, and AutoExcel was the subject of nonstop media attention.

Two years before Jones stepped down, AutoExcel was listed on NASDAQ. Since that time, however, the business had become sluggish. The board stood in awe of Jones for his personal integrity and his ethical treatment of employees. His charismatic persona was charming, if sometimes unmistakably intimidating.

As a measure of their respect and appreciation, the board voted to make Jones a lifelong member and participant in executive sessions of the board. They soft-pedaled their discomfort with the company's declining fortunes, expecting the young, vigorous new CEO to give the company a strong vitamin cocktail.

Shortly after Franks moved into the executive suite, his CFO warned him of rough financial seas, urging him to "tighten the ship." According to the CFO, things were much worse than Franks had been led to believe during his corporate courtship. In fact, without serious surgery, the company was headed for a precipitous end.

Unfortunately, the best strategy for setting things aright, according to the CFO, called for personnel cuts. The most dispensable positions belonged to the stable of highly paid executive vice presidents, who cost the company dearly but added little value. Franks resisted mightily. He truly wanted to honor AutoExcel's highly touted no-layoffs tradition. Besides, these senior executives had been with the company for decades. They were practically family. In fact, at least two of them were the former CEO's brothers-in-law. Over the years, despite previous ups and downs, Jones, his father, and his grandfather had always kept everyone on the payroll. That was one of the firm's accomplishments most applauded by the business media, and Franks didn't want to kill that sacred cow.

Franks managed to keep things going the first year. During the honeymoon period, he, too, received ecstatic accolades from the press. In fact, in one major business publication, the author of the article wondered if Franks was "outjonesing Jones." Mostly the article spoke of Franks's inspirational leadership, his integrity, and his concern for employees. In the bleak economy, AutoExcel's weak growth was largely ignored.

By the first quarter of the second year, Franks concluded he had to take his CFO's advice. There simply was no alternative unless he wanted to take the company into bankruptcy. Franks put together a twenty-four-month plan designed to put the company on a stronger footing. This, however, involved eliminating most of the senior executives whose divisions weren't producing.

Respecting the organizational culture, Franks had welcomed Jones's continuing role on the board. More than that, he hadn't moved to change the composition of the board, all of whose members had been appointed by Gibson or his father. He felt they represented the combined history and wisdom of the organization.

The short story: When the vice presidents learned of their impending terminations, they turned to Jones and the board, their longtime associates. Franks never quite knew what hit him when the board voted to buy out his contract.

When the next CEO came aboard, his first act was to shift the balance of the board by introducing "new blood" and retiring the majority of the old guard. His second act was to implement Franks's turnaround plan. Two years later, the company was back on track, just as Franks had predicted.

Is it fair to call those vice presidents malevolent followers? Perhaps, perhaps not, except from Franks's perspective. In some cases, the malevolent followers are far more malevolent, driven by envy of the leader's position or by greed. In organizational succession cases, an unsuccessful internal candidate for a leadership position may actively or passively undermine the new leader.

One deposed leader shared the following story about how malevolent followers used a passive strategy to ambush her:

> Three senior executives in a manufacturing firm were among the finalists for the CEO position. After lengthy deliberations, the board brought in an outsider from another industry. The new CEO decided to keep these experienced executives as her team to draw upon their immense combined knowledge.
>
> On the surface, the three also-rans seemed relieved to have retained their positions and looked eager to help the new CEO. The CEO's decision to keep these senior executives appeared to be a win-win situation for everyone. After all, combined, these three represented more than sixty years of company history and experience.
>
> Actually, the three contenders were disgruntled and angry. They were aware of one another's strategies, but they acted independently to undermine the new CEO. They didn't proffer misinformation. They simply withheld critical information. In addition, they isolated her from other sources with alternative views within the organization.
>
> Without critical intelligence and help, the new CEO never found her footing. When the board ousted her, one of the trio was appointed interim CEO.

The next example demonstrates how a very effective, subtle, and ambitious vice president subverted a series of bosses:

> The first CEO of a fledgling economic research organization was a young Washington neophyte. As an economist, he had experienced a meteoric rise in a quasi-academic think tank. That success catapulted him into the top position of this new firm. The organization depended largely on government contracts. So he was pleased to have Dan as his special assistant, an individual with long-term Washington experience in the Office of Management and Budget. Over the years, Dan had developed many connections on the Hill. He knew what the Congress wanted and exactly how to package it.
>
> Despite this expert coaching, the young CEO proved a disaster in his first congressional testimony. With each response to his congressional questioners, the neophyte CEO provoked their escalating fury. In an unprecedented journalistic decision, the *Washington Post* printed the CEO's inept testimony on the front page. Not long after that, the CEO "resigned."
>
> Over the next six years, four more CEOs held that position, all ultimately exiting without distinction. Each of these CEOs—one had come from academia, the others from the not-for-profit sector with numerous congressional contacts of their own—counted on the

special assistant's wisdom and experience. Between CEOs, Dan served as acting CEO, sometimes for months. In fact, Dan's total tenure as acting CEO was longer than any single regular CEO's time in that position.

Not surprisingly, under the acting CEO, the organization flourished, with increasing numbers of government contracts and cordial congressional relationships. Eventually, the board appointed him to the permanent CEO position. Ironically, the special-assistant-turned-CEO also maintained congenial relationships with each of the CEOs he had so subtly undermined.

Malevolent followers often leave their prey unaware of the source of the poisonous arrow. Malevolent types can show up just about anywhere among the leader's followers, occasionally even within the leader's entourage.

Pushing the Leader to Play God—Even Without Crises

In our discussion of leaders in crisis, we saw how the needs of followers may drive them to look for an omniscient, omnipotent figure, someone willing to play God. In crisis, as well as at other times fraught with ambiguity, followers commonly want the leader to promise not to abandon them. Some leaders, eager to meet their followers' needs, take the bait, even when that means the leader is in danger of falling over the toxic cliff.

Sometimes the call to play God meets certain needs of the leader as well. We saw in Chapter 5 how Mayor Rudolph Giuliani, after 9/11, was pushed by enthralled and anxious followers to try to override the legal two-term limit on his mayoralty. Traumatized New Yorkers' desperate need for reassurance and Giuliani's equally desperate need to repair his pre-9/11 tattered credibility were a perfect match. Only the strenuous objections of the City Council and one possible contender for the role prevented Giuliani from taking this illegal step.

Followers, anxious for reassurance, urge the leader to speak with a certainty that the circumstances simply don't warrant. Fearful followers want reassurance from a leader with a confident mien, much like the feverish child who looks to her worried parents to tell her she'll be fine. When leaders respond to this invitation to play God, they are teetering on the ledge of toxicity. They begin to act more certain than they are or can be, given what is actually known about the situation and how to handle it. This trap can destroy not only the leader's credibility but, in extreme circumstances, the followers' lives as well.

Even in noncrisis times, a deadly circular dynamic can take shape: The leader becomes impatient for "clear evidence" on which to base a decision and, in turn, pressures the staff to come up with the data. Feeling the hot breath of the leader's urgency, staff members rapidly scrape together tenuous data, presenting them as more substantial than they really are. Or the staffers feel pressured into vouching for them. The result: The leader makes the decision based on flimsy evidence, inevitably leading to poor results.

Ceding Personal Responsibility to the Leader

As we saw in the previous chapter, some followers are only too willing to cede personal responsibility for their fate to the leader. That allows the followers to escape any blame—from others or themselves—for failing to live up to the organization's (or society's) achievement norms. In addition, followers use control myths to avoid responsibility when things go wrong. "I was only following orders" or "It was the leader's decision to do things this way" are familiar songs sung by followers who want to sidestep responsibility.

Criticizing the leader may mean taking a chance. Yet not calling the leader to account creates an even greater risk, since the fate of the entire organization may be on the line. Let's remember that ABB executives were reluctant to find fault not only with the celebrated Barnevik's acquisition strategy but also with his decentralized matrix structure, despite the massive miscommunication and other snafus they clearly created among units. When a yes-man mentality takes hold of the followers, even well-intentioned leaders are likely to keep galloping off in the wrong direction.

Some followers, devoted to their own interests, are reluctant to set aside their valued pursuits to develop the counterarguments or rewrite the memo or come up with an alternative budget. That requires taking attention and time away from their own projects. They might see the leader starting down a dangerous path, but the control myths conveniently come into play (e.g., "The leader probably has a good reason for this decision. She undoubtedly knows something we don't know that prompts her to make this seemingly bad choice"). Saving another staffer's job can take weeks of work behind the scenes to line up appropriate evidence of the leader's bad judgment as well as support from associates. Looking the other way when the leader starts to go astray allows lethargic or self-centered followers to avoid responsibility for the leader's bad decision, since they have not intervened in the decision-making process.

∾

This chapter considered several different groups of followers—two types of benign followers (type A and type P), the leader's entourage, and malevolent followers. Each type, in its own way and for its own purposes, can push an otherwise nontoxic leader into toxic action.

Two additional groups figure in this drama. They start out not as followers but as chroniclers and overseers of the leader. Through various circumstances, however, they become the malleable, intimidated, sometimes corrupt votaries of the leader. In Chapter 9, we shall see the unexpected and nuanced role the media and boards of directors play in creating toxic leaders.

9

The Odd Couple: The Media and Boards of Directors

The media and boards of directors make up the last two categories of followers. This pair often turns good leaders into bad by unwittingly colluding with them in a mutual seduction or by silently standing by as good leaders transform themselves into Mr. Hydes. On the surface, these two groups don't seem to have much in common, either with one another or with the other followers described in the previous chapter, any more than Felix and Oscar of *The Odd Couple* did. Yet, oddly enough, they do.

Ordinarily, we do not think of the media and corporate boards as followers. Instead, we expect the media to be the leaders' chroniclers and critics and corporate boards to be their overseers. Sadly enough, in a displacement of roles, this odd couple frequently slips into something more comfortable: the robes of the hagiographer and the champion, respectively. In both cases, the media and members of the board all too often fail. They dwindle into devotees of the leaders they are supposed to cover as their journalistic beat or to advise and control in the boardroom.

That role change does not prevent the media and members of the board from taking a sharp U-turn when the leader's golden halo begins to dim. Then they turn with a vengeance, partly to assuage their own anger, embarrassment, and self-recrimination for allowing themselves to have been duped.

Corporate boards of directors, with myriad subcommittees, are responsible for serious oversight functions. Their role demands keeping the CEO and the entire leadership team on the straight and narrow. While advisory boards don't have the same legal power to change the corporate traffic light from green to red, their advisory function does call for them to hold up the yellow diamond with the squiggly lines when they sense dangerous curves ahead.

The roles of oversight and certifying bodies, including accountants, demand that they exercise their critical faculties as they review the CEO's plans and action. All too often accountants, responsible for certifying the validity of corporate leaders' financial statements, succumb to pressures that transform them into followers rather than upholders of the public trust. Similarly, boards of directors commonly turn from shepherds into sheep.

Internal audit boards confront comparable challenges. Conflicts of interest that arise when the same accountants serve as consultants to the leader's firm contribute to the problem. We all witnessed how this disastrous game played out in the Enron case, when the energy giant's external auditor, Arthur Andersen, failed to keep the Enron board's internal audit committee properly informed. It seems a very long time ago that young accounting graduates jockeyed for jobs with the Big Eight accounting firms, whose very names—like Arthur Andersen—bespoke straight-arrow integrity.

The complex dynamic between leaders and the media, as well as between leaders and boards of directors and/or their accountants, results in a curious distortion of roles. The chroniclers, controllers, and certifiers transmogrify into followers. The leaders, for their part, become either the manipulative Svengalis or the myopic Mr. Magoos, so inflated with confidence that the first strong gust can blow them off their corporate perches.

The No-Touch Tango: The Special Dance of the Media and Leaders

With the exception of answering to their own media-mogul bosses, media folks are not under the control of the leaders they cover in the same way that the leaders' employees or political constituents are. Nonetheless, members of the media often become so enamored of the leaders on their beat that they might as well be counted as regular—nay, far more powerful and thus rather dangerous—followers.

As guardians of the public trust, we expect the media to retain and protect their roles as objective observers and critics. In those roles, the media run the double risk of seduction or exclusion by the leaders whom they are assigned to cover. Leaders and the media find themselves in a delicate, no-touch tango of mutual need. One wants adulatory coverage; the other wants full access or, better yet, a major scoop. Consequently, they often engage in a reciprocal courtship, each seeking to create a "friend," while forgetting the wise old Washington aphorism that advises, "If you want a friend in this town, get a dog."

Consider the case of the political reporter assigned to cover presidential candidate X. (We'll come to corporate leaders shortly.) That reporter frequently flies on candidate X's plane, along with the campaign staff. If the staff and the candidate are media-savvy, they quickly welcome that reporter as one of the family. And the reporter, for her part, nourishes her access to the candidate.

Any misstep by either partner can bring the dance to a disastrous halt. One critical story and the reporter loses her access. One snub and the leader bids adieu to the possibility of an admiring story in the next day's paper. Worse yet, when the door to candidate X's inner sanctum slams shut in Ms. Fourth Estate's face, Ms. Fourth Estate may have to fall back instead on interviewing candidate X's critics for their opinions of his character, his campaign, or, heaven forbid, his cavorting.

In an earlier era, the crusading reporter may have been the representative of one ideologically positioned newspaper or radio station. Today, that journalist is more likely to be the more wary employee of a media conglomerate ruled by a powerful media titan, such as Rupert Murdoch. And if the reporter is wary, so is the public, whose confidence in the media is not much greater than its weak faith in the Congress, if we are to believe public opinion surveys. This shift further complicates the measured dance between corporate leaders and the media.

Much as reporters and corporate leaders may want it otherwise, a media interview is no longer simply a meeting between two individuals, each with his or her own agenda. Willy-nilly, the no-touch tango becomes a dance between the representative of a giant media operation with its own commercial interests at risk and the leader of an organization whose stock could rise or fall precipitously with the utterance of an injudicious phrase or the hint of a five o'clock shadow. This and the sound-bite packaging of news can push an otherwise thoughtful leader to worry more about form than substance.

One CEO painfully recalled the time he had misplaced his notes before an appearance on CNBC and, as a result, couldn't remember the talking points he had planned to hit. He dreaded his staff's inevitable critique of his performance. Yet imagine his astonishment when

> [i]nstead, and not because they wanted to flatter him, they were full of compliments: "You looked calm, authoritative, presidential." None of these qualities should necessarily change anybody's mind, he said, but, hey, television works that way. "You looked young," they said to him, a compliment he took as ludicrously irrelevant to the formation of anybody's informed opinion, yet, in practice, it counted, and the CEO must never forget that it counts. If it counts for a trained, informed, and sophisticated staff like his, it surely counts even more for the general public.[1]

A Complex Courtship

In this media-dependent world, it is no secret that political and corporate leaders, as well as their staffs, court the media. Long before television, President Franklin D. Roosevelt was known for artfully granting certain favored reporters exclusive interviews. During the Kennedy administration, the president and his brother, attorney general Robert Kennedy, manipulated the press so skillfully that it took decades before many of the journalists fully understood how thoroughly they'd been beguiled.

A journalist friend of mine in Washington recalled the day when, as a twenty-five-year-old cub reporter for the *Washington Post*, he was assigned to write a story on the charismatic young president. He took his assignment very seriously and wrote what he believed was a first-rate analysis of a presidential initiative. The day after the story appeared, my friend was nonplussed to receive a call from the attorney general, Bobby Kennedy, telling him how pleased the president had been by the young reporter's "brilliant analysis" and how the president hoped to have an opportunity to discuss various policy issues with him sometime soon. Imagine any cub reporter's reaction to such a call! Then the attorney general suggested that my friend just might want to join the Kennedys for Thanksgiving in Palm Beach. Even twenty years later, even after he understood that he'd been manipulated, this now seasoned reporter looked back nostalgically at playing touch football with the Kennedy clan that balmy November day in Florida so long ago.

Many leaders of for-profit and not-for-profit organizations, along with their public relations staffs, are very adept at courting the press. They feed their media contacts choice bits of news that the reporters can't get elsewhere, and over time a relationship—notwithstanding some mutual guardedness—begins to develop. Still, strong connections with members of the media can lead usually nontoxic corporate leaders to violate, quite unintentionally, their relationships with their internal followers.

One corporate leader recalled how she was caught off guard by a telephone inquiry from one of her close media contacts about an impending downsizing within her company. Although this information was known exclusively by the for-your-eyes-only crowd on the tenth floor, the executive blurted out, "How did you know?" By noon, this inadvertently confirmed rumor was being aired on the local TV channel as "breaking news." The hundreds of employees whose pink slips had already been processed were pretty upset about hearing the news first from the media rather than from their own executives.

Even within seemingly remote academia, the outreach of leaders to the media can be surprisingly impressive. Many colleges and universities routinely retain public relations firms, in addition to their in-house PR departments, to place their institutions in the best public light. Some academic experts, leaders in their own fields, who become media stars maintain a wide network of media contacts. We see them repeatedly on CNN and other nightly radio and TV news broadcasts. Academic leaders are no more immune than corporate toxic leaders to the ego inflation that celebrity status can bring. We frequently witness academic experts who, under the glare of the TV studio lights, trip into the pothole of expounding authoritatively on subjects far beyond their area of expertise in the hope of being invited back by a TV host who favors "articulate" guests.

Selling the Business News Is the Business of the Media

The business media, too, are hard pressed to avoid being seduced by the leaders whom they track. After all, cover stories on corporate titans sell magazines and newspapers—"mugs sell mags," as the expression goes. The faces of corporate leaders, revered and reviled, smile out from the covers of numerous glossy newsstand publications. Bill Gates has graced the cover of *Fortune* magazine no less than eleven times since 1996. Among certified toxic leaders, Tyco's Dennis Kozlowski, Enron's Kenneth Lay, AOL Time Warner's Robert Pittman, hotel magnate Leona Helmsley, and many of their compatriots have appeared on the covers of business publications. As I noted earlier, some corporate leaders who currently top the charts for unethical and criminal practices previously showed up, time and again, on the annual Ten Best Leaders lists published by these same magazines.

Bottom-line concerns commonly push reporters who write for media conglomerates (and today there are few who don't) to grab the public's attention as fast and as hard as possible. The purpose of this frantic competition is to corral the largest audience—and quickly.

> Audience size plays into the bottom line, which plays into the stock price, which is monitored quarter by quarter. Everybody fears punishment by the market if [you are] not quick to react to a developing story and grab the audience before anybody else does. Nobody is punished for any other failing: not for being too superficial, not for being too conservative, not for being too liberal. You can tell them anything so long as you can get them to show up to read or watch the ads.[2]

After all, to stay in business, the media need to produce an audience for their advertisers. Whoever is first to assemble the largest audience keeps the greatest share. So competition for the scoop or the "big get" is rampant, even among friendly colleagues such as Barbara Walters and Diane Sawyer.

This rush to publication creates another problem: the many errors that, often as not, remain uncorrected. Twenty-four-hour news channels suffer seriously from the disease of instantaneous news, which has spread to other media venues. And, as we shall see, leaders may be loath to demand corrections.

The Dilemmas of the Business Media: How Dry Is Dry?

Several years ago, three academic sponsors—the Peter F. Drucker Graduate School of Management, at Claremont Graduate University, with the Marshall School of Business and the Annenberg School for Communication, both at the University of Southern California—convened an international conference on media and corporate leadership. Their purpose was to consider how the media—print, broadcast, and entertainment—shape the public's opinion of business leaders.

A high-powered group of media reporters and editors, corporate leaders from different industries, including several media CEOs, and a cadre of academics met in Los Angeles to analyze what the media did and how they did it. They examined the relationship between leaders and the media from three perspectives: the media's, the corporate leaders', and the public's.

At this meeting, media reps complained that business news by itself was too dry to attract any sentient audience. This sorry condition, they argued, prompted journalists to put a human face on the news. By starting their story with the dilemmas or achievements of real-life business leaders, they argued, print and broadcast media could then draw their audience into the more arid business issues.

One participant explained the strategy through a well-known, if apocryphal, tale concerning the cub reporter who filed a story about a town inundated by flash floods. Allegedly the reporter wrote, "The heavens opened yesterday, and God sent Mudville a flood of biblical proportions." The editor sent back the following urgent message: "Forget the flood. Interview God."[3] Setting the corporate leader as bait not only hooked the intended prey but also commonly resulted in CEOs being portrayed as God or the devil. According to these savvy members of the media, the audience had little interest in the lesser-known members of the celestial corporate hierarchy.

Some business as well as political reporters specialize in leadership profiles, repeatedly interviewing the same leaders. That's their bailiwick, and their charge is to create exciting copy. Many leading business publications insist that "all business stories are personal stories." Without the personal, there is virtually no political story, either.

In the process of describing their feats to eager media reps, well-meaning, nontoxic leaders may suffer the same fate as Narcissus examining his reflection in the pool. They fall in love with their own image. Simultaneously, the most seasoned journalists frequently develop myopia from the stardust that charismatic leaders adeptly sprinkle in their eyes. In this delicately choreographed seduction of self and other, both leader and media metamorphose in ways that prevent them from functioning effectively in their intended roles. In fact, the media unwittingly join the ranks of the leader's admiring followers.

The media sometimes create great hoopla about a previously unknown leader, only to work equally hard later to knock their own celebrity creation off that pedestal. Anita Roddick, founder of the Body Shop, was brought to worldwide attention by the press, who lionized her socially responsible approach to business. Roddick's trade-not-aid strategy, her environmental consciousness, and her humanistic treatment of employees made the "mediagenic" CEO the focus of great adulation. That thralldom eventually was followed by equally great skepticism. The press began a negative drumbeat after a 1992 documentary falsely attacked Roddick's much-publicized opposition to testing cosmetic ingredients on animals.

Roddick successfully mounted a libel suit, winning more than $400,000 in damages. Accused of not living up to her espoused business practices, Roddick astonished media critics by commissioning an independent ethics researcher at Stanford's Graduate School of Business to conduct a "social audit" of the Body Shop. Roddick published the unedited report, thereby earning plaudits from a temporarily satiated media. Controversy continues to swirl around Roddick, but on balance she seems to stick to her values, even after yielding leadership of the Body Shop to new management.

During an intense day and a half of debate, the Los Angeles conferees explored why and how this strategy of first building up and then tearing down leaders had become so popular. One well-known business writer explained ruefully that the media were only interested in "rising stars, gurus, and fallen angels." The drama of a corporate leader's rise and fall has "legs." It builds readers' interest, sells newspapers and magazines, and attracts TV viewers. Al Dunlap provides the perfect case study of a business leader trumpeted by the media as he rose to dizzying heights and was later shouted down by the very press that had idolized him. Entrepreneur Donald Trump's larger-than-life existence and near-death financial adventures continue to make intriguing copy.

Less exotic corporate birds remain in the shadows beyond the circle of intense media attention. As the conference's rapporteur noted succinctly, "Ordinary executive competence"—and, I would add, character—"is not news."[4] The corporate "plain folks" simply don't sell copy—that is, not unless they happen to get caught up in a crisis not of their own making.

Earlier, we met Aaron Feuerstein, CEO owner of Malden Mills in Lawrence, Massachusetts. Feuerstein, you may recall, watched from the parking lot as a fire reduced his factory to smoldering ashes. That disastrous fire also put Feuerstein's three thousand employees at risk for pink-slip syndrome. Before that, Feuerstein was hardly a media celebrity, despite years of the same commitment he demonstrated that disastrous night. Helplessly witnessing the flames engulf his factory and his employees' livelihoods, Feuerstein softly swore to keep going.

In fact, for the media, that was only the beginning of a stirring corporate saga of how the self-effacing, stubborn, deeply religious CEO refused to take the insurance money and run. Instead, against the advice of financial experts, Feuerstein selflessly—some said foolishly—determined to keep his workers employed and protect the Massachusetts mill town that had brought workers to his factory through the years. But Feuerstein was the exception to the media's build-up-and-then-tear-down rule—at least, more or less.

The New England entrepreneur resurfaced in the news several years later, when another crisis sent Malden Mills into bankruptcy and threatened to wrench day-to-day operational control from Feuerstein. A double whammy—several unseasonably warm winters that reduced orders for Polartec, and the burden of debts incurred from Feuerstein's earlier decision to maintain his workforce—pushed Malden Mills into Chapter 11 bankruptcy. Nevertheless, the redoubtable CEO remained convinced that his earlier decision to protect his workers and the community was the ethically appropriate decision, bottom line be damned. At this writing, Feuerstein is struggling to raise sufficient capital to regain control from GE and run the company in tune with his commitment to his workers. He, too, makes fascinating copy.

Who Intimidates Whom?

At that same conference, several experienced media representatives expressed genuine shock when some CEOs admitted that they felt intimidated by the media. One entertainment CEO explained how his general counsel advised against demanding a retraction of an incorrect story that had cost his company millions. The general counsel insisted that a retraction, no matter how deserved, would leave the company vulnerable to future bad press by an embarrassed and resentful reporter who held the power of the pen. Other CEOs present, nodding in agreement, recounted similar legal advice. Thus, in a distinctly unleaderly way, leaders are urged to shrink from confronting the media on issues of truth and accuracy. Another step toward toxicity.

Not all leaders are deterred by the media. Jack Welch, former CEO of General Electric, was renowned for his meticulous efforts to control his image, and thus GE's, in the media. Nor did he stop there. Welch even worried about how experts who were consulted by the media perceived him. Some years ago, two of my colleagues were quoted in the same story on Welch in one of the major business magazines. In both cases, these management scholars offered what they thought were very positive but balanced comments about Welch's leadership. Shortly after their comments appeared in print, both of these academics were amazed to receive handwritten notes from Welch, expressing his "disappointment" in their comments.

Nor is Welch the only leader, corporate, political, or nonprofit, who has tried to exert control over the media. In numerous cases, it is the media who find themselves intimidated by a convincing leader with whom they have a close—perhaps too close—relationship. When this causes the media to soft-pedal or quash legitimate news, the fallout can create serious consequences for everyone: the media, the leader, and the leader's followers. Leaders whose ill-considered plans are critiqued in the press are far less likely to proceed with a questionable strategy, as President John F. Kennedy found out much too late.

The details of Kennedy's efforts to convince the *New York Times* to downplay, if not suppress, the Bay of Pigs story before the fiasco occurred have been so oft told that they hardly bear repeating here. Yet the story teaches us the importance of the media's maintaining their role as the guardians of public information. Several weeks after the ill-fated invasion, the embarrassed president told Turner Catledge, managing editor of the *Times*, at a meeting in the White House:

> "Maybe if you had printed more about the operation you would have saved us from a colossal mistake." More than a year later he told [publisher Orvil E.] Dryfoos, "I wish you had run everything on Cuba. . . . I am just sorry you didn't tell it at the time." Clifton Daniel [assistant managing editor of the *Times* at the time] speculated that "the Bay of Pigs operation might well have been canceled and the country would have been saved enormous embarrassment if the *Times* and other newspapers had kept the public more fully informed."[5]

Had the media refused to be bullied by Kennedy, the neophyte president might have been spared his darkest political and diplomatic moment.

From Mutual Seduction to Self-Destroying Prophecy

The media's lionization of leaders often spins those leaders' heads. First the leaders begin to believe their *own* press releases. Then they start to take seriously those glowing accounts that the media write about them. The heady cocktails that the media serve up can intoxicate even nontoxic leaders. And intoxication with one's own inflated image can easily turn to delusional grandiosity and arrogance.

At that point, the leader believes she can do no wrong, that whatever she does will be greeted with applause by a fawning media who hang on the leader's every word. The sense that "I can do no wrong," the delusion that "the organization or my followers cannot do without me," or the belief that "I'm so clever that I'll never get caught" spell arrogance and pomposity. These two conditions easily escalate into toxic leadership. Michael Milken, wunderkind of Drexel Burnham Lambert before its ignominious demise, agreed with the media's and the Street's opinion that the young, obsessed financier warranted the label "genius." In fact, Milken allegedly believed that his convoluted financial arrangements so far exceeded the intellectual grasp of government investigators that he was quite unstoppable. The same misperception plagued Jeff Skilling and Andrew Fastow of Enron.

When the seduction between the media and leaders is mutual, and the media fall victim to the leaders' or their PR department's spin, nontoxic leaders can be pushed off course. This is not to say that the media are the only ones who engage in this process. Other followers, as we have seen, can have the same effect. The point is merely that in this mutual seduction, the media abandon their role as chroniclers and join the ranks of the leaders' followers. When the media come too close too often in an effort to get the scoop and maintain access, they court the danger of dulling their objectivity.

Another danger lurks: The media can push nontoxic leaders into toxic inaction. Drawn by visions of a scandal-thirsty public, the media may conduct interviews with corporate and political leaders that feel much like a romp through a minefield. Wary of condemnation by journalists sniffing for scandal, a leader may become virtually immobilized in the headlights of the media. In this case, media-induced risk avoidance can inhibit a leader from taking bold action when the situation absolutely calls for it. Critics of President Bill Clinton's limping second-term foreign policy attribute his inaction largely to earlier media criticism of the dramatic military strike he had ordered against Iraq in the midst of his impeachment hearings. The media characterized Clinton's action as nothing more than a political diversion. Of course, Clinton's well-documented penchant for dealing casually with the truth made him an inviting media target. Nor is this to suggest that unrelenting media criticism by itself was to blame in the Clinton case; it is merely to say that media criticism can make nontoxic leaders reluctant to engage in needed action.

Thus we have seen that the media are as likely to succumb to leaders as the rest of us—although perhaps for somewhat different reasons and with different results. The media's vulnerability stems largely from their need for access and from the moonbeams with which the leader clouds their vision. We have also seen how leaders, whose PR can send the stock price skyrocketing or plummeting, assiduously court the media. This reciprocal courtship between leaders and the media frequently becomes a self-destroying prophecy.

Governing Boards, Advisory Boards, and the Like

In all organizations with boards, the board's primary purpose is to subject both the leader and the executive team to serious oversight. They are there to set both policy and limits. They have the responsibility for selecting the CEO, as we saw in Chapter 4. When they function properly, boards provide a bulwark against toxic leadership. Although the exact nature and functions of boards vary among for-profit corporations, not-for-profit organizations, and public agencies, all boards are charged with maintaining the ethics and prudence of the organization.

Given the vast literature on boards, this is hardly the place for a systematic review of their similarities and differences.[6] In fact, the point of this section is deliberately different. It is to explore how and why boards, designed to set limits on executive action, so often allow corporate leaders to spin them around in a game of organizational blindman's buff.

In the post-Enron era, we are witnessing major efforts to reform board structure, composition, and practices in corporate America. The Sarbanes-Oxley Act of 2002 is designed specifically to address some of the most egregious toxic corporate governance behavior, including conflicts of interest and intimidation of auditors.[7] Before the Enron debacle, however, we saw quite the reverse: an ongoing epidemic of corporate boards that transformed themselves from overseers to applauding or silent audiences—Enron, WorldCom, Tyco, Global Crossing, Adelphia, Tyson, Apple, Gap, Cendant, Qwest, Xerox, Waste Management, and the Walt Disney Company, for starters, and the list goes on.

During the 1990s, for example, Disney repeatedly appeared on

Business Week's list of America's worst corporate boards, by virtue of some board members' minimal management experience and cozy connections to Disney CEO Michael Eisner. The Disney board blew off criticism by pointing to the company's stellar economic performance (which it barely noticed was part of a rising economic tide that was lifting all ships). Former board members Stanley P. Gold and Walt Disney's nephew Roy Disney are the exceptions. As of this writing, Disney and Gold have mounted a vigorous campaign, aided by a website, to unseat CEO Michael Eisner, whom they charge with mismanaging and distorting the company.

Even as I am writing this chapter, Donald Carty, CEO and chairman of AMR, parent of American Airlines, has resigned. The cause: the uproar created by concealing extravagant retention bonuses and $41 million in funding to a pension plan for seven senior executives while union employees were being asked to take significant pay cuts that would continue for five years. The executive largesse to management included Carty and former American president Gerard Arpey, who, ironically, then received the board's nod to replace Carty as CEO. Within days, the board named Edward Brennan, former CEO of Sears, as chairman of AMR. Brennan, the *International Herald Tribune* notes, "sits on the board's compensation committee, which approved the [executive retention and pension] plan."[8] Following the protest from union leaders, American Airlines announced that the executives had agreed to forego the retention bonuses, but not the contribution to their pension plans.[9]

Considerable academic research reveals a robust link between strong, ethical governance and corporations' performance on a host of measures. Governance that puts the well-being of shareholders, employees, and customers ahead of the financial interests of the top management team and the board seems to pay off in a host of ways. According to a 2003 study by GovernanceMetrics, an independent corporate governance ratings agency in New York, the relationship between ethical governance and corporate success is alive and well today. In GovernanceMetrics' study of one-, three-, and five-year returns of companies in Standard & Poor's five-hundred-stock index,

> stocks of companies at the top of the [firm's ethics] ranking outperformed the index in a meaningful way. Those ranked lowest significantly underperformed the index. In the S&P 500, the average decline of a stock for the three years ended March 20, 2003 was 2.3 percent. . . . But the five companies earning the [firm's] highest score

rose 23.1 percent on average. The top 15 companies averaged total returns of 3.4 percent. Top-ranked companies also outperformed their peers in measures like return on assets, return on investment and return on capital.[10]

Despite the poor performance of so many boards, others boast a roster of impressive intellectual and professional credentials. In fact, the stellar qualifications of many board members, including, oddly enough, certain members of the Enron board, make this issue all the more puzzling. Why and how did so many corporate boards fall so completely under the spell of these toxic corporate leaders? How come, even as the economic tide turned, they continued to rubber-stamp management's proposals, legal and fraudulent, and to pay CEOs astronomical salaries? Richard Grasso, chairman of the New York Stock Exchange, became the poster boy for outsize CEO corporate action. This came about despite plummeting shareholder value and waves of downsized employees in their own companies.

The clubby composition of these boards appears to be one major factor in boards'—for-profit and otherwise—inability to maintain their oversight objectivity. Other factors also contribute to poor board performance: too many insiders, including current and former executives; too many members with business connections to the company or the CEO, who earned consulting and legal fees as well as other perks from the company; too many members with relatives who worked for the company; too many audit, compensation, and nominating committee members who either were responsible for hiring the CEO or vice versa, as in the Grasso case, or had other close connections to the leader.

Taken together, these features of the board's composition create an in-crowd atmosphere, where the chosen meet to decide how the organization should be run. As I have suggested earlier, perceiving oneself or one's group to be among the chosen leads to serious myopia and the risk of groupthink. As board turnover occurs—and it does so only sluggishly—suggestions for new board members traditionally come from the existing board.

Even in those cases where there are multiple nominees for each open board position, those nominees tend to be drawn from a common pool. The possible candidates all bear a striking resemblance to one another and to the current board. Consequently, the individuals who constitute the slate of candidates are virtually interchangeable. So even if the shareholders do technically vote on the board members, the voting is more apparent than real. In not-for-profit organizations, the problem is compounded by the fact that the board usually nominates and elects other board members, without any shareholders to worry about. Both the International and U.S. Olympic Committees suffered from this inbreeding, with dire results.

Given these conditions, even when they might wish to object to a leader's proposed action, board members face serious obstacles. Taking a critical stance incurs pressure from other board members who share not only corporate backgrounds, values, and connections but also the same uncritical mind-set. Let's not forget the multitude of research on conformity that demonstrates the power of an apparently unanimous group against a lone would-be dissenter.[11] Broad and clear role expectations of individuals in related roles—such as friendship roles—that are integrated into the larger social context place additional structural pressures on potential dissenters.[12]

Many times directors sit on several of the same corporate boards, thereby creating interlocking directorates that spread the contagion throughout a large corporate network. In addition, the names of corporate board members appear among the ranks of not-for-profit community boards as well. Ken Lay, former chairman of Enron, was well known and beloved, in fact, for his philanthropy to not-for-profit organizations in his Texas community. Edward Brennan, recently named chairman of the AMR board mentioned above, sat on five other boards at the time of his appointment as AMR chairman: Allstate, McDonald's, Exelon, 3M, and Morgan Stanley. Reportedly, he planned to "resign from some of the boards he sits on to concentrate on the struggling airline," although a spokesperson noted that "Brennan had not determined which board seats or how many seats he would give up."[13] The *International Herald Tribune* also noted,

> Of [Brennan's] directorships, his seat on the board of Morgan Stanley presents the greatest potential for conflict. . . . Morgan Stanley serves as a financial adviser to AMR, and its chief executive, Philip Purcell, sits on the AMR board. Morgan Stanley could not be reached for comment.[14]

Brennan's pattern of board memberships is far from unusual; in fact, it is merely par for the course.

Working within a common corporate context, there is much to lose in the long term by risking the disapproval of the group. Nor is it particularly unusual for personal and social bonds eventually to overlay relationships that began simply as governance-focused board members, thereby strengthening the linkages among these corporate directors.

I interviewed one board member after he had stepped down from the board of a not-for-profit institution. He talked about how difficult it had been to approach other members of the board with his concerns about the corrupt behavior of the president. This was a member who had done his homework, who understood that the leader, charming and persuasive, was nonetheless milking the organization for his personal gain. As he told it:

> Many of these people are my social friends. We go to dinner together; we travel together. For example, Frank [another board member] and I are real close. Yet when I tried to approach him with my concerns, he simply didn't want to hear any of it. We've been friends forever, even before we were both members of the board. In fact, Frank was responsible for bringing me aboard. So after a while I decided it was best to get out. It was clear that I wasn't going to persuade anyone, and I couldn't continue on that board without feeling my own integrity was being diminished. It was the only way I could see to maintain my personal integrity without disrupting my long-term friendships and the rest of my personal life.

When I asked this former board member if other members were aware of the leader's flaws, he said:

> Some were, but they didn't want to make waves. I think the chairman of the board had serious political ambitions. So he didn't want any mess on his watch. He didn't want anything that could be used against him later. He thought he could deal with it indirectly, by moving some of the president's responsibilities to other people in the front office. That way, Michael [the president] could be the outside person and Jack [the vice president] could run the inside operation. He was a good outside person, charismatic and all, and people were very attracted to him. He was very articulate, even eloquent, so that took him a long way.

In the wake of so many corporate meltdowns, *Business Week* conducted a year-long study "to determine which boards were getting it right and which weren't."[15] In addition to the lack of independence, the poll found that the poorly performing boards were characterized by too many members with limited equity stakes, excluding options; too many without experience with the organization's primary business or with companies of comparable size; too many with a plethora of other board memberships; and too many with poor attendance records at board meetings. The combination of these factors increases the likelihood that board members will have far less at stake and know substantially less about the company than the leader and his or her management team. Under these circumstances, the probability that the board will switch roles with management, becoming its follower rather than its overseer, increases exponentially.

The amount of time and depth of inquiry into management's decisions are crucial if the board hopes to avoid operating as a rubber stamp. In his testimony before the U.S. House of Representatives, the chairman of Enron's finance committee, Herbert S. Winokur Jr., reported that "the Finance Committee met regularly five times per year for 1½–2 hours typically the afternoon before each regular Board meeting."[16] Readers can judge for themselves the adequacy of the time spent on reviewing and guiding the complex financial arrangements that ultimately proved Enron's undoing.

The Board's Role in Selecting the Leader: Real or Unreal?

In the previous section, we reviewed the difficulties, particularly the clubbiness, that beset the selection of board members. We also noted, too briefly, that the current CEO often has a large hand in the selection of his successor. This is particularly the case when the CEO is regarded as highly successful. When the current CEO plays a significant role in selecting his or her successor, the probability is great that the individual chosen either will very closely resemble the incumbent or will be someone the retiring leader finds suitable.

When Sanford Weill, CEO and chairman of Citigroup, the world's largest financial services company, announced his retirement as CEO, effective at the end of 2003, he simultaneously named Charles Prince, his "longtime confidant," to succeed him as CEO and Robert Willumstad to step up to the COO position.[17] Weill described his relationships to Prince and Willumstad in the following way: "We are really good friends, the three of us. . . . I think we know each other very, very well."[18] In response to Weill's announcement, Ben McGrath of the *New Yorker* noted: "Look closely at his announcement, however, and you will notice that he is staying on as chairman until 2006; that he has handpicked his successor, with little input from the board; and that there is no guarantee that, when 2006 rolls around, he will actually leave."[19]

In some cases, like GE's unusual six-and-a-half-year search for

CEO Jack Welch's successor, the board actively participates in the process. Yet when it is a current and admired CEO, such as Welch, who is directing the board's search, there's still little likelihood of a radical departure in the type of leader who will be chosen to replace the well-regarded incumbent.

Board Compensation

If we take the amount of time spent by the Enron directors as a rough index of board effort, the compensation directors receive takes on new meaning. Much has been made in the media of board compensation in for-profit companies, and rightly so. By 2000, the average total compensation of outside board members of S&P 500 companies averaged $100,807, according to a study by Towers Perrin, an international management consulting firm. Board members presumably attended eight meetings annually, served on at least two committees, and chaired one committee.

> "The $100,000 hurdle really does represent a milestone of sorts," says [Ted] Jarvis [a consultant at Towers Perrin]. "Years and years ago," a seat on the board cost the company a mere "20 bucks a year." Back then, explains Jarvis, ["]most board members embraced their titles because of what that position bestowed and opportunity it offered to network."[20]

Shaping the News

Organizational leaders and their executive staffs serve as the pinched waist in the hourglass of information flow that the board receives. Boards often hear only what the leader wants them to know. They may be kept far from the ordinary folks at lower levels who know everything that's going on but are organizational light-years removed from the board.

Many executives interviewed for this study, who served on different types of boards, emphasized how common it was for the leader and his or her executive staff to shape and package the information that the board received. The alleged reason: to avoid "wasting the board's time" on what were "more appropriately staff matters."

The testimony of Robert K. Jaedicke, chairman of the audit committee of the board of directors of Enron since the mid-1980s, a man whose integrity as dean of Stanford University's Graduate School of Business was universally respected, bears tragic witness to this modus operandi. Jaedicke's testimony suggests that despite strenuous efforts to examine an organization's practices, boards can be kept in the dark and deliberately deceived by both the senior management and their outside consultants. According to Jaedicke:

> Arthur Andersen representatives attended each meeting of the Audit Committee. At each meeting, they made reports to us about issues of interest or concern. Further, it was my invariable practice to hold an executive session with the Arthur Andersen representatives, or at the very minimum offer one, where they could meet with us without management present. Arthur Andersen was free to report to the Committee any matters regarding the corporation and its financial affairs and records that made the auditors uncomfortable.... At each of these sessions, Arthur Andersen was given the opportunity to meet privately with the Committee outside the presence of management to discuss any of these matters. It now appears that Arthur Andersen had significant concerns about Enron's financial practices, at least as early as February 2001, but failed to raise those concerns with the Audit Committee at that time.[21]

Later, Jaedicke argues,

> In reading the "report" [of the special investigative committee], I was deeply disturbed to learn of the marked lack of candor of both company management and our professional advisers concerning these transactions. The lifeblood of an effective Board is the ability to receive full and candid information by its outside advisors and management. It is clear now that substantial and critical information was in many instances concealed from the Board—and in others was affirmatively misrepresented to us—by both company management and its outside advisers. This lack of full disclosure severely undermined the Board's effectiveness and oversight ability. No Board can properly execute its duties or make informed decisions without it.[22]

The chairman of the audit committee later describes how other employees knew about the chicanery that was afoot, but failed to inform the board.

Yet many organizational leaders, with boards they hope to control, routinely keep the board securely insulated from any contact with employees other than the trusted entourage. And in some organizations, the culture is totally infused with the values of the adulated leader, even when those values shade into the unethical. Assuming the board did have contact with inculcated lower levels of the organization, it still would learn little that would be useful. Finally, Jaedicke offers a sad conclusion that should serve as a warning to board members in all organizational settings:

> Considering the amount and seriousness of information that was concealed from us and misrepresented to us, I am not confident . . .

that we would have gotten to the truth with any amount of questioning and discussion. . . . They had plenty of opportunity to tell us the complete truth, we imposed numerous controls that required them to report to us fully and honestly—but they chose not to do so.[23]

Tripping the Light Fantastic

One unobtrusive way in which boards become followers of the leaders they are appointed to oversee is frequently evident in not-for-profit boards, from those of the U.S. and International Olympic Committees to hospital and opera boards. Membership on these boards gives the members access they might not otherwise have to an impressive array of world leaders and other celebrities. For some members, it is a gold-plated invitation to a glamorous life they might not enjoy under other circumstances.

The board of the opera dines with the world-renowned tenor at special board-only banquets. The board of the university is invited to spend a "just family" weekend with the president and five Nobel prize winners as the culmination of a high-visibility conference where the Nobelists have presented their latest research.

One very adept university president made certain that her board members were treated to special "power breakfasts" and galas with leaders from the world stage who came to campus to present commencement addresses and receive honorary degrees. Despite the fact that most board members are independently wealthy and travel in prominent social circles, few had access to such an array of dazzling world figures otherwise. Bathed in the glamour of these events, board members and their spouses, who were included in most social activities, felt the full force of the moonglow treatment. That the leader could pull off such events earned her reverential respect and appreciation from the board. As the board watched the president being flattered by visiting dignitaries, their awe for their leader expanded.

Groomed in this way to see the leader in the best possible light, board members have a difficult time perceiving the president's less-than-exemplary organizational decisions as just that. In this and many other ways previously described, most board members cling to their membership on the board, even as their roles gradually shift from overseer to overseen.

∼

In sum, this odd couple—the media and governing boards—commonly, but imperceptibly, loosen their grip on their positions vis-à-vis the leader. They slip from their respective roles as chroniclers and overseers of organizational leaders into postures of acquiescent and adulating followers. When leaders no longer receive tough-minded feedback from the media and hard-nosed critique from their boards, even the very best of nontoxic leaders can lose their way.

In some instances, followers recognize the leader's toxicity but find solace in the dubious art of making lemonade out of lemons. Still, a serious question remains: What, if any, benefits can followers ethically derive from tolerating a toxic leader? In Chapter 10, we'll examine this strange question.

IV

LIBERATING OURSELVES FROM
THE ALLURE OF TOXIC
LEADERS

10

Is There Any Silver Lining? Can Any Good Come from Tolerating a Toxic Leader?

Until now, I have emphasized the seemingly endless negatives that flow from putting up with toxic leaders. Still, many people—particularly older benign pragmatic followers with children's college bills to pay or with retirement too close at hand and too few realistic options—feel generally stuck. In the political arena, too, followers beaten down by a powerful despot may believe that the leader's overwhelming resources and leverage make escape quite impossible. Much of the time, their anxieties, as much as or more than their external constraints, keep followers under the toxic leader's sway. But for the moment let's set aside what entraps these followers and consider what good, if any, can come from tolerating a toxic leader.

In an effort to address the misery of those followers who feel they simply have to grin and bear it, let's examine whatever thin silver lining there may be to tolerating a toxic leader. As you might expect, this chapter will necessarily be noticeably shorter than most of the others.

Five Thin Layers to the Tarnished Silver Lining

There are at least five thin layers to the tarnished silver lining of tolerating a toxic leader:

- Opportunities to exercise leadership

- Opportunities to sharpen one's own ideals and learn what *not* to do from negative role models

- Opportunities to build self-esteem and discover one's superior moral authority

- Opportunities for sufferers to vent their complaints and bond with one another

- Opportunities to learn how to resist and organize resistance

Opportunities to Exercise Leadership

Toxic leaders, particularly as they slip deeper into paranoia and toxicity, frequently devote the lion's share of their energies to controlling their followers (despite the evidence that followers often control themselves). Encouraged by the lack of restraint from the outside, much of their attention is devoted to developing new, more grandiose projects, courting the media, and imposing increased measures of repression. These measures include the shaping of new policies and structures to keep the followers from unseating the toxic leader.

With the leader's efforts now trained on control instead of growth, the system begins to suffer from neglect. In every crevice of the organization, ordinary but necessary functions degenerate. Shoddy products, sloppy service, sagging employee morale, deteriorating infrastructure, and dissatisfied customers all leave much work to be done by others. In the public arena, too, services are impaired, and constituents feel ignored and stifled. Innovation, the lifeblood of growth, comes to a grinding halt. The result: Everywhere one looks, leadership gaps appear.

When a toxic leader fails to keep the system operating, informal leaders have the opportunity to emerge, to attend to these neglected problems. With no choice but to slough off their dependence, these new leaders arise as unfettered, independent individuals. Buoyed by their newfound independence, these emergent leaders can give full vent to their own creativity and leadership potential.

Mary Ellen Thompson, who headed up the marketing division of a large paper company, spoke about her own experience with a toxic boss:

Greg, the VP for marketing before me, made all of our lives miserable. He was a control freak. He only cared about controlling us. He spent more time checking on where we were every minute and whether our travel vouchers were accurate than worrying about our budget for the next fiscal year or any of our customers. Morale dropped to an all-time low. It looked like some of our best people were on the verge of leaving.

At one point, I realized something had to be done, and fast. So I invited everyone in our small group—excluding Greg, that is—to come together at a restaurant for lunch to discuss what we could do to improve things. So much wasn't getting done, you wouldn't believe it. At that lunch, we talked about how to organize to get the budget done, as well as how to respond to customers who had really been totally neglected. It was amazing. The energy around that table could have moved a mountain.

We mapped out a plan to work as if Greg didn't really exist. We each took assignments and set milestones and deadlines. We actually put a pretty good budget together and presented it to Greg, who hemmed and hawed, added a few touches, and then passed it off as his own work. I think we caught him by surprise with that one.

The best thing was that we didn't feel so powerless anymore. We all learned how to step up to the plate and make things happen. It was very exciting. We continued to work that way even after the budget was submitted. We found one not-so-small advantage. When Greg was asked how he arrived at the figures, he really couldn't answer. So he was forced to call us in, and it became obvious that we had done the work. Although Greg stayed in that position for another six months, the staff's morale was high. So was our energy. We bonded. We felt good about what we were doing, about ourselves as capable people who didn't have to wait for a leader to tell us what to do, and about one another. When Greg left, I was promoted to his position, and, as you can imagine, I had a crackerjack team already in place.

For many individuals who have never undertaken leadership roles, from either lack of opportunity or lack of self-confidence, the urgency of these unmet needs presses them into action. The realization that they can lead dawns on some individuals who, without the pressure of the void created by the toxic leader, would never have recognized their own leadership potential. Once they begin to function as leaders, these fledgling leaders may discover that their talents and skills fit quite well with the organization's needs.

Oftentimes individuals have had the skills and wisdom to perform these leadership tasks all along but were never given the chance to flex their leadership muscles. Other times the leadership hollows created by the toxic leader's neglect provide a valuable fresh training ground for emerging leaders.

Sometimes an added benefit surfaces. Because these new leaders are virtually beyond the toxic leader's field of vision, they can avoid being stuffed into an existing but inappropriate leadership mold. Forced by circumstances to take their first leadership steps without any coaching by a mentor, these untutored novices learn to dance to their own internal leadership rhythms. A happy result occurs: These new leaders have more latitude to try innovative strategies, from which they otherwise might have been deterred by an experienced but controlling leader bent on reproducing his or her own image.

These special circumstances also provide the emergent leader with opportunities to learn her way around a daunting hierarchy. Navigating in both internal and external waters is a key strategic skill that most emergent leaders, given time, can learn to do well. In the process, these new leaders learn to widen their own network of potential colleagues inside, close around, and outside the organization.

Followers who become informal leaders can learn the ropes of creating temporary coalitions for various organizational purposes. These same skills will prove useful in formal leadership roles as well. Emergent leaders can learn the skill of creating shifting co-alitions, that is, forming "hot groups" that come together for a time-limited purpose and subsequently disband.[1] These hot groups often fly under the radar, so they are likely to escape the toxic leader's ire.

One senior editor in a large publishing house reported his work with such a hot group, despite the suspicions of the CEO. The group, he recalled, was able to continue by calling itself a "lunch group" (never a "team"), since it always met at lunchtime. After creating the first coalition, it is an easy step to link unrelated co-alitions into a larger network for one set of purposes and then recombine some or all of them later to achieve other common goals, as connective leaders usually do.[2]

Opportunities to Sharpen Ideals and Learn Positive Lessons from Negative Role Models

A vast literature exists on the topic of positive role models, as noted in Chapter 2. Positive role models, as the late sociologist Robert K. Merton first noted, help others who identify with them to "approximate the behavior and values" of those individuals.[3] All kinds of people can serve as role models. For example, role models can be as diverse as athletes, political figures, rock stars, and other celebrities. Younger people, still in the throes of socialization to various roles, are particularly vulnerable to the influence of these larger-than-life figures, whom they learn to emulate. Role models appear closer to home in the guise of parents, other family members, teachers, and clergy members.

While the term "negative role model" routinely appears in popular culture, until relatively recently the research literature paid less attention to this powerful phenomenon as a source of positive lessons. In the popular culture, the term usually refers to individuals whom others regard as role models but whose behavior fails to live up to the exemplary standards expected of them. There is much public hand-wringing about negative role models, those individuals whose inappropriate behavior presumably influences their malleable, would-be emulators to replicate their dysfunctional antics.

Negative role models, however, also serve a relatively less noticed but equally important function.[4] As Julian Lennon understood, they teach individuals who recognize their negativity how *not* to behave and which values *not* to espouse. Seen from this perspective, the negative role model's dysfunctional features prevent most followers from developing a psychological identification with them. Without that sense of identification, potential emulators see little that they admire or wish to imitate in their own lives. In fact, it is quite the reverse. That is not to deny the fact that a negative role model can serve as a teacher for those individuals who deliberately choose the path of toxic leadership, as noted in Chapter 2.

Negative role models are easy to find. Ask any employee with a dysfunctional boss. Ask any volunteer in a political campaign that engages in "dirty tricks." Ask any altar boy who has been the target of abuse by a trusted priest. Positive role models may inspire followers to succeed because they represent a desired self. By contrast, negative role models may represent a feared self that helps those who are more concerned with avoiding failure.[5]

Toxic leaders, acting as negative role models, teach their followers many lessons about how *not* to lead. Those of us who have observed a toxic leader firsthand learn the negative effects of such dysfunctional leadership. When we are the actual target of a toxic leader, we feel the brunt of that leader's negative behavior and his inappropriate values. Those unforgettable experiences may traumatize us, but they may also teach us *not* to touch the hot plate of toxic leadership.

In one not-for-profit organization, the employees felt their executive director had little interest in the mission of the organization, only in his own career. He held elaborate events for donors. He insisted that, to convince these outside supporters to part with their money, the organization needed to entertain them in their accustomed style. The staff complained that the executive director (let's call him Rogers) was away more than he was in the office. They saw these external activities as largely devoted to building the executive director's own network for future career moves. One of the executive director's assistants put it this way:

> Rogers is always tooling around. Presumably in the name of "managing for the mission." Sounds good, doesn't it? But most of us see that as a thinly veiled excuse for him to do his own thing. If you ask me—and many of the other insiders who pay attention to his activities—it is simply to increase his already huge network of contacts. We all think this is just a way station for him. He's looking for something far bigger than this.
>
> Rogers is a glad-hander par excellence. You never met a slicker self-promoter. Maybe worst of all, you can never believe anything that he says. Eventually, we all recognized him as a first-class exaggerator. And that's putting it politely.
>
> Around here, we began to describe anyone who was a self-promoter or an exaggerator as a "Rogersian," or we call it "pulling a Rogers." Besides, for all his frantic hobnobbing, he never seems to raise any money. Mostly he keeps telling us some big donation is in the works. Then we never hear anything more about it. Being around him makes me appreciate my own circle of straight-shooting friends and family.

The values of integrity, respect for others, self-respect, commitment to goals and ideals that transcend the self, compassion, and altruism are felt by their very absence in the arenas where toxic leaders operate. The noticeable lack of these values diminishes the quality of life in the organizations they run. Although followers may have taken those qualities for granted in previous, nontoxic environments, in their absence these values take on new meaning and increased importance.

One scientist who worked in an R&D firm with a leader whose first act as CEO was to purchase a Learjet described his own heightened awareness of values:

> When Hennings, our new CEO, came on board, the first thing he did was buy a Learjet with company funds. He insisted he and his staff needed it to save time at airports, to serve our customers rap-

idly, and to create the image of a substantial, cutting-edge firm. He kept insisting that it wasn't for him alone. He said he had come here to make money and that that was good for everyone, because the rest of us would make more money, too. He sent the HR people out to calm the rest of us natives by giving us all these rationalizations. I don't think anyone believed what they were trying to sell us. We certainly didn't believe any of that baloney.

In fact, I don't think anyone believed him. Most of the professional employees are scientists and engineers. Most of us don't stay up nights thinking about piling up money. We all drive beaten-up cars. That's our form of reverse snobbery, I guess. Cars and other signs of affluence don't mean much to us. Research and publications do. So we were very turned off but mostly grumbled among ourselves. It was a poor use of company funds that could have been put to better purposes, like research in new areas. Still, it made us think about our own values. Were money and the jet-set life important, or were research and advancing science what mattered? I think that Learjet was a symbol of all the values that were missing now that Hennings was running the place. One good thing that came of that was my buddies and I began to think more seriously about our own values, what was important to us.

It is easy to see how the inappropriate behavior of toxic leaders can serve as a clear example of what the followers should avoid. The toxic leader's negative object lesson may stimulate followers to reconsider their own values, previously taken for granted under the aegis of a more positive leader. Of course, for those followers bent on taking the path of toxic leadership, negative role models offer a ready road map.

Opportunities to Build Self-Esteem and Discover One's Superior Moral Authority

The opportunity to build one's self-esteem is a rather strange, even oblique benefit of enduring the tyranny of a toxic leader. So is the opportunity to recognize and experience one's own superior moral authority. Those I interviewed who had chosen, for whatever reason, to remain under the toxic leader's sway described how that process helped them to gain a better understanding of their own strengths and significance. Their resolve to continue their own positive development boosted their self-esteem.

The negative example of their toxic leader made several interviewees recognize how their own and others' dedication to the moral high road gave them an important internal authority. They understood that their moral authority enhanced them not only in their own eyes but in the eyes of others as well, including their opponents. These presumably "stuck" followers began to understand how their greater moral authority was not only admirable and worthy in its own right but also powerful in a Gandhian manner. Some interviewees who had served under toxic leaders began to view their own talents and character in a more positive light. Some seemed to gain new self-respect when they compared their own nontoxic behavior to that of their dysfunctional leader.

Tom Ketry, a service manager in a computer company, described the lessons he had learned about himself as he dealt with a toxic boss:

> I grew up in poverty. I was the first person in my family to graduate from college. Although I was pleased to have accomplished that much, I never thought of myself as particularly outstanding. I was brought up by a mother who put a lot of emphasis on ethics and morality. I absorbed that from her, but I never thought it was particularly unusual. Since I've worked under Tim, who is a very destructive manager, who will do anything to make himself look good, I have learned that I am a better person than I realized. I've come to understand that I should value more who I am as a person. I would never do the things Tim does—lie, backstab, slack off, take credit for work other people did, and much more. I think that, in an odd way, my self-respect has gone up when I compare myself to him. I'd rather lose out on a promotion or a pay increase than do some of the things he does routinely. I'd rather feel good when I look at myself in the mirror.

Still other followers who had no aspiration to be leaders suggested that they had always looked up to leaders and felt that leaders were somehow superior to ordinary people. Their experience with toxic leaders seemed to teach them otherwise. One graphic designer who worked in a large studio explained her perspective this way:

> Since I've always thought of myself as an artist, I never had any desire to become a leader. But I also never thought I had what you need to be a leader. I've always admired leaders. At least from a distance, they seemed very admirable to me. I don't think that way anymore.
>
> When I came to this company, I was very excited to be part of such a famous organization. I felt privileged to say I worked here. That was then. After being here for fifteen years, I feel very different. I see what it takes to become a leader in this place, and I

wouldn't trade what I do for any of that. Most of the people who move into leadership positions in this company are very political. They spend more time sucking up to the people they think have a say around here than doing their work. That mostly fills me with disgust. But then, they aren't the ones with any artistic talent.

For some constituents, the very model of a toxic leader turns them against the entire leadership process. They see the rise to leadership positions as tantamount to giving up valued facets of their own character, including their prized integrity. And, as I have noted elsewhere, the process by which we select and appoint leaders, in many cases, tends to provoke the emergence of the more neurotically ambitious individuals, who elbow their way past their more balanced, less obsessed peers. So it is not particularly surprising that some constituents would be turned off to the entire leadership process.

Al Boynton, a senior manager in a high-tech company, explained his perspective and why he stayed:

> I'm sixty years old. I have only a few more years to retirement. I'm good at what I do as a systems analyst, but I don't kid myself that, at my age, I could get a comparable job elsewhere. Most companies are trying to get rid of their older, better-paid people. So I'm realistic. My wife has diabetes, and we need our health insurance. When I first came here, quite some time ago, I thought about bucking for a high-level executive role. I was young and eager. But as I watched how people made their way into the front office, as well as those who came from the outside, it didn't look so good to me. I think the people who did that gave up a lot of themselves—their souls, that is. They had to sing the party tune, stuff a lot of things that they didn't like or knew weren't right, if they wanted to stay on the fast track. That takes a certain kind of person. And I'm not that kind. I guess I'm lucky. I like the work I do. Watching people move up the ladder in this organization and what they had to do to succeed didn't seem worth it to me. I think the process stinks. I'd rather be master of my own soul.

Working under a toxic leader, as we have seen, can help followers to recognize their own character strengths. That experience can boost the followers' self-esteem. Comparing themselves to a toxic leader who rarely takes the moral high ground can teach followers who have higher ethical standards another lesson: not to misprize their willingness to sacrifice material gains to preserve their moral authority.

Opportunities for Sufferers to Vent Frustrations and Bond

As social psychologist Leon Festinger demonstrated, one of the strongest forces for producing group cohesion is the presence of another group.[6] Perhaps even more mobilizing is the appearance of a common enemy. Those who are suffering from a toxic leader should take heed of these findings. Once sufferers recognize they have a common oppressor, *les misérables* can join forces to draw solace from one another. Once they discover the commonality of their experiences and feelings, the possibility begins to emerge that they will find the strength to withstand, if not outright oppose, the toxic leader.

Harriet Zoft, who worked in the public relations department of a consulting firm, spoke to this issue:

> Frank, the vice president for public relations, was a real ass. He took credit for everyone else's work and did little himself. He didn't appreciate anything we did unless someone else complimented him on it. I don't think he knew good work from bad. Then, as I said, he took the credit. The rest of us in the office—there were four other women and myself—became a band of compatriots. We developed our own special language, so we could talk when he was around and he didn't even know what we were saying. We could be insulting him to one another, and he couldn't understand what was being said. That injected a lot of humor in our work. It made us laugh a lot.
>
> Otherwise, I think we might have cried a lot or gone crazy instead. We did everything we could to get rid of him. It took us several years, but we eventually succeeded. I don't think he ever knew what happened. We didn't want to leave, even though all of us could have gotten other jobs. We liked one another. We worked well together, and we didn't want to go our separate ways. So we put up with him, but there were times it was really rough. That was when having one another was a huge source of comfort and energy.

Sometimes these bonds strengthen those individuals so that they can act in concert to oust or undermine a toxic leader, as Harriet's group eventually did.

Mike Lentil was a senior VP in an advertising firm. According to Mike, the CEO was grossly incompetent and provoked repeated crises for the firm. Apparently the governing board was in the CEO's pocket, so the other ad executives were largely on their own. As the firm lurched from crisis to crisis, members of the different divisions that ordinarily competed for resources began to see one another as allies. The cauldron of turmoil transformed many of these would-be competitors into desperate collaborators. Their repeated crisis interaction brought them new respect and appreciation for one another. Mike reported the situation this way:

> Jonathan, our CEO, was a gigantic incompetent, but he had some great social skills. The board thought he walked on water. Those of us who worked with him daily and saved his ass on a routine basis saw him in a different light. He got us into one crisis after another. We had to look to one another to get ourselves out of these ditches he kept digging for us.
>
> The interesting thing about all these crises that he stirred up was that they brought us together as a group, almost like family. This was true even with people you didn't particularly like. There were so many times that we worked over the weekend and through the night in desperate situations that we got to know and trust one another in a very special way. Crises can do that, you know. For example, there was one fellow in the accounting department whom I never used to trust. I thought he was always out for himself. But I saw the way he came through in a pinch. That made me see him in a different light, too. After that, I could live better with that other side of him because I knew I could count on him in a crunch. I think we all had a sense that we needed to work together as a team to keep the ship from going down. Eventually, as you can probably imagine, the Peter Principle worked, and Jonathan moved on to a different company.

Misery not only loves company, as the old adage tells us. Misery also creates appreciation for fellow sufferers. Working under the leadership of a toxic boss brings us together in a special way with others who have lived through or currently share the same negative experience. We become a community, with a shared history. Our membership in this community reduces the pain of isolation and unshared misery. It provides a sense of warmth and comfort even within the larger context of distress. Amidst this sense of shared identity, competition among former competitors can wither, and collaboration may begin to flourish as fellow prisoners recognize they all hate the same prison menu.

The tight bonds that develop among followers who suffer at the hands of a toxic leader are long-lasting. They usually endure far beyond the time of actual common misery. These bonds of shared suffering, under the right circumstances, may develop into cudgels for breaking the toxic leader's hold.

Opportunities to Learn How to Resist and Organize Resistance

When toxic leaders prevail for any reasonable length of time, the four previous ingredients—opportunities to exercise leadership, to sharpen one's own ideals and learn to avoid the dysfunctional behavior of negative role models, to build self-esteem and discover one's own superior moral authority, and to vent frustration and bond with fellow sufferers—can simmer into a heady stew of resistance. Each of these complex opportunities can strengthen those individuals who construe their situations as opportunities to learn, rather than simply suffer.

- Seizing opportunities to take the lead in an ignored but relevant component of the organization provides a training ground for leadership. Within this context, you can throw off the shackles of the toxic leader and gain a new measure of independence and autonomy. Shedding the bonds of followership, you can seize the chance to express your own autonomy and creativity. You can learn to inspire and organize other followers.

- Sharpening your own ideals and analyzing the pitfalls of negative role models can help you avoid the destructive behavior into which toxic leaders lapse. When you not only search your own soul but engage in deep discussions with others in the same situation, you begin to discover whether or not you share the same values. This, in turn, leads to bonds and connections that can flourish into support groups.

- Grasping that you know how to take the high ground, as well as guarding and nurturing your own talents, can build your self-esteem and give you the leadership edge. Gandhi eschewed weapons of violence. He relied primarily on taking the moral high ground, which ultimately defeated his heavily armed military opponents.

- Bonding with others in the same situation can create trust, strength, and collaborative practices that will serve you well as an organized group of resisters.

Taken together, these opportunities can serve as boot camp for an organized revolt. On the other hand, organizing to overthrow a toxic leader can be quite risky. So resisters should think ahead to a fallback position or a workable exit strategy.

I have already noted the importance of support groups among bonded fellow sufferers. Support groups can come to the aid of a beleaguered colleague in ways that enable that individual to keep going. By closing ranks, they can work together to protect a particular colleague or the entire group from a toxic leader's attack. Savvy support groups also can prevent the leader from dividing and conquering individual members.

Support groups play a special role when the toxic leader must be confronted. If the group acts together in that confrontation, the leader will have much more difficulty brushing off the group's complaints. This strategy is particularly valuable when the matter to be discussed affects the entire group. Sending a lone representative into the lion's den only gives the lion an opportunity for a delicious private snack behind closed doors. The very fact that there are multiple witnesses to the encounter may keep the toxic leader in check and possibly force him to change his behavior.

Linda Ambrose worked in the human resources division of a hospital, where the HR director was a classic toxic leader. Linda described the strategy that the group developed:

> We learned how to resist the hard way. We saw how our strongest member got picked off by the head of HR because she was always willing to speak up as an individual. Her name was Helen, and whenever she saw the HR director acting in ways that were destructive to another individual or the group, she would make an appointment and confront the director. Helen did that on several occasions. We all respected her guts.
>
> At first, the HR director listened as if she were going to change. Later, it became obvious that she wasn't interested in Helen's complaints, even though Helen was representing the group. Eventually she told Helen she should begin to look for another job. Helen eventually left. She didn't really have a choice. The director began to write up a whole set of false complaints about Helen, so she didn't have much chance. That was a huge loss to us, but we learned something important from it: Never let a single individual who is representing the group meet one-on-one with a bad manager. Now we go as a group. That makes us pretty formidable. We've also learned that the same tactic works when you are going to talk to an untrustworthy supervisor simply about your own job, et cetera. You should bring someone else with you. That makes it much harder for the supervisor, with a witness present. Of course, it creates tensions, because it makes it clear that there is no trust between you and the supervisor. But that's a small price to pay. Besides, the ten-

sions were already there before the meeting or we wouldn't have needed to meet that way in the first place.

Support groups can grow into planning groups for strategizing about how to deal with, reform, or possibly unseat a toxic leader. Multiple support groups, both inside and beyond the immediate domain of the suffering followers, can be linked together to create a widespread network of potential resisters. Sometimes, when followers have not yet amassed either the psychological or logistical resources for ousting a toxic leader, passive resistance can work as an effective alternative. Dragging one's feet, as Gandhi taught his oppressed constituents, can bring a toxic leader's operation to a halt.

On occasion it becomes apparent that a confrontation with the leader is in the making. Forcing a three-way confrontation among the distressed followers, the toxic leader, and another party who has some oversight responsibility for the toxic leader—that is, her boss, or (if the toxic leader is the CEO) one or more board members—can be useful. But, again, this is risky business, and there is much homework to be done before such a confrontation is arranged.

Doing your homework is the cardinal rule for success in dealing with a toxic leader. Know and document all relevant details that you can about the leader's toxic behavior. Learn as much as you can about the general political landscape. Engage in what lawyers call "discovery" or "due diligence" about the relationship between the toxic leader and any third party you might wish to bring to the confrontation. Be sure that the third party is not in the toxic leader's camp or at least can serve as a neutral broker. That is part of the intelligence that you will need about the political landscape.

Not all individuals who remain under the toxic leader's baton will join in an underground resistance movement or an outright revolution. Under the right circumstances, however, both types of action may be possible. But just what are the right circumstances? What does it take? How do followers—both those who feel they simply have to grin and bear it, as well as those who have toughened into dry tinder, just waiting for the lit match to ignite them—begin to resist a toxic leader?

How do followers of a toxic leader recognize the tipping point, that synthesis of circumstances that leads to change? How does the group develop the necessary psychological and emotional strength to resist, as well as the rational understanding and planning skills? How do followers perceive when the political climate is ripe, when their economic and technological resources are adequate to stage a successful revolt? Let's turn to these bedrock questions in Chapter 11.

11

What Are Our Choices? How Can We Deal with Toxic Leaders?

The challenge of this book has been twofold: first, to understand why we follow toxic leaders, and second, to determine how to free ourselves from their grasp, be it bare-knuckled or suede-gloved. This chapter focuses on the second of those concerns: how and what we, as individuals and groups, can do both to avoid seduction and to stand up to toxic leadership.

Most of the earlier chapters have been about tolerating the abuses of toxic leaders. To some degree, we have come to take abuse and corruption for granted. Daily media accounts describe the excesses of toxic leaders in business, politics and government, athletics, the church, academia, and even other not-for-profits presumably designed for altruistic purposes. Many cynics feel that is simply the price we pay for living in societies replete with organizational and social hierarchies whose upper levels are served goodies piled high on silver platters. Some turn a blind eye to the chicanery, if it is not totally over the top, in the hope that, as the faithful followers of toxic leaders, they might share some of those perks. Power relationships have always carried that hidden—if usually unfulfilled—promise.

When Someone Speaks Out

Yet tolerating toxic leaders is not the only way we can respond to them: Others make a tougher choice. Janine Drysdale (another pseudonym, of course) found herself and her colleagues in a serious quandary. Marianne Perkins had just been appointed the executive director of their not-for-profit agency. Janine had been a member of the search committee. At her candidate's interview, Marianne stood head and shoulders above the other contenders. She had done her homework; she understood the budget as well as the out-standing service that had won the agency many accolades. She seemed like the perfect choice—until she arrived on the job.

Marianne's opening talk to the staff took the wind out of every-body's sails. She dwelt on her expertise as a "fixer of broken sys-tems." That, she announced, was just what she planned to do in her new post. Janine and her coworkers were speechless. How had this sterling candidate changed into such an arrogant know-it-all? How had she come to believe that this agency, known throughout the community for its outstanding record, was broken?

Things only went downhill from there. Marianne, it turns out, had appallingly poor people skills. Janine kept asking herself over and over how could she have been so taken in at the interview.

The story is a long one, too long perhaps for this chapter. So let me try to shorten it somewhat by telling you that, after that first meeting, Janine decided to write Marianne a letter. This is how Janine describes her approach:

> I tried to look for a common thread, and the common thread that I saw was, number one, she's a new person, and she wants to be successful. We want her to be successful. We want the agency to be successful. So we had a common thread right there, and that's kind of the angle I started off with. I said [to my fellow staff members] that we want to do whatever we can to be successful, but in order to do that, we need to be honest with Marianne and fill her in on the background of the agency and so forth, so she knows where we're coming from. And she knows what she's getting into and that we're not like the broken agencies that she's been so used to fixing.
>
> So I wrote her a letter just telling her that before I was on that interview panel, our staff had gotten together to outline the qualities that we wanted to see in an executive director. And I listed every-thing in there of what we expected from our executive director. I didn't tell her what we didn't like about her behavior, because I didn't want her to feel I was attacking her. I gave her the letter, and

I told her, "If you want to discuss it at the next staff meeting, we could do that."

Well, she never answered. She acted as if she never got it. Things kept getting worse. People were meeting secretly to figure out ways to get rid of her. Time went by, and one day she called me into her office and accused me of saying something to another staff member that I had never said. That really got me. She did that a lot, telling people that other people had accused them of bad things, but without ever identifying their accusers. I insisted that she produce the accusers, which of course, she couldn't do, since I hadn't done what she was accusing me of.

The next day she called me to her office again. This time, she said, "What's wrong? I thought you were strong enough, that you could handle this." It was really ridiculous. The whole thing was just totally ridiculous, and I told her, "I need time to digest this. Let me talk to you tomorrow about this." And so the next day, I came in, and I decided—I mean I really, really had to think about this, because I thought the staff is really ready to topple her because she's done so many bad things, like accusing people of things they hadn't done and a lot worse.

You have to realize, too, that our staff has been there for a long time with the same executive director, and change is difficult. It's hard. For anybody to come in and fill in the shoes of somebody who's been there for thirty-two years, that's hard. That was going to be a difficult thing to do. But she totally screwed it up.

So people were very upset, and I just thought, the only way that I can reach her is that I knew she was a Christian, and she knew that I was, too. And I thought the only way I can talk to her is if I go through that angle with her. I really, at that point, could have just totally hated her if I wanted to. But I thought, "What do I need to do? What do I need to model for her?" And I thought I need to model love for her, and I needed to show her how to treat people.

So I just went in and asked her if I could talk to her. I just walked in, and I said, "Can I close the door?" And she said, "Fine." She was sitting behind the desk. And I said, "I need you to come out from behind your desk." So she came out, and she sat way across the room, and I said, "I don't want you sitting over there. You're too far away. I want you sitting closer to me." And so she went, and she sat in a chair that was kind of close. Then I said, "Now, bring the chair and put it in front of me." She was looking at me, and she said, "Are you telling me what to do?" And I said, "Yes, I am." She says, "Okay." So then I told her, "Give me your hands," and I looked at her right in the eye, and I told her, "I have a conversation that I want to share with you, but I don't want to do this without starting this in prayer with you." And so I did that with her, and I just prayed about what our conversation would be, how our conversation was going to go and the things I had to say to her, and how I did not want to be hurtful to her but these were things that needed to be said because I wanted her to be successful. And I wanted this agency to be successful.

At that point, I told her everything that she was doing wrong. I mean everything. I deleted nothing. I came right out and I said, "Your people skills suck." I just came right out, and I said that to her. I said, "You know that you cannot be talking about some employees with other employees. You know you're the leader. You need to keep [your thoughts about people] confidential. You cannot make comments under your breath." I said, "What you say and what your body language is saying are two different things." I said, "Whatever you say you're going to do, you need to do it, and you need to model it for the employees, and you're not modeling it."

I said, "Your staff doesn't want a buddy. They want an executive director." Because she kept trying to have lunch with everybody every day and just trying to be one of the gang, you know, but people were really uncomfortable with that.

Although that was pretty tough talk, that one heart-to-heart with Marianne was just the beginning. A long road lay ahead for Janine, who talked about how hard it was for her to take this role:

I have to say it wasn't something that I would normally do, and I've never experienced anything like that before. But there was something inside of me that knew that I had to do this. You know, it's like a calling for me that said, "This is what you are here for. You are put here in this situation. You're the one that needs to take care of this, and you're the one that needs to do this." . . . I don't think that this was something I normally would have done because when I went into her office and started telling her to come out from behind her desk, and I mean I would never be brave enough to do that.

I asked if she had planned it before she came in.

No, it just came to me as I did it. And it was something I knew I had to do. . . . I was put here at this time to be here for this woman and to help her out. Don't ask me how I know this. I just know that that's why I'm here right now for her, and its not something I normally would want to take on. I don't have the time or the, you know, the expertise to take on something like that.

Janine worried that the rest of the staff would be angry because she seemed to be taking Marianne's part, particularly when Marianne was being pretty heavy-handed about it. She forged ahead nonetheless, with the courage that Harvard lecturer Brian Little describes as "acting out of one's character."[1] When Marianne stepped on someone's toes, Janine moved in to soothe and explain.

Toxic Handlers, Whistle-blowers, and Confronters

Janine was what Peter Frost and Sandra Robinson call a "toxic handler."[2] Toxic handlers are people who absorb, dilute, and otherwise handle the negatives that are naturally generated in organizations by toxic leaders, as well as by toxic policies and practices. Toxic handlers seem naturally drawn to heal people who have been traumatized. As Frost and Robinson note, toxic handlers may be chewed up in the process.

In this case, although Marianne seemed to take the advice and began to work hard to undo the problems she had caused, the situation has not yet been resolved. Yet Janine seems quite optimistic and determined to keep trying. Finding a basis of trust—in Janine's case, a shared religion—can ease the way for both the advice giver and the toxic leader to establish a constructive dialogue. Janine also confided that one of Marianne's most vehement opponents had thanked her for what she perceived to be a rather miraculous turnaround in Marianne's approach to her leadership role. So perhaps there is hope after all.

Some, like Janine, are confronters. They go directly to the toxic leader without going public. What makes them do it? Why did Janine act? Why did Carol Sosan and her coworker Louise in the aerospace company protest the improper treatment of their boss by confronting his boss? What pushed Dillon at the World Bank? What made well-known whistle-blowers such as Roger Boisjoly, Cynthia Cooper, and Coleen Rowley speak up? Most of them said they had no choice; they simply had to act. They described what drove them in different words—their "conscience," their "sense of right and wrong," "that's just what you do." Yet each was touching on that aspect of character that makes us act not for our own advantage but for others or for an important principle, like truth or justice.

Speaking Out on Your Own Behalf

Speaking out against toxic behavior for the sake of others does not mean that speaking out on your own behalf is somehow a lesser good. Sometimes your personal good coincides with what is also good for others.

By now, the case of *Fred Korematsu v. United States* is a well-known embarrassment in the annals of U.S. law. An American citizen of Japanese descent, Fred Korematsu, a twenty-two-year-old defense plant worker, refused to obey Executive Order 9066 (generally known as the Exclusion Order). That executive order, signed by President Franklin D. Roosevelt, served as the basis for interning Japanese Americans during World War II. Rather than sign up for internment, which would separate him from his Caucasian girlfriend, Korematsu, an Oakland, California, high school graduate with an unblemished record, ran away.

Arrested and convicted in a federal district court of knowingly violating the Exclusion Order, Korematsu appealed the decision to the U.S. Circuit Court, which upheld his conviction.[3] Korematsu was interned in Utah in a relocation center along with thousands of other Japanese Americans. From there, he appealed his case to the U.S. Supreme Court. The Court refused to overturn his conviction.

Decades later, at the urging of the American Civil Liberties Union and several young lawyers imbued with the zeal of a noble mission, Fred Korematsu agreed to reopen his case. In 1983, Korematsu's conviction was reversed. In 1998, President Bill Clinton hung the Medal of Freedom around Korematsu's neck in a poignant White House ceremony. Korematsu received an official apology from the U.S. government. Moreover, thousands of Korematsu's fellow internees each received $20,000 compensation—small but symbolic evidence that it is rarely too late to confront a leader's hurtful decision.

Although Korematsu acted initially for personal reasons, he saw the larger issue of injustice for people incarcerated simply on the basis of race. Eventually others who had been similarly harmed also benefited from Korematsu's courage. That initial injustice came from President Franklin D. Roosevelt, a leader whom historians have given high marks but whose decision in this case was clearly toxic. Janine, whom we met a few paragraphs back, had understood Marianne's negative impact on the whole agency, but it took a personal injustice to mobilize her. Her coworkers, like Korematsu's, reaped the harvest of Janine's actions.

A Conspiracy of Goodness

One last story, documented by Pierre Sauvage in an extraordinary film, *Weapons of the Spirit*, reveals much about why some people can maintain their integrity in the face of tyrannical leaders, even at great risk to their own lives.

During World War II, at Le Chambon-sur-Lignon, a small town

in the mountains 350 miles south of Paris, a community of five thousand Huguenot farmers hid five thousand Jews, mostly children, from the Nazis. Without any formal decision or even much discussion among the villagers, except for their pastor's sermon denouncing the Nazis, these descendants of religiously persecuted Huguenots quietly engaged in what the filmmaker described as a "conspiracy of goodness." Sauvage, himself one of the children born during those dark days in Le Chambon, interviewed the rescuers some four decades later. The filmmaker was still trying to comprehend what drove their extraordinary spiritual opposition to toxic leadership. When asked why he and his family had taken such a risk, one of the villagers replied simply, "That's just what you do."

Several telling factors emerge in this film: the Huguenot villagers' awareness of their own ancestors' history of religious persecution; their strong religious faith; the leadership of their pastor; and their belief that an individual's conscience must be one's true guide.

The Lessons to Be Learned: What Makes People Speak Out

What are the lessons to be learned from such stories of resistance to toxicity? What are the conditions that prompt some people to resist toxic leaders, be they their boss at the printing company, a despotic political leader, or possibly an abusive spouse?

There are several factors that can make a difference. Many years ago, renowned social psychologist Kurt Lewin put forth his field theory of social behavior.[4] It may be applicable here. Some forces acting upon us in situations involving toxic leaders can be thought of as *driving forces*—pressures, internal or external, that drive us to take action. Other, *restraining forces*—such as our fears and anxieties—may restrain us from taking action. When the driving forces grow stronger, they may overwhelm the restraining forces, and vice versa. But the process is dynamic. As the driving forces push us hard in one direction, the countertension on the restraining side becomes stronger, like pushing against a strong spring. The spring pushes back.

Let's consider some of the driving and restraining forces that affect followers' decisions to protest.

- *Proximity.* When followers are close to the grievous act, they are more likely to speak out. That's a driving force. If we work in the same department, live in the same neighborhood, or see the event take place, we are more likely to act.

- *Information*. When we only know the bare outlines of the problem, we are probably unlikely to take on what we perceive as somebody else's issue. With each increment of knowledge that we receive, the more we are drawn into the problem, the more we feel the drive to act relative to the restraining forces of avoiding trouble, and consequently the less we can excuse our inaction. Not long ago, at an economic conference in Davos, Switzerland, Holocaust survivor Elie Wiesel and *New York Times* writer Thomas Friedman spoke about the importance of technology in spreading the word about toxic deeds. While I would certainly agree that the Internet and TV can help convey information quickly and far, they are no panacea. Yes, the Chinese students at Tiananmen Square got the word out to the world through the Internet and TV, but the Chinese government still brutally put down the student revolution as the world, for the most part, stood by and watched.

- *Cost*. Cost is a curious factor, because we can calibrate cost in so many different ways. The residents of Le Chambon didn't see the risk to their lives as a great cost, while many of the people who stood close by while Kitty Genovese was stabbed clearly did. Proximity drove toward action, but fear and other cost factors were so strong that they restrained the witnesses. Nonetheless, some confronters, whistle-blowers, and toxic handlers see that the risks are great but feel that the real cost of not acting is greater. That real price is the damage to their souls.

- *Identification with the victim*. If we identify with the party being hurt, we are more likely to act. Sharing a similar history, even though we share little else, may be enough to create the bond of identification that drives us to act. The inhabitants of Le Chambon, with their own legacy of religious persecution, could identify with the Jewish families the Nazis sought to destroy. If the victims of the toxic leader are unlike us in nationality, race, age, gender, history, and ideology, their plight is less likely to move us to action.

When Treasury Secretary Henry Morgenthau Jr., of Jewish descent, tried to intercede on the part of Jewish victims of the Nazis, first with President Franklin Roosevelt and later with his successor, President Harry S. Truman, he met with little success. Roosevelt refused to order the bombing of either the train tracks to the

Auschwitz concentration camp or the camp itself, although American planes were hitting targets only five miles away.[5]

When Morgenthau later entreated Roosevelt's successor, President Truman, to allow a vessel carrying young, parentless Jewish refugees to land in the United States, Truman still turned the ship of orphans back to certain death in Europe. Several newly discovered pages from Truman's diary describe his intense negative reaction to Morgenthau's request.[6] In his diary, Truman describes his anger and psychological distance from these Jewish victims. Lacking the ability to identify with this group, Truman also lacked an important basis for action. The strength of restraining forces kept both presidents from acting.

- *Size and power of the knowledgeable group.* When only a few people or groups, particularly not very powerful ones, know that a leader is acting in a toxic manner, there is probably small likelihood of stopping the leader. Sadly enough, there is considerable evidence that powerful groups who see the victim as the Other will also acquiesce to toxic action toward them. This is especially true if the leader either seduces or threatens those around him or her into collusion and silence. Toxic leaders often initially seduce their followers with what I call "dangerous gifts," personal or political, that benefit the followers and place them in the leader's debt. Later, the rule of reciprocity kicks in, and the followers feel more obliged to go along with the toxic leader's action. In political cases, the objectors may be injured, jailed, or killed. In the corporate context, we see various analogous scenarios.

In the Tyco case, former CEO Dennis Kozlowski seduced a small inner circle by sharing his ill-gained profits with them—a sad example of such dangerous gifts. In the Westar Energy case, CEO and chairman David Wittig not only included his executive vice president, Douglas T. Lake, in his shady dealings, but managed to drive out all his various critics, including two directors.[7] There is some comfort in knowing that after Wittig's and Lake's departures, the ousted critics were back and running Westar.

- *Qualities of character: courage and the willingness to take risks, integrity, sense of responsibility and service, compassion.* In virtually every case where someone speaks truth to power, qualities of character were powerful driving forces toward action. Courage and the willingness to take risks always seem to be involved. Sometimes, although the risks are objectively great, the confronter either sees them as relatively inconsequential or, as we've seen, feels that the risks associated with not acting are even greater. Integrity, another key quality of character, comes up again and again. For many of those who decide to take action, their integrity is laced to a strong sense of responsibility or service, either to their group, their organization, their god, or their country. Preserving their integrity and standing up for truth may be worth more to them than their lives. Presumably this was the case with David Kelly, the microbiologist who blew the whistle on British prime minister Tony Blair's estimate of Iraq's access to weapons of mass destruction. Compassion is still another quality of character that appears repeatedly as we analyze accounts of people who are stirred to speak out to toxic leaders on behalf of their victims, as well as in the name of truth.

• *The emergence of someone who protests and/or a critical event.* The appearance of someone who protests the decision of a toxic leader can galvanize resistance that is simmering just below the surface of a group. Rosa Parks's refusal to sit in the back of the bus ignited the civil rights movement, which was ready to erupt but needed the spark of a critical event and the appearance of a credible protester. Although other candidates had been considered by civil rights organizers to take such a galvanizing step, the strategists of the nascent movement knew that the protester should not be someone whose political or personal baggage could be exploited by the opposition.[8] Whistle-blowers can, but often don't, serve this purpose, since they commonly act alone.

During World War II, Gloria Leavitt, a shipyard welder, courageously broke an illegal and racist strike by striding through the picket line while her coworkers hung back. Only then did they follow. When circumstances are right, public action can be more effective than private confrontation or whistle-blowing.

The Choices We Have as Individuals

Although I have focused largely on why we tolerate toxic leaders, even to our own detriment, that is not the total picture. Clearly, there are other choices we may be able to make, even though we live and work under the aegis of a toxic leader. Here are some to consider:

- *Counsel the toxic leader; help that leader to improve.* That is the choice that Janine made, with some success. In many cases, however, that avenue is simply out of the question—or is it? That choice may, in more instances than we initially realize, be worth a serious try. Perhaps if key opinion shapers both within and outside the leader's group are brought into the process, they can have a serious impact on the leader.

- *Quietly work to undermine the leader.* This is a difficult choice, because it can put the underminers in danger of taking toxic measures themselves. When, if ever, is toxicity deserving of countertoxicity? Nonetheless, despite that difficult moral dilemma and the personal dangers that may be involved, when all other avenues are blocked and the toxic impact of the leader is high, it may be your only possible route. In a famous incident, several of Hitler's generals tried to assassinate him with a bomb one of them brought in his briefcase to a meeting. Hitler, of course, escaped, and his surviving would-be assassins were executed, but their courageous attempt lives on.

- *Join with others to confront the leader.* Coalitions are extremely important in confronting toxic leaders. When a single individual confronts the toxic leader as the representative of the unhappy multitudes, that individual is in danger of being ousted, as we saw with Carol Sosan and Louise in the aerospace company. Single challengers may also realize their efforts have failed and subsequently leave, often after retribution by the toxic leader. Still another danger is that they may be subtly bought off and, worse yet, may interpret the bribe as a breakthrough. Seducing the leader of the opposition can decapitate a resistance movement, as one feminist group discovered in the 1970s. That group had sent its lead spokesperson to confront university administrators on behalf of female faculty, who were routinely being denied tenure. The administrators rather cynically arranged for the spokesperson to receive tenure and sit on various committees to represent the untenured female faculty. The spokesperson took her advance as evidence that the university had capitulated. Here we have another example of "dangerous gifts."

The newly minted full professor with tenure then owed her own debt to the administration, which she consciously or unconsciously paid by trying to cool out the group she was meant to represent. In early unionization efforts, management frequently tried to seduce the leaders of the rank and file. To eliminate workers' opposition, managers would identify the leaders of blue-collar groups and quickly promote them into management positions.

• *Join with others to overthrow the leader.* Here, too, coalitions are the key to success. This means both coalitions within the organization that the leader heads, as well as coalitions that cut across internal/external lines. Joining with outsiders who represent important constituencies, be they shareholders, customers, consumers, voters, legislators, or other relevant parties, can serve as a powerful lever. The media can play a powerful role here, yet including them can create its own complex costs.

Organizing a major protest is not easy, and sometimes it takes more than one serious protest to get the leader's attention. On July 1, 2003, a half million Hong Kong residents marched to demonstrate against the strict internal security legislation proposed by the government. The legislation would have mandated lengthy prison terms for individuals convicted of sedition or even of handling documents that the government considered seditious.

That show of organized protest forced Tung Chee-hwa, Hong Kong's chief executive, to back down somewhat and agree to defer for several days the vote on the controversial measure. Two subsequent rallies at which speakers demanded greater democracy, followed by the resignation of two top government representatives previously thought to be close to high-level Beijing Communist officials, pushed Tung Chee-hwa to agree to another round of public consultations. A harried Tung insisted that he had no plans to step down.[9] At this writing, the situation remains in flux, a victory for the protesters that would not have occurred without their organized efforts.

There are precautions to be considered by those contemplating the overthrow of a toxic leader, be it in a small business organization or a large nation. The first attempt is potentially the most dangerous. Much depends upon the resources—supporters, finances, intelligence, legal and political resources, and, in the case of governments, military and police forces, and possibly munitions—available to the leader and the rebels. The degree to which the attack catches the leader off guard is also a critical factor.

Leaders who succeed in putting down the first attempt to unseat them quickly move up the learning curve. By contrast, their defeated opponents usually withdraw in disarray, disband, or are eliminated. By the next attempted overthrow, the leader is more experienced, more prepared. The new opponents are usually just that—new—and therefore less likely to be experienced than the leader in such matters. So in addition to considerable institutional resources, the leader has the advantage of more experience, along with a reputation for the ability to withstand attacks.

A leader's reputation for formidability only grows more intimidating with each new foe vanquished. As Tom Peters's dissertation research showed, even small but consistent wins by a toxic leader can cow would-be challengers.[10] Fidel Castro, who has maintained his stranglehold on Cuba for half a century despite repeated attempts to overthrow him, provides a case in point.[11] Thus most subsequent attacks come from new, less experienced groups, which the seasoned leader has learned to repel more efficiently and effectively than previous adversaries.

Consequently, it is not surprising that it can take years, even decades, for opponents to regroup, gather sufficient resources, rethink strategy, and learn as best they can from their own and others' experience before they succeed in overthrowing a toxic leader. The opponents of former Yugoslav president Slobodan Milosevic— among them many intelligent, educated, dedicated, professional individuals—had to bide their time until their numbers, resources, and experience increased sufficiently to overthrow a toxic leader who seemed to grow larger and stronger with each assault on his power.

- *Avoid entrapment by friends and family.* Individuals whom we may count as our personal friends or close associates, even family members, may entrap us if we are not careful. There is no denying the pain we face when friendships or family ties threaten integrity, but taking the straightforward tack with those close to us can perhaps save them as well.

You will recall that Betty Vinson, an accountant and senior manager at WorldCom, fudged the numbers for eighteen months despite the fact that she was beset all the while with grave misgivings. Yet Vinson found it difficult to refuse the requests of her boss, Buddy Yates, with whom she'd been friends since they had worked together at a previous company. That friendship did not protect her from criminal charges.

Timothy and Michael Rigas allegedly conspired with their father, John, founder of Adelphia Communications, to engage in securities fraud. So even parents may not stand as a bulwark against entrapment.

- *Leave.* This option is a very personal one. It means you leave knowing others are still trapped in the clutches of the toxic leader. Sometimes leaving is your only alternative, particularly when the leader has the power to oust you from the group. Some people depart when the negatives outweigh the positives; when they feel physically or psychologically ill; when they are so personally undermined that they can't work effectively; when they have determined there is no support for resistance; and most of all when their self-respect begins to ebb. Leaving is not necessarily accompanied by a sense of defeat. For example, scientist Robert Beyster left what he considered servitude in a large firm to build Scientific Applications International Corporation as a model of freedom, based on employee ownership.

The Policy Choices We Have: The Safeguards Against Toxic Leadership

While it is difficult to create policies single-handedly, the impetus for changing toxic policies can be initiated by a single individual. Ultimately, however, developing or changing policy is the work of a group, and here, too, coalitions come into play. Let's consider some possible safeguards, not all appropriate in all situations:

- *Term limits.* The processes by which we select and keep leaders in public and private office often attract the wrong candidates for the wrong reasons. Thomas Jefferson described his perspective on the danger this way: "Whenever a man has cast a longing eye on offices, a rottenness begins in his conduct." And even when leaders enter with respectable levels of competency and integrity, many remain in office so long that they eventually reach their level of incompetence. The result is that they dwindle into mediocrity or worse. And, of course, Lord Acton's famous dictum applies here as well, since long terms of office tend to concentrate inordinately the leader's power: "Power tends to corrupt, and absolute power corrupts absolutely." In fact, it is virtually a truism that even nontoxic leaders who hang on too long commonly go from good to bad.

The desire to cling to power is so common that we need to consider for a moment just why it happens. Undoubtedly, many factors contribute, including the very obvious one of becoming accustomed to the perks of power. Some years ago, I heard former Boston mayor Kevin White, initially elected on a reform platform, reflect on why voters had unseated him, not once but twice. That is, after initially ousting the mayor, the voters subsequently re-elected him, only to defeat White a second time. Although, according to White, he had entered politics idealistically to "uplift the downtrodden," the former mayor ruefully acknowledged he had "gotten too used to having the door held open for me." We should hardly be surprised that leaders—who, after all, share our human vulnerabilities—can be seduced by the attractive perks and ingratiating retainers that come with power.

Still, one less obvious but perhaps more compelling reason why leaders often hang on too long is worth considering: For some leaders, giving up power means losing their path to immortality. In short, relinquishing power becomes symbolic death. Besides, except for the most cynical, as time passes, leaders become increasingly committed to their goals, which they try with increasing desperation to achieve. But they, too, can lose their perspective. So again and again we see leaders step back from vital but unpopular tasks lest they lose their hold on power.

Not too long ago, a meeting of several former prime ministers and academics shed some light on this issue. As these political leaders ruminated about the lofty goals they had set out to achieve but then failed to pursue, several academics asked the obvious question: why? To a person, the former prime ministers insisted that such actions would have cost them their office. Not one indicated he had seriously considered sacrificing power for principle. Thus, holding on to power can gradually become an end in itself, albeit with strong rationalizations. Is there any antidote for this serious toxin?

Term limits can act as one protection against toxic leadership in several important ways. First, they put everyone—would-be leaders and their supporters, as well as opponents—on notice that the leadership position is *not* a lifetime possession. Leaders then know that at some designated future date they will have to return to the ranks of followers and nonfollowers alike, simply as a peer. That helps to reduce high-handedness in power.

At the same time, both followers and nonfollowers realize that they need not cozy up to the leader to prevent being permanently left out in the cold. The knowledge that the leader has a limited term provides insurance against the leader developing unlimited power or arrogance.

A predetermined length of service in a particular leadership role may also light a flame under incumbents. It may remind them that time is of the essence, that this is their one big chance to achieve their most highly prized goal.

- *Repair the flawed process for selecting leaders.* We need to address the larger issue of repairing the entire flawed process for selecting leaders—in public and private leadership roles. Until we do, those individuals most neurotically driven to achieve power will continue to elbow everyone else aside in their rush to leadership. That issue, too, is a worthy topic for encyclopedic treatment elsewhere—certainly in relation to elected office, but in the private sector as well.

Nonetheless, we'll address this topic more fully in Chapter 13, when we'll focus on how we might induce reluctant, but capable, candidates to enter leadership roles. We'll also discuss how the addition of midlevel employees to selection committees can help put forward nontoxic leaders.

- *Create respectable departure options.* Many leaders cling to their role because they can't bear giving up the comfortable perks that leaders usually enjoy. When we let leaders remain in office too long, we also stifle the talents, ingenuity, and enthusiasm of other leaders with fresh ideas. We also block the emergence of younger generations of leaders waiting in the wings. So we need to develop respectable exit options.

Thomas Jefferson's concept of leadership in the public sector called for serving in high office, presumably in Washington, for a limited period of time, then returning home to serve one's own community. The returning leaders would then apply their experience to other roles. This model could work effectively beyond the halls of government as well. In fact, one variation on this theme—

the Experience Corps—brings the expertise of retired executives on a volunteer basis to communities and fledgling businesses.

Still other attractive options need to be developed to entice long-term leaders to depart in a respectable manner. Not too long ago, Boston University began to experiment with a rather unconventional option for dealing with democratically elected African leaders who have been at the helm too long. BU offers these leaders an honored place in the Lloyd G. Balfour African Presidents in Residence Program, where they can write their memoirs within the shelter of a university setting. These long-term leaders receive a generous stipend, housing, an office, and secretarial help, as well as the informal honorific benefits that come with a university affiliation.

The first recipient of this sinecure was Zambian president Kenneth Kaunda, who served "under less than democratic circumstances for twenty-seven years, but ultimately left office of his own accord when an election was held and he lost."[12] Serious ethical considerations need to be addressed before arranging such departures for leaders, including CEOs and university presidents, who have been known to overstay their usefulness. Presumably, such options would be designed for long-term leaders in an effort to prevent toxic consequences from an overdrawn leadership career. An important caveat: The case of noncriminal but toxic leaders generates ethical issues, which undoubtedly call for other, more complex solutions. Preventing toxic leaders from contaminating any new institutions that they might join must be dealt with in a thoughtful and ethical manner as well.

- *Mackerels in the moonlight: corrupt but effective leaders.* Sometimes we allow leaders to stay on too long because we stand in awe of their genius, despite their other evident toxic qualities. In the 1880s, John Randolph, a Virginia aristocrat, complained that presidential hopeful Henry Clay was such a genius and yet so corrupt that "like a rotten mackerel in the moonlight, he both shines and stinks."[13]

Earlier we met Charles Dutoit, music director of the Montreal Symphony, who controlled the baton there for twenty-five years. Dutoit was renowned not only for his musical brilliance and his signature Garbo-like sunglasses, but also for his arrogance and rage. The misery that his temper and haughtiness showered on the musicians finally tipped the delicate balance between genius and toxicity and ultimately led to his ouster. Financier Michael Milken,

Providence mayor Buddy Cianci, and Boston mayor James Michael Curley are just a few other examples of toxic leaders whose toxicity was joined to effective leadership. Oftentimes the brilliance of certain toxic leaders not only intimidates followers into silence but convinces them that no one else can possibly replace them or bring to the organization the benefits—like contracts and fame—that they can.

The bottom line in the choice between the organization and the "toxic genius" or even the "great toxic leader" seems self-evident: Toxic brilliance is still toxic. Is any toxic but brilliant individual's contribution truly worth the serious destructive impact he or she has on the organization and its people?

- *Open and democratic policies, practices, and procedures.* In those systems fortunate enough to exist within a democratic tradition, the culture of an open democracy must be scrupulously maintained. Even in the face of crises, when we are tempted to introduce authoritarian measures to "protect" us from future harm, let's not forget the importance of safeguarding the group's traditions of openness, individual rights, and democratic procedures.

- *Educated constituents who can deal with their anxieties.* Educating constituents sufficiently to deal with their anxieties is no cakewalk, since most of us prefer to avoid the pain of dealing with our angst. Nonetheless, education that leads to insight helps to free us from narrow thinking, from stereotypes, and from self-delusions. Yet education is a long-term strategy that must be maintained by sequential leaders. If successors are disinclined to support such educational endeavors, the followers must exert adequate pressure to keep these efforts in place.

- *Protecting whistle-blowers from reprisals.* Although whistle-blower protection policies and programs exist at the federal level and in numerous states, various informal kinds of retribution are common. The National Whistleblower Center, in Washington, reports that informal, on-the-job harassment of whistle-blowers commonly persists.[14] To deal with this ongoing problem, more protective policies, within organizations as well as in legal statutes, need to be developed and enforced.

Much more than policies are called for at the informal level, where reputations are created and crushed. For example, the "whispering war," fueled by rumors passed through e-mail and conversations around the water cooler, as well as at professional meetings, is virtually impossible to combat.[15] Reputation, that most precious of intangible gifts and most difficult to protect from rumor, can quickly be tarnished beyond repair. Here, too, the exercise of integrity and courage is necessary to combat unfounded rumors about others, since speaking up on our own behalf in such situations is usually both difficult and futile.

- *Accountability forum.* Leaders, even nontoxic leaders, can make serious mistakes. No one seriously expects that leaders involved in a multitude of complex decisions will always get it right. The issue is not simply the substance of the decision, right or wrong, but the process. "How was the decision made?" "On what information?" "At whose insistence?" and "On whose counsel?" are just a few of the salient questions that leaders should be willing to address in an open accountability forum. Leaders who cannot confront their own mistakes, both privately and publicly, are probably not leaders we can trust with decisions that affect our lives.

Too often, we have made it de rigueur for lower-level members to fall on their swords to take the blame for a leader's bad decisions. We need to ask ourselves what that says about the courage, integrity, and accountability of the leaders to whom we entrust our safety. The political uproar that followed President George W. Bush's and Prime Minister Tony Blair's use of what proved to be incorrect intelligence to justify the preemptive attack on Iraq led to various lower-level officials being smoked out on both sides of the Atlantic. Even when they deny their culpability, these lower-rung individuals may not be spared.

Sometimes little distinction is made between those actually responsible for the poor decision, from the leader's staff to the leader who makes the final decision, and those who blow the whistle on it. That was certainly the case with the infamous "sixteen words" in Bush's State of the Union address, where one lower-level staffer after another at the CIA (not even counting CIA director George Tenet) and the White House were forced to take the hit. An object lesson from across the Atlantic: Dr. David Kelly, the microbiologist who spoke off the record to a BBC reporter, was called before a government inquiry board to explain his "leaking" information about the validity of the intelligence used by Blair. Asked if he felt the Blair government was "throwing him to the lions," the soft-spoken Dr. Kelly stoically responded that he "accepted" his situation. The next day, Kelly took a solo walk in the woods behind his home, where he quietly slit his wrists.

In this chapter, we have explored some pragmatic options that followers may select for dealing with toxic leaders. There are more available than you might think: confronting them, helping them to change, quietly undermining them, blowing the whistle on them, and organizing to oust them. There are undoubtedly still others. Most of the action required for dealing with toxic leaders is not for the faint of heart. The costs of *in*action, however, may be even greater.

These options represent a set of possible cures for toxic leadership. Yet the old adage about an ounce of prevention being worth a pound of cure may apply to toxic leaders. In Chapter 12, let's consider how we might detect the early signs of toxicity in leaders and their visions. Let's also explore some techniques of prevention that just might work.

12

Detecting the Early Signs of Toxicity in Noble Visions and Leaders

When the toxicity of a leader is full-blown, we easily recognize it. In many cases, we can avoid these obvious characters. Escaping the magnetic pull of more subtle toxic leaders or those in the early stages of toxicity is far more difficult, for they attract us with challenges and visions that excite and entrap us before we perceive their negative potential. In this chapter, let's explore how we might detect the nascent signs of toxicity in leaders and their noble visions.

When We Take Heroism to the Extreme

Noble visions commonly entail promises of heroism. Taken to its extreme, our unexamined longing to be heroes can leave us responsive to the toxic leader's dark call to battle, to genocide, and to unjust wars. War, just or otherwise, may be the quintessential example of the noble vision that leaders identify as the doorway to immortality.

What lessons can we learn from war? First, war offers immense opportunities to act heroically. Again and again, combatants report they felt most fully alive when they were facing death. In those moments, their adrenaline pumped wildly, leaving them simultaneously terror-stricken and superhumanly strong.

Many veterans look back nostalgically on their wartime experiences as moments of electrifying, noble, heroic action, infused with brotherhood for their own colleagues but gut-wrenching hatred for the enemy. War is probably the greatest expression of hating the Other. Hate can fuel heroism. At the same time, combatants are commonly willing to sacrifice their lives for one another, their country, and the cause.

Poet Wilfred Owen, in arguably the best-known poem of World War I, conveyed that pernicious connection between the euphoria of war and the search for glory when he wrote:

> If in some smothering dreams, you too could pace
> Behind the wagon that we flung him in,
> And watch the white eyes writhing in his face,
> His hanging face, like a devil's sick of sin;
> If you could hear, at every jolt, the blood
> Come gargling from the froth-corrupted lungs,
> Obscene as cancer, bitter as the cud
> Of vile, incurable sores on innocent tongues,
> My friend, you would not tell with such high zest
> To children ardent for some desperate glory,
> The old Lie: Dulce et Decorum est
> Pro patria mori.[1]

The Exhilaration of Living Intensely

Toxic leaders, particularly those who push us into unjust wars, are on to something. They know that the exhilaration of feeling totally alive is addictive and that people can do amazing, even valiant things in that state of mind. So it is hardly surprising that leaders— both good and bad—create enterprises in which we can feel we are living most intensely, where we are completely present in the moment.

In another context, Harold J. Leavitt and I described this state of mind as characteristic of "hot groups," those short-lived, high-achieving groups in which people engage in challenging tasks for what they perceive to be exalted purposes.[2] In virtually every case, hot groups are imbued with the belief that what they are doing will make the world a far better place. A sense of flow colors their actions.[3] Hot groups can enter that mind-set without toxic results, but let's remember that hot groups themselves are not totally immune to toxic leaders.

I mention hot groups because they are a relevant example of

what we need to learn how to do on a larger, longer-term, nonwar basis. That is, we need to discover how to feel most alive—experience the exhilarating meaning in our lives—in *other* ways, without war, without annihilating other groups, without resorting to the we/they dichotomy, and without engaging in the serious harm that the visions of toxic leaders routinely create.

If we can grasp why that extreme moment of danger we face in war is so invigorating, we might make a useful discovery that goes something like this: We feel animated because, in that instant, we allow our submerged terror of death to come to the surface. Once our terror is palpable, we can consciously put it to good use keeping us safe and infusing us with direction and strength.[4] If we could face directly and deliberately our multilayered anxieties about daily life, as well as our terror of death, without letting them control us from the slumbering depths of our unconscious, we probably would feel more alive more regularly. We could also savor life more intensely. We could put our fears to other, more constructive uses, which would sharpen our direction and invigorate us, even if they didn't promise complete safety. Then we could live that intensely without the stimuli of enemies and daily wars, small and large.

This sense of living fully occurs at other moments besides wartime. For one, it happens when we confront other great dangers that spark our anxiety, including potentially fatal illnesses. For another, we also feel that incredible intensity of life at times of immense joy—at the first sight of our newborn child, at the accomplishment of a long-desired feat, at the moment when we win that do-or-die contract, at the sound of great music, at the announcement of our candidate's success—and at other highly emotional moments. We sustain that intensity and appreciation of life at least for some short time afterward, until the quotidian demands of daily life reanesthetize us.

Perhaps our longing for exhilaration and intense experience is what lies at the heart of Goethe's insight: that safety itself is no bargain. In fact, seeking safety puts us directly in the path of another, perhaps greater danger: failing to live life fully. Helen Keller, who lived her entire existence in physical darkness, could see more clearly than most that "[a]voiding danger is no safer in the long run than outright exposure. Life is either a daring adventure or nothing."[5] That is why the chance to participate in a noble vision seems most attractive. But it is that very yearning for exhilaration that positions us within the grasp of toxic leaders.

The Noble Vision Revisited

When we seek the exhilaration of life and strive for immortality without consciously understanding why we do, we make ourselves perilously susceptible to the noble visions of leaders, good and bad. We know that sorting out these noble visions before they plunge into disaster is no simple exercise. We only have to turn on CNN's international news coverage to see how difficult it is to distinguish the villains from the victims.

When noble visions conflict with one another—as they have in the Middle East, Kosovo, Northern Ireland, and parts of Africa— each new assault provokes an escalated response by the victims and their leaders. That retaliation, in turn, begets another, more desperate and barbaric round of vengeance. Every day, the conflict between the Israelis and the Palestinians provides heartbreaking scenes of the endless cycle of "noble visions" locked in deadly combat, blindly killing off the next generation of both sides.

Detecting the Toxic Seeds Within the Vision

Discerning the danger, perhaps the potential toxicity or evil, in a leader's vision is a subtle and complex challenge. By what criteria must leaders and followers measure weighty decisions, particularly those draped in the cloak of lofty enterprises, to prevent a toxic outcome? How do we detect deception when we want so desperately to be convinced and ennobled by an exhilarating mission? At what point in the arc from articulation to implementation can we begin to recognize the vision's toxic potential? What are the warning signs, those early symptoms, of impending toxicity? I raise the following questions not just for followers, but for leaders, too. After all, leaders would do well to worry about being drawn into the abyss, along with their targets and their willing followers.

Perhaps we can begin to pose a set of useful questions. I don't for a moment presume that these are the only questions or even the most relevant ones. I present them mainly as a starting point so that the reader may add to the list.

- Is the vision noble and positive for you and your group but detrimental to innocent others?

- Have multiple groups, with different needs, vetted these choices and subjected them to second and third opinions to determine whether there is benefit to most and harm to none or very few?

• Does the vision promise to make us large at the cost of making others small?

• Does the vision turn evil into moral virtue or moral virtue into human weakness? Does the vision cloak evil in self-sacrificial or virtuous garb, like Heinrich Himmler's speech "thank[ing] the members and leaders of the SS for shouldering the terrible but unavoidable task of exterminating millions of people"? He said:

Most of you will know what it means to have 100 or 500 or 1000 corpses lie before you. That we have endured this has hardened us, and—with a few exceptions of human frailty—we remained decent. It is a victorious page in our history that has never been and never will be written.[6]

• Does the vision involve the leader as your group's savior who destroys your enemy or competitor? According to the leader's vision, must your opponent be crushed for you to survive? Is that a necessary outcome?

• If the leader/savior destroys your enemy, commercial or political, what are the guarantees that those same destructive forces will not be turned next against those who are *not* your foes, like your colleagues, your friends, your family, and ultimately you?

• Does the vision require you to see others as enemies or tainted Others who must be ostracized or eradicated? Or does it provide the chance for antagonistic groups to start small, working together on limited mutual goals, so that they may build enough trust to move forward together gradually? Does it offer the possibility for different groups to specialize and thus work together interdependently? At a minimum, does it allow room for divergent groups to live and let live economically, commercially, politically, religiously, racially, sexually, and philosophically?

• What kinds of sacrifices does the vision demand from you and others: money, labor, time, integrity, character, truth, justice, freedom, family and friends, or your very life? How large and how deadly must the cost of the noble vision be to others and us before we recognize its toxicity?

- Will the vision stand the test of time and the judgment of history?

- Does the vision withstand the "illusion test"?

Noble visions that call for force and harm are obviously suspect. But what about the ones that merely call for gallant deeds, like saving the world or improving life? Do they also promise to enhance life for us at great risk to others? Too often in the past, we have enthusiastically pursued technological solutions to problems without seeing the secondary and tertiary effects that the very solution we welcome is silently gestating. And where do they go from there? The same holds true for human problems.

No simple answers exist, only difficult questions. But we shrink from confronting these questions at our own peril and all of civilization's.

Detecting the First Symptoms of Toxicity in a Nontoxic Leader

At the outset of this book, I tried to outline the behavioral characteristics and the personal qualities that distinguish toxic leaders. The research for this book has convinced me that most people easily recognize full-dress toxic leaders. Diagnosing the early symptoms of toxicity in a nontoxic leader, however, calls for some additional direction. Besides, we need to guard against our own blindness.

It might be useful to have a rough checklist of signs by which we can detect when a previously nontoxic leader is beginning to exhibit the signs of toxicity:

- Does the leader, who may have appeared initially as the organization's or your personal savior, first inflict harm on your enemy or your competitors, then gradually on others? Does your own sense of indebtedness, safety, and relief prevent you from recognizing the leader's toxicity? Once committed to a leader, are you too convinced of the leader's goodness and strength to read correctly the toxic signals and renounce your old commitment? Do you then resolve your cognitive dissonance by ignoring the leader's growing toxicity?

- Does the leader begin to display arrogance and excessive pride, like Shakespeare's tragically flawed general, Coriolanus? Does the leader become self-important and disdainful of others? Does the leader dramatically change his or her lifestyle and circle of friends, becoming inaccessible to old colleagues and intimates?

- Does the leader begin to keep his or her own counsel or take counsel only from a few advisors or only from yes-men and flatterers, like Shakespeare's King Richard II and U.S. president Richard Nixon?

- Does the leader use others to do his or her dirty work and then disown them? That, of course, was how Shakespeare depicted King Richard II, who first directs Mowbray to kill Lord Gloucester and then, when challenged by Bolingbroke, exiles Mowbray for life while ignoring his own complicity in the murder.

- Does the leader begin to mistreat the lowest or weakest members within the group?

- Does the leader fail the "golden mean" test? More specifically, does the leader begin to engage in excesses or fail to demonstrate sufficient leadership capacity? Mathematicians and philosophers consider the golden mean the "ideal rate of growth."[7] Both Confucius's Doctrine of Mean and the golden mean of Aristotle's *Nicomachean Ethics* recognize that violating the golden mean leads to dysfunctional deficits— that is, lack of effective action on one hand and destructive excesses on the other.

- Does the leader become evasive, refusing to explain his or her decisions or even lying outright? Does the leader begin to reject the legitimacy of being held accountable for results?

- Does the leader begin to blame others for his or her decisions and deeds?

- Does the leader begin to act in his or her self-interest instead of the interest of the whole organization or a larger group, thereby destroying the possibility of authenticity?

- Does the leader begin to disguise dubious actions or decisions as noble and altruistic?

Undoubtedly there are other warning signs of the leader's impending toxicity. These ten symptoms, however, may offer the observant follower some advance notice of more toxic things to come.

The Partially Toxic Leader: What's a Follower to Do?

Even essentially nontoxic leaders have their toxic moments. And toxic leaders are not toxic all the time. They might interact toxically with some individuals and not others; they might behave toxically in some situations and not others.

We might think of those leaders who act toxically for a substantial part of their lives but do so in a selective manner as *partially toxic leaders*. In their nontoxic phases, they can be quite effective.

Those followers—employees and others—who have to deal with such leaders must make a difficult decision: to stay or to leave, to take it on the chin or to try to reform or perhaps overthrow the leader. That presents a serious existential question for employees and constituents whose daily lives are bruised by their encounters with partially toxic leaders. Let's briefly consider two examples, one from the political world, one from the business arena.

On several notable occasions, President Franklin D. Roosevelt, generally admired as an effective, ordinarily nontoxic leader, clearly exhibited serious toxic characteristics. To wit, as we saw, he ordered the internment of Japanese-American citizens during World War II. He refused entreaties to bomb the train tracks to the Auschwitz death camp or the camp itself. He also ordered trials by a military tribunal, without the possibility of appeals, for German saboteurs who landed on U.S. soil in World War II. In addition, he tried unsuccessfully to pack the Supreme Court. Yet, on balance, most historians give FDR's leadership behavior a nontoxic grade.

In the second example, an editor described working at a publishing house where the CEO was a partially toxic leader. In much of his work, the CEO exhibited many toxic characteristics. Yet he had a positive effect on the firm in other ways. Under this partially toxic leader, the publishing house flourished financially but not editorially. The editor who had felt the brunt of the CEO's toxicity reported:

> I faced a choice of whether to leave or stay—changing the character
> of the CEO was not possible. I decided to stay and told myself that

it was recognition enough that I knew I was doing a good job and didn't need his approval. I am convinced this was the right choice. It took considerable courage, and I had to look to myself for direction.

Eventually, I am happy to report, that CEO's contract was not renewed by the board.

Working under partially toxic leaders is never easy. The choice to stay or leave, reform or revolt requires a complex calculus. These choices are difficult and highly individual. Yet, as we have seen in our discussion of negative role models, dealing with partially toxic leaders can teach us to draw on our courage and self-reliance, whatever our choice. Still, leaders who are more exemplary, albeit disillusioning, also offer us chances to learn courage and moral self-reliance, without the toxic side effects.

Leaders Who Disillusion

Although many toxic leaders deal in illusions, it would be unfair to characterize *all* leaders as dream merchants. Leaders committed to their supporters' well-being, rather than to their own power—and such leaders do exist—are more likely to help followers forgo many of their illusions through painful but strengthening doses of reality.

This approach calls for leaders to deal with their own anxieties as well as those of their followers. Max DePree, former CEO of Herman Miller, the office furniture design firm, recalls a story about how his father, D. J. DePree, confronted his own anxieties when the Depression cut profits to the quick. In an effort to comfort his employees as well as himself in those dark days, the elder DePree visited his workers at home during the Christmas season. When he called upon Jim Eppinger, one of DePree's most devoted employees, DePree discovered the family had no Christmas tree. Money was too scarce. (Ironically, many years later, when DePree apologized for that time to his old friend, Eppinger had absolutely no recollection of the missing Christmas tree. In fact, Eppinger had remembered that Christmas as "one of the highlights of his life" because DePree had assigned him to the New York territory, "the greatest opportunity" he had ever had.)[8]

The process of disillusionment is painful for leaders as well as followers. Nontoxic leaders have their own strategies for coping with anxiety, theirs and ours. Constructive leaders refuse to succumb to illusions or offer them to us. Indeed, they may insist on shattering even those we create for ourselves.

Initially, leaders who disillusion us may seem quite unappealing. They demand too much. They push us to stand eyeball to eyeball with unsettling truths, even as they stand by and firmly support us. Yet that was what we all saw New York City mayor Rudolph Giuliani do in a press conference immediately following the 9/11 terrorist attack, when he candidly told CNN, "The number of casualties will be more than any of us can bear ultimately."[9]

The Valuable Inconvenience of Leadership

Leaders who disillusion us do not claim to know all the answers. In fact, they may not claim to have *any* answers. More often, they expect us to help create the solutions for which we so desperately look to them. They may even ask us to set aside our current activities in which we are happily immersed and instead put our shoulder to the wheel of community leadership. I call this the *valuable inconvenience of leadership*, because it teaches us what we otherwise might never have learned.

Leaders, toxic and nontoxic, understand on some level that the enterprises they invite us to join are related to our hierarchy of needs. They also perceive the connection between those needs and the control myths that keep us in check. Toxic leaders, however, deliberately manipulate us in ways that keep the control myths in place so that we, as followers, will prevent ourselves from confronting these dysfunctional leaders, from demanding that either they change their behavior or recuse themselves.

By contrast, leaders who disillusion us ask us to face up to two unpleasant tasks. First, they insist we unbundle our needs—even those at the highest levels of our hierarchy of needs, like self-actualization and transcendence—from the control myths that keep us in the toxic leader's grasp. Second, they urge us to confront our existential angst and let it rise to the level of consciousness, where we can put it to positive, creative use. These are not trivial undertakings. And, to be sure, they can cause us great pain and suffering, particularly in the short run.

So it is not hard to understand why we commonly prefer toxic leaders. We respond to them because they offer us free lunches, while nontoxic leaders expect us to help prepare the meal and clean up besides. Toxic leaders work hard at reducing our existential anxiety and obscuring their clay feet. They promise to take over what are rightly *our* responsibilities to the group so that we can concentrate on our own egoistic pursuits. They free us from the valuable inconvenience of leadership. But as an old Tammany Hall politician reportedly warned, "There ain't no such thing as a free lunch." Only later do the bills arrive, in the currency of stunted growth, stifled creativity, and, quite imperceptibly, the silent evaporation of our freedom.

Facing Reality Despite Anxiety

Illusions cushion us from reality and the anxiety that attends it. That shelter from the thunderstorms of life heartens us temporarily, but that's about it. In fact, Freud wisely argued that anxiety actually represented a healthy response to danger.[10]

Anxiety has other benefits as well. Facing up to reality, difficult as that may be, sets us on the path to maturity and clear-eyed confidence. It seasons our anxiety with hope and offers us the possibility of deeper understanding and creativity. As Hungarian sociologist Elemér Hankiss put it so well, "the 'existential' environment, that is, . . . the world or universe . . . [is] the framework of existence: an environment of anxiety and hope in which one must find freedom and peace of mind, roles and identities, faith in oneself, dignity, meaning, and purpose."[11]

Dealing with reality forces us to take responsibility for ourselves and develop new coping strategies. Indeed, the sober recognition that the leader's promises are, in fact, little more than cotton-candy illusions is a necessary condition for self-assured constituents—and the society in which they live—to survive and flourish. Ronald Heifetz suggests that the role of the leader is to create a holding environment while the group figures out how to deal with a new challenge, rather than to promise to solve the problem for them.[12] That is how Aaron Feuerstein, CEO of the family-owned Malden Mills, dealt with his serious challenge.

You'll recall the story of the December 11, 1995, fire that leveled the Malden Mills factory, when employees in the parking lot heard Feuerstein vow, "This is not the end." It is now a well-known story—almost a legend—that Feuerstein kept his entire roster of three thousand employees on payroll with full benefits for three months after the devastating fire idled every one of them. Dealing with his own anxiety, Feuerstein managed to put his employees' concerns above his own.

The dedicated employees knew that without the factory, Feuerstein couldn't support them permanently. He was not promising a lifetime sinecure. This white-haired CEO, who'd seen it all, was simply creating a temporary safe haven where he and the workers would each do their part to figure out the next step. Faced with the opportunity to retire on the insurance money, Feuerstein chose instead to rebuild the factory, even if his mounting debt ultimately would force him from the CEO position. He made the choice without illusion. The workers, as we saw, increased production to help offset the serious financial blow that they all had suffered.

Lulling followers with the illusion that the omnipotent leader can protect them from all harm prevents their facing and coping with the inevitable threats that reality brings. Only when we confront our difficulties and come to terms with them—perchance prevail over them—can we grow strong enough to face up to the inevitable next trial. It is primarily in the crucibles of life that we find our own strength. That was certainly the case with many of the outstanding leaders whom leadership experts Warren Bennis and Robert Thomas interviewed, as we saw earlier.[13]

The Search for Truth

We have seen that truth in an unfinished world is always a work in progress. Yet what first appears to be a quixotic search for the most current discernible truth ultimately turns out to be not only important but unavoidable. As humans living in an unfinished world, our stubborn, life-supporting curiosity compels us to continue that uncertainty-reducing search for truth. In fact, one way of dealing constructively with our anxiety in the face of uncertainty and chaos is to use it in the pursuit of truth, imperfect as that truth may be.

Engaging in that quest drives us to push back the borders of the unknown and create knowledge not simply for ourselves but for the rest of humanity. Steven Weinberg, one of three 1979 Nobelists in physics, has an interesting take on the scientific search for truth: "The effort to understand the universe is one of the very few things that lifts human life a little above the level of farce and gives it some of the grace of tragedy."[14]

Nonetheless, we must accept the reality that at any specific moment in time we may not be able to determine a final and complete truth. We may simply have to live with the knowledge that much uncertainty inevitably remains in an unfinished world. That stubborn reality does not diminish the significance of our search.

Acting in the Face of Uncertainty: The Positive Role of Fear

Only when we accept that life is uncertain, that its meaning may never become totally clear, that anything can happen, but that we must go forward nonetheless, can we feel the true exhilaration of living. That is the fundamental noble enterprise in which each and every one of us must knowingly engage if we wish to come face-to-face with our own capacity for heroism and to break free from the shackles of toxic leadership.

Only when we are living on the verge of uncertainty, moving forward, making our best judgments as we step out into the unknown, will we be avoiding the danger that Goethe perceives in safety. That is what philosopher of history Eric Voegelin called "an adventure of decision on the edge of freedom and necessity."[15] Freedom from subservience to leaders coupled with the necessity to take action despite our fears may, in the long run, be far more important than finding an elusive truth.

Our anxiety is there, but this time it is where we can see it, where we can keep an eye on it; it is not driving us mercilessly from the deep waters of our unconscious. When our anxiety is up front, as wild as it may be, we can rope and tame it to help us live a full, even heroic life, a life that enlarges us not by crushing others but by lifting them high.

Fear need not be inhibiting. In fact, fear and anxiety can play an extremely positive role. Hankiss argues that fear

> challenges us and prompts us to build up, and maintain, our civilization or to change it if necessary. It prompts us to live more intensely. It reminds us of our human situation and the precariousness of our existence. It may protect us against submerging into Heideggerian "oblivion."[16]

As we struggle to understand and shape the meaning of our lives, that anxiety can be transformed into creative energy and direction. It can help us come to grips with—in fact create—new important symbols through which we can better understand the world in which we live and act. It can assist us in completing one more piece of our unfinished world. Voegelin put it very well:

> [Man] is an actor, playing a part in the drama of being and, through the brute fact of his existence, committed to play it without knowing what it is. . . . The role of existence must be played in uncertainty of its meaning. . . . The ultimate, essential ignorance is not complete ignorance. . . . The concern of man about the meaning of his exis-

tence in the field of being does not remain pent up in the tortures of anxiety but can vent itself in the creation of symbols purporting to render intelligible the relations and tensions between the distinguishable terms of the field.[17]

Clearly, we can transform anxiety into creativity and meaning. Søren Kierkegaard, Sigmund Freud, Otto Rank, Rollo May, and Ernest Becker have all insisted we need not simply be victims of our anxiety. Another part of human nature—our openness to life—dilutes our anxiety and shapes our responses to reality. When it is joined to our fear and angst, our receptivity to new experience promotes growth and sparks creativity.

Edgar Schein writes about "learning anxiety," the positive face of fear that we experience when we open ourselves to new situations.[18] Fear has often served as the midwife to creativity. Delumeau, in his discussion of "creative anxiety," focuses on the role fear plays in heightening creativity.[19] And as Hankiss writes:

> Fear has two sides . . . it can be either salutary or destructive. As a modern philosopher wittily puts it, "Timeo, ergo sum," and it is true that, when viewed in clear focus, fear is a "call to being." It is "creative of being."[20]

Those nontoxic leaders who insist upon opening our eyes to reality often increase our pain and anxiety, at least for the moment. Over time, however, by forcing us to confront life's uncertainties, they are more likely to teach us courage and moral self-reliance. After all, courage requires taking effective action despite the continuous glimpse of death from the corner of our eye.[21] And then, perhaps only then, can we move beyond our search for truth and focus on the importance of freedom—not only freedom from fear, but freedom from illusions by which toxic leaders hold us tightly in their grasp.

This chapter has considered how to detect the seeds of toxicity in the leader's noble vision. The focus has been on experiencing, in more positive ways, the exhilaration that we derive from the toxic leader's vision. In addition, I have tried to identify the early warning signs of toxicity in previously nontoxic leaders. If we recognize the first symptoms of toxicity, we have a chance to avoid or confront it, both in leaders and their lofty visions. That done, where do we look for constructive, nontoxic leaders?

In the next and final chapter, let's turn to that very question. In fact, let's explore not only how we might free ourselves from toxic leaders but also how we might identify and encourage both non-toxic reluctant leaders and the potential leader within every one of us.

13

Freeing Ourselves from Toxic Leaders: Nurturing Reluctant Leaders and Finding the Leader Within

In this book, I have tried to explore why and how we continue to endure, seek out, and sometimes create leaders, particularly toxic leaders. If such relentless activity moved us toward a world where more and more good leaders led followers into worthwhile enterprises, that would be just fine. And, of course, some leaders—like Alfred P. Sloan Jr., Martin Luther King Jr., Aaron Feuerstein, Anita Roddick, Mohandas K. Gandhi, Nelson Mandela, Desmond Tutu, and Václev Havel—have taken us on some remarkable journeys. Unfortunately, though, such inspiring outcomes occur more seldom than we wish. Consequently, our search for leaders continues.

In this chapter, I want to consider a set of possible strategies for freeing ourselves from toxic leaders with their destructive illusions. Because anxiety plays such a major role in our vulnerability to toxic leaders, let's examine not only the positive aspects of anxiety but also several other sources of nontoxic leadership. Let's also touch again briefly on the benefits that flow from leaders who free us from illusion, who make us deal with our anxiety, and who impose on us the "valuable inconvenience of leadership."

In this final chapter, let's also take a few moments to think about how to kick the vision habit and the we/they dichotomy, and just how the Zulu concept of *ubuntu* and a more connective model of leadership come into play. Let's consider in some depth two important, related alternatives to toxic leaders: reluctant leaders, recognized for their leadership qualities by their peers, and the "leader within," that is, the potential for leadership that we all harbor. We'll also try to clarify the special challenges of businesses in contrast to other types of organizations. And finally, let's turn our attention to the connections among democracy, autonomy, freedom, and the rejection of toxic leaders. But before we get to that, in this final chapter let's take a quick look backward.

A Quick Look Backward

To simplify what we have concluded so far: The major attraction of toxic leaders stems from their readiness to promise us simultaneously the possible and the impossible. That is, they assure us they can both calm our fears *and* keep us safe. Toxic leaders offer us this grand illusion of security to quell two stubborn types of anxiety: our existential angst, sparked by our awareness of death's inevitability, and our situational fears, instilled by a world marked by economic meltdowns, downsizing, illness, accidents, blackouts, earthquakes, wars, and terrorist attacks that can erupt with no advance notice. And because these leaders frequently manage to soothe our anxiety, we begin to believe they probably can indeed keep us safe, as well.

The illusionary promises of toxic leaders fit, tongue in groove, with the complex existential, psychological, and social forces their followers confront. That is, they jibe with the challenges we followers face in an unfinished world. In that world, we try to quiet our fears through successful competition, through heroic action, measured against the society's achievement ethic. The outcome of our daily strivings can enhance or diminish our self-esteem. Leaders' promises also suit our complex personal needs, colored by our yearning for immortality or at least a small slice of heroism. Buffeted by the powerful interaction of these personal and social forces, we followers become supremely vulnerable to authority figures—good, bad, and middling.

The Power of Illusions

Toxic leaders ply us with several additional illusions that neatly meet our complicated needs. They assure us that we are not simply insignificant croutons tossed about on the salad of existence. They offer us an important, perchance heroic, role. If we participate in the toxic leaders' noble visions, they promise we shall earn eternal life or at least an honored place in the history books to boggle the minds of future generations. So we can—at least symbolically—overcome death.

Illusions play a powerful role in the dynamic between most leaders and their followers. Effective leaders—good and bad—understand their followers' deep need for illusion. Exactly how they use those illusions distinguishes constructive leaders from their toxic counterparts. Non-toxic leaders focus on dreams *we* need to fulfill.

Toxic leaders manipulate the power of illusions to corral anxious followers. They play on their followers' concerns, which they claim only *they* can handle. We see that the toxic leader may first emerge as our savior, vanquishing our enemies—be they our business competitors, a faltering economy, our political opponents, or our global neighbors. Only later do we realize that the leader is using the same power, unchecked, against our associates, our friends, our families, and eventually against us.

Immortality and the Call to Heroism

The promise of immortality is a potent anodyne for the fear of death. It also assuages many earthly woes. Proving that we are worthy of immortality, however, is a monumental task.

Many observers of the human condition have proposed that we all seek immortality in various ways.[1] The major qualification for attaining it is heroic action. So it is not surprising that all kinds of leaders advertise their visions as noble. These visions, they claim, offer a path initially to heroism and ultimately to immortality.

The hero is always engaged in something beneficial to society, making it better, stronger, healthier, richer, purer, more beautiful, and more predictable. Heroism requires exceeding society's highest standard of achievement, thus marking us as worthy competitors.

Working together, the call to heroism and our anxiety-driven need for self-esteem sweet-talk us into the arms of toxic leaders. Urged on by a toxic leader, we seek heroism so that we may outdo others and feed our hunger for self-esteem. If we can't meet those challenges by ourselves, we often feel the need to join the hero's entourage or her mass of followers. In this way, we attempt to placate our deep-seated anxieties about our worthiness for eternal life.

Napoleon Bonaparte reminds us, "There is no immortality except in the memory in the minds of men," as we saw earlier. Because Napoleon wisely knew that numbers don't really matter in this exercise, he didn't differentiate between the memories of our neighbors and those of the whole world. There is a saying that "you don't have to do great things, you can do small things with great love." So despite the fact that we usually think of heroic action as jumbo-size, heroism can come packaged in many sizes, from individual to world-shaking.

While we often reach for considerably more, we probably can achieve immortality via small daily acts of thoughtfulness and saintliness. If Napoleon's insight is valid, we can live on in the memory of others for practicing philanthropy of the spirit as well as the purse—for urging our employees to become Big Sisters or Big Brothers to lonely children, for singing holiday carols for residents of nursing homes, for ensuring our company's waste products don't pollute the environment, for providing our low-wage workers with reasonable health care, for repairing the local park, and in many other ways, small or medium-sized. Grand-scale accomplishments, like developing a vaccine for Alzheimer's or charting the trajectory to a newly discovered planet, worthy though they may be, are not the only way.

Enterprises, of various sizes and shapes, can serve as legitimate "immortality projects."[2] While our immortality projects hold out myriad benefits, both to others and ourselves, they also make us resonate to toxic leaders who feed us the illusion that *their* vision is the surest route to immortality. And that danger is all too real.

Strategies for Freeing Ourselves from Toxic Leaders' Illusions and Becoming Self-reliant Constituents

Given the seductiveness of illusions and the toxic leaders who proffer them to allay our layered anxieties, just what options do we have? How do we free ourselves from those illusions and become self-reliant constituents? Let's consider a few possible strategies.

Strategy One: Matriculating in the School of Anxiety

Tolerating toxic leaders is a fearsome price to pay to avoid confronting our anxiety.[3] Instead of letting our existential angst and situational fears hold us hostage, followers can enroll in what Søren Kierkegaard called "the school of anxiety."[4] There, we can learn new ways of connecting to our own creativity, becoming more resilient, and growing from the confrontation with our complex anxiety.

While anxiety may be prompted by *external* social change, it also stimulates *internal* psychological and cognitive change, provoking us to think differently. Anxiety nips at our psyches when we recognize that innovation as well as change and disruption all call for serious responses. Here, Kurt Lewin's concept of *freezing, unfreezing,* and *refreezing* comes into play.[5] In a frozen state, we feel a sense of certitude, false or otherwise, but a sense of certainty nonetheless. In the next stage, an unfrozen state, we experience anxiety as certainty evaporates and new uncertainties appear. In this unfrozen state, we do not quite know what will happen next. The anxiety of that unfrozen state makes us more open to change, newness, experimentation, and learning. We are more willing to test ourselves and the world around us. This unfrozen condition galvanizes us to search for new solutions and thereby restore and create symbols and institutions that reduce our fears. Eventually, we refreeze at this new level. We usually remain in this rather impermeable state until the next discombobulating event unfreezes us once more.

While anxiety invariably accompanies serious change, its appearance does not necessarily signify that we are in trouble. Rather, it may indicate that change is under way.[6] In fact, anxiety compels us to expand our identity and authenticity. By facing up to anxiety and the accompanying pain, we become emboldened to take the next step—even in the face of fear and uncertainty. Acting *despite* fear and trembling is one definition of courage, the very stuff of true heroism. Then we are most likely to take risks, to act as our own leaders, even to reach for the stars.

The process is painful, but it can strengthen us enough to stop relying upon false gods. The school of anxiety helps us gain the strength to break out of the control myths that have immobilized us, making us the captives of toxic leaders. After that, we can recognize the inadequacies of toxic leaders. Only then can we confront such leaders and urge them to change.

Nor is this all bad for the toxic leader. As good leaders know very well, encouraging their people's insight, critical thinking, and courage to criticize enlarges the leader's vision and strengthens the whole organization. Warren Bennis has wisely noted, "Perhaps the ultimate irony is that the follower who is willing to speak out shows precisely the kind of initiative that leadership is made of."[7] Accepting the responsibility to speak out is an important step in creating more democratic organizations that need able leaders at every level. And if confrontation doesn't yield the desired result, the liberated followers ultimately may have to consider ousting the toxic leader.

By matriculating in the school of anxiety, we learn to take risks, to call upon our own leadership potential, "the leader within," and possibly to create our own noble visions. This is the curriculum of leadership.

Strategy Two: Seeking the Leader Within and Strengthening Democratic Organizations

Followers need to rethink their stance vis-à-vis *all* leaders. This calls for abandoning our roles as passive, obedient followers who wait for the leader—any leader, even the best—to direct our action. Moving from the dependency of a follower to the independence of a proactive constituent is another important step in the intense journey of seeking our own aptitude for leadership, that is, finding the leader within.

As constituents, we independently (or sometimes with consultants' help) evaluate problems and determine what, if anything, *we* can do versus what requires the help of *others*. In the process, we begin to think of ourselves not as followers but as leaders in our own right. We become active constituents who support a solution acceptable both to the leader and us. Or as consultants, we advise the leader on relevant strategies and solutions.

In this way, we can learn to forego our dependence on leaders and the debilitating illusions we have demanded from them. We can begin to look at our lives, our tasks, our organizations, and ourselves more realistically. We can develop our own leadership potential, reduce our personal neediness, and, as a welcome by-product, stop pushing good leaders over the bad line.

When many individuals discover the leader within, an entirely new and larger cadre of potential leaders emerges in organizations. When a sufficient number of individuals tap into their own human potential, organizations become stronger and more democratic. In this way, we build organizations in which the many, not the few, share the burdens, the responsibilities, and the rewards of leadership. Ultimately, students who graduate from the school of anxiety are likely to foster more democratic organizations.

Curiously, however, democracy itself stimulates anxiety because it requires that we look to ourselves for leadership. On the organizational landscape, we rarely see democracy practiced in its un-diluted form. Participative management in organizations, a bold experiment in democracy, often generates so much anxiety—in both leaders and followers—that it quickly dwindles into thinly disguised authoritarianism.[8] Ask any middle manager who has experienced the nightmare of conflicted authority and responsibility.

Democracy requires patience and strength. It is a responsibility, not a privilege, to assume some of the leadership burdens of our society, both within and beyond for-profit and not-for-profit organizations. Democracy calls for far greater portions of ego strength and confidence than ego. Not only does it demand the ability to criticize the leader. It also insists upon a far more painful capacity: the willingness to criticize ourselves and accept—at times solicit—critiques from others.

As if that were not difficult enough, democracy is time-consuming, messy, and inefficient. Yet its longer-term effectiveness is well worth the price.[9] In the short run, admittedly, it may be easier to turn the organization over to someone who will make the trains run on time. In the longer run, however, those trains may carry people to the death camps of demoralization, downsizing, and dead ends before grinding to a rusted, depleted stop.

Whatever the other weaknesses of democracy may be, when it comes to the problem of toxic leaders, democracy has one incontrovertible plus: It provides a clear, legal mechanism for removing bad leaders. Although most business organizations are far from democratic, they exist within a broader democratic environment, amid a widespread general ethos that supports democracy and abhors tyrants. That democratic ethos also values merit. To the extent that their participants matriculate in the school of anxiety, for-profit, not-for-profit, and political organizations can become less vulnerable to incompetent and malevolent leaders. Facing our anxiety, albeit an arduous process, helps us to acknowledge our responsibility for leading and nurturing a democratic society.

Strategy Three: Demanding Leaders Who Dis-illusion Us and the Valuable Inconvenience of Leadership

As followers, we need to learn to accept—in fact, seek out, support, and if necessary create—leaders who refuse to provide illusions, leaders who may even insist upon puncturing the illusions we have fashioned for ourselves. These leaders are likely to place weighty responsibilities upon followers that will make us learn, grow, and develop resilience.[10]

Consequently, we often prefer toxic leaders to those dis-illusioning leaders, who would press our noses to the dark window of life. Discomfortingly, good leaders pull the scales from our eyes.

They demand that we face difficult truths. Long before Martin Heidegger and Karl Jaspers, Søren Kierkegaard exhorted us to confront our anxiety and our immutable human mortality in order to achieve "authentic experience."[11]

Electing this strategy requires kicking the illusion habit. Illusions that toxic leaders feed their followers may turn into murderous self-delusions. Let's work instead toward "authentic existence," which may take a more complex, indirect route. And, perhaps most important, we need to *create*—rather than find, seek, or ask others to give us—the meaning of our life. As psychiatrist Thomas Szasz says, "The self is not something that one finds. It is something that one creates."[12]

Learning to tolerate nontoxic leaders in not enough. We need to embrace and support these dis-illusioning, demanding leaders. Unlike the Jim Joneses and the Osama bin Ladens of the world, nontoxic leaders rarely promise us eternal paradise. Nontoxic leaders do not allow anxious followers to hoist them onto pedestals of omnipotence. In fact, such leaders are more apt to call upon constituents—despite their palpable fears and uncertainties—to share the hardships of leadership. In that way, they teach us the valuable inconvenience of leadership. This strategy also promotes democratic organizations and societies, where the rule of the majority serves as an imperfect bulwark against the tyranny of the few.

Strategy Four: Kicking the Vision Habit and the We/They Dichotomy

Followers also need to kick their addiction to leaders with grand (or, worse, grandiose) visions. Not that having a leader with a vision is necessarily bad. Some leaders' visions inspire us to be better than we ever thought we could be. Yet when a leader's vision calls not simply for self-improvement but for perfect purity, something is often amiss. Such purity usually means removing the stain of a tainted Other or becoming great at the expense of making others small.

Besides, even those leaders who begin with the loftiest intentions are not immune to these corrosive effects. In the act of seeking legitimate noble ends, leaders can inadvertently slide all too easily down the slope of toxicity, dragging their admiring followers along behind them. So large doses of caution are appropriate.

Another important lesson comes from rejecting the we/they dichotomy. Let's remember William Faulkner's wisdom, cited earlier: "Apprehending the other in terms of mutual humanity is the task and the trouble."[13] Defining ourselves as the chosen generates immense problems for everyone—for leaders, for their supporters, and for nonfollowers alike. For leaders, moving beyond those easy strategies that pit their followers as the chosen people against the external, tainted Other takes psychological and intellectual strength and moral courage. It also calls for fresh ideas and innovative leadership strategies.

For followers, forgoing the comforting illusion that we are the chosen is not any easier than it is for leaders. It requires facing up to our anxiety and learning from it. If we choose this path, we must abandon our psychological crutches and learn to walk courageously with the pain of accepting uncertainty about everything except the inevitability of death.

It is no trifling challenge to relinquish the shelter of the chosen and begin to see the Other as part of ourselves, perhaps the needier and most important part of ourselves, to whom we should devote our most heroic efforts. For that is what it takes to move beyond our own narrow egos and the control myths that keep us enchained.

Albert Nolan, the South African theologian, noted the hard-to-travel continuum from simple empathy to complete identification with the Other.[14] While Nolan's focus is primarily on service to the poor, he provides a framework that can be applied more generally to perceiving and relating to those who differ from us in various ways. At the near end of the continuum, *compassion*, we ask, "Am I my brother's keeper?" The next way station, which requires *structural change*, answers, "Yes, I am my brother's keeper." The third point on the continuum, *humility*, says, "No, I am my brother's brother." Only when we manage to feel both *solidarity* and *reciprocity* with the Other, the far anchor point of the continuum, can we say, "No, I am my brother." For leaders, this ability to see the Other as self requires a willingness to share power and authority with other leaders, with constituents, even with nonfollowers and potential successors.

Only when we see other people as part of ourselves can we understand their motives, their strengths, and their frailties, even their darkest needs and actions. When we, as the chosen, see that we have the same capacity for darkness (whether or not we have acted upon it) that we attribute to the Other, then our need to annihilate the Other diminishes. In a similar process, we sometimes recognize that our anger at someone else's negative action evokes our special edge of fury because it contains an unrecognized portion of our anger at ourselves. Sometimes this specially fueled anger arises from wittingly or unwittingly tolerating, colluding with, or not preventing the other party's toxic behavior.

Ubuntu: A Basis for Building Consensus

This ability to see others as ourselves is embedded in the Zulu concept of *ubuntu*, which has been defined as

> [t]he principle of caring for each other's well-being . . . and a spirit of mutual support . . . Each individual's humanity is ideally expressed through his or her relationship with others and theirs in turn through a recognition of the individual's humanity. Ubuntu means that people are people through other people. It also acknowledges both the rights and the responsibilities of every citizen in promoting individual and societal well-being.[15]

The concept of *ubuntu* was pivotal in the extraordinary South African Truth and Reconciliation Commission, the postapartheid process of reconciliation designed and infused by the incandescent leadership of Anglican archbishop and Nobel peace prize winner Desmond Tutu.

This unifying perspective is contained in the Zulu proposition *umuntu ngumuntu ngabantu*, which can be translated as "a person is a person through other persons" or "a person is a person through the otherness of other human beings."[16] Finding the common core of humanity in ourselves and others, even in those others whose actions we condemn, is the starting place for empathy and identification with people who appear to differ from us in significant ways. Only then can we begin to break out of the shackles of the we/they dichotomy, which toxic leaders manipulate to spark cohesion among their own followers and bind them to the leader.

Connective Leadership: *Ubuntu* in Action

The capacity to see even the smallest sliver of mutuality in the needs and agendas of others is a significant hallmark of *connective leadership*.[17] It is *ubuntu* in action. The ability to foster interdependent relationships among diverse parties distinguishes connective leaders. These unusual leaders connect their visions, their tasks, and their goals to those of their supporters as well as to those of other leaders, even to those of traditional opponents and *their* followers.

Connective leaders have an eye for discerning the mutuality in what others only perceive as opposing groups with competing needs, ideologies, and agendas. Connective leaders look for the overlap, however small, among diverse groups and work to enlarge it. Nontoxic connective leaders help their constituents to forge realistic strategies for dealing with their mutual problems, despite the distress provoked by their differences. They foster the leadership potential of others and avoid manipulating their supporters' anxiety through illusions.

The Costs of Seeking Truth and Meaning

Followers need to look to themselves to seek the deep meaning or (to adapt Clifford Geertz's cultural term) the "thick description" of their lives.[18] We all need to feel that the grand struggle we call "our life" makes us significant beings in a meaningful universe, as Becker, Rank, and Kierkegaard all have claimed. This heroic striving in the name of the Other is one possible strategy for dealing with our mortality. Through our own efforts, we try to leave behind some small trace that makes a positive difference in the world, a difference that is based *not* on annihilating the Other but on enhancing the Other. In this way we enhance ourselves as well— by living up to the most noble part of our being.

Even as we seek truth and the meaning of our lives, a serious caveat is in order. Our pursuit of truth and meaning is a two-edged sword. On one hand, such a quest can drive us to the loftiest of actions. Just as easily, however, as Senator Bob Kerrey and his squad discovered too late, it can push us beyond the limits of human decency and integrity, all in the name of hoped-for honor and heroism.

Our search for truth and meaning frequently cloaks itself in the multicolored garments of achievement, righteousness, justice, and purity. Those worthy goals can also lead us astray, as most religious wars—from the Crusades to the conflicts in Northern Ireland and the Middle East—amply demonstrate.

The "truths" for which we would willingly die can turn out to be merely death-dealing falsehoods. Even scientific facts devoutly believed at one moment can eventually prove to be incomplete or incorrect. As the late physicist Max Born observed, "The physics of one era is the metaphysics of the next." Clinging tenaciously to our own group's algorithm for truth, justice, or righteousness often goads us to obliterate those who believe in competing concepts. As

Born noted, "The belief that there is only one truth and that one-self is in possession of it seems to me the deepest root of all the evil that is in the world."[19]

Consequently, we should welcome the discomfort of competing "truths" in our schools, in our politics, in our organizations, and in our lives. These alternative truths stretch us, make us seriously ponder new ways of thinking, and help us to conceive creative solutions. With the complexities of the world as we know it, don't know it, and perhaps can never know it, we shall understand one another and ourselves better by seeing the world, from time to time, through one another's spectacles.

Strategy Five: Drafting the Next Generation of Leaders: The Nature and Nurture of Reluctant Leaders

"Where have all the good leaders gone?" is a question posed all too frequently. That question is closely entwined with the main concerns of this book. The dilemma of identifying appropriate candidates for leadership roles stems directly from our definition of leadership. Traditionally, we have defined leadership as a *privilege* to be competed for by a few. Instead, we should reconceptualize leadership as a *responsibility* to be conferred upon and shared by a large cadre of individuals who demonstrate the requisite qualities to act in the name of the entire group. Great difficulties and distortions flow from our traditional but flawed perspective.

Reconceptualizing leadership as a responsibility to the social group—be it a nation, a company, a volunteer organization, a neighborhood, or a family—that all members must undertake for a delimited period of time would change the fundamental way we perceive and evaluate leaders. It would also vastly change the candidate pool, the selection process, constituents' attitudes toward leaders, and leaders' attitudes toward authority, power, honor, and office.

Instead of the self-selection process we now have, where leaders insinuate themselves into the ranks of candidates, leaders would be *drafted* by their peers. Leadership candidates would be drawn from every sector and layer of society, based upon their peers' recognition of their qualifications for the role. This would address the current thorny issue of the disproportionate number of the entitled elite and the psychologically driven among the ranks of aspiring leaders, a condition that overexposes us to the candidacies of toxic leaders. Drafting reluctant leaders would also catapult us beyond servant leadership into an ethical and altruistic, but basically politically savvy, kind of leadership.

Because we have traditionally conceptualized leadership as a privilege, with many associated perquisites and powers, leadership roles tend to attract primarily individuals who thirst for power and personal glory. Despite and even because of the Herculean ordeal that the quest for leadership has become, ordinarily only the most driven, competitive, thick-skinned individuals are willing to subject themselves to the brutal trial. The leadership selection process has become so distorted and destructive that stable, nonneurotic, intelligent, more reserved potential leaders are increasingly disinclined to throw themselves into the leadership fray. The media add to the subversion of leadership, as we have seen, first by adulating celebrities and certain leaders-in-the-making and then searching for the clay feet of those very same leaders once they assume the leader's role.

Leadership as responsibility would entail a different method for selecting leaders. It would foster the selection of reluctant leaders, whose leadership potential (i.e., character, authenticity, integrity, wisdom, courage, and connectiveness) was recognized by constituents. Gandhi, Martin Luther King Jr., Václav Havel, and Nelson Mandela were all reluctant leaders. They were selected by their peers and convinced by circumstances—sometimes an epiphanous experience—of their responsibility to assume the burden of leadership, not its glory-encrusted mantle. In business firms, too, we easily recognize colleagues whom we'd all be willing to follow.

The selection process would more nearly resemble a draft than a contest, with individuals serving for a given period of time in any one leadership position. Leaders would be relieved of their regular responsibilities for the period of their "drafted" service. In addition, to the degree feasible, they would not be obliged to endure any greater financial hardship than they were experiencing in their customary role. Conversely, they would not expect or accept the astounding multimillion-dollar contracts of many current CEOs. Their terms would be limited, although at a later time, if their constituents drafted them, they could be selected for leadership at other levels or in different sectors (the neighborhood, the community, the corporation, a start-up, academia, or the state or federal government).

Returning to the general citizenry or pool of followers after a term of leadership service has important virtues. It can build a cadre of strong, experienced leaders who support and groom—

rather than annihilate—their potential successors. It would also leave former leaders much more sympathetic to the difficulties and pressures their successors experience. When their term is up, these experienced leaders could serve as advisors, as they often do now, to current, neophyte, or emerging leaders.

This approach to leadership reflects the Jeffersonian notion of leaders drawn from the citizenry, who would serve for a delimited period and then return to their previous roles. By defining the length of service in a given position, the leader's sacrifices would be limited and shared by many. In addition, the leader would be less likely to settle into the comforts and privileges of office that tempt many office holders to convert a single term of service into a career of pomp and power. To paraphrase Lord Acton's famous dictum about absolute power, endless power corrupts endlessly.

Moreover, when constituents realize that the current office holder will return to the group after a specified term, there will be much less temptation to treat that individual as a special, more worthy being whose long-term favor must be courted by less powerful individuals or groups. The presumed need to curry favor with an embedded power figure and to seek inappropriate access through unethical or illegal means would also sharply diminish.

The drafted leaders' awareness that their current power positions were not sinecures would have a similarly salutary effect on those individuals. It would heighten leaders' awareness that even-handed treatment of *all* constituents would have long-term positive consequences for their eventual return to the ranks of their former followers. Consequently, the seeds of corruption and cynicism would be less likely to germinate, unwatered either by the leader's invitation or by the constituent's seduction of the leader. Arrogance, too, would more likely be held in check.

In the case of political leadership, because leaders would be drawn from the general population on the basis of their recognized qualities, they would not have to fight for resources to propel them into office. Nor would there be any need for protracted and expensive, not to mention increasingly tedious, election campaigns. Let's remember that in many countries political campaigns are limited to a few short months or weeks. Rather than being beholden to those special groups who had contributed major campaign resources, leaders would recognize their responsibility and accountability to all. This would reduce uneven access and distribution of power to special-interest groups and place primary focus on the greater interest of the whole.

For leaders in every arena—from the corporate and political to the academic and athletic worlds—contributing to the good of the larger group, rather than stockpiling one's own power and wealth, would emerge as a more appropriate grail to be sought. This model of leadership would present constituents with a blueprint for contributing to the society, a joint enterprise offering all participants the opportunity to do something lastingly significant—dare I say ennobling—with their lives.

In this view of reluctant leadership, the selection process requires that we educate not a small elite but the broadest spectrum of our star-spangled diversity, particularly our young people, about their responsibilities for leadership. Education for leadership should teach us that we are accountable to the entire group, not just to ourselves, our kin, or our neighborhood. Dedication must be directed toward causes that benefit the entire community or networks of organizations. This approach demands leaders who practice a politics of commonalities, that is, focusing on similarities, rather than a politics of differences, which attracts followers by emphasizing the we/they dichotomy.[20] Competitive partisanship and divisiveness will decrease in the face of a system or group perspective, that is, the commitment to the larger good.

This approach to grooming and selecting leaders has the potential for producing a very large pool of able candidates. Over time, it can generate leaders in every cranny of society, leaders with a depth of experience and the ego strength to bring other leaders into the process from top to bottom. Such leaders, acting from a sense of responsibility and authenticity, can go far toward healing the social corrosion bred by cynicism. They can inspire us to confront the enormously complex problems bedeviling society. Those with experience can serve as mentors to tenderfoot leaders. The problem of leadership succession evaporates. The query "Where have all the good leaders gone?" will no longer need to be sounded in the land.

Business Organizations: Their Special Challenges

Before closing the book, I want to address the special challenges of coming to terms with toxic leaders in business organizations. But let me say at the outset that while there are several fundamental differences between businesses and other types of organizations, there are also more similarities between them than we usually recognize.

Thus, dealing with a toxic leader in the business arena is often not all that different from interacting with the toxic leader who manages a government agency or with a toxic dean or president in academia, where appointments are not necessarily subject to term limits or democratic overturn. Moreover, in the last decade, government agencies and nonprofits, like universities, have been moving rapidly toward a business model, where the bottom line has become increasingly relevant. As a result, the differences between businesses and other organizations are gradually blurring.

In businesses and other types of organizations where the hierarchy rules—and, according to Harold J. Leavitt, it rules in virtually all large organizations despite much theoretical wishing to the contrary—toxic leaders can wield the authority and resources the hierarchy vests in them to keep themselves in power.[21] So they can entrench themselves, despite the despair of their employees.

By their nature, companies are rarely run democratically in the way that some nations are. Yet we should remember that even democratically elected political leaders sit atop government and other organizations structured as nondemocratic hierarchies. Earlier, I noted how participative management—that is, businesses' attempts to inject democracy into business organizations—often morphs into window dressing for a benign (or not so benign) type of authoritarianism. Business employees cannot simply vote a toxic corporate leader out of office. But then neither can the government employee who reports to a toxic midlevel civil servant or politically appointed agency head or cabinet secretary.

Russell Ackoff has described the "democratic corporation," that is, a circular organization, structured as a democratic hierarchy, where all individuals in positions of authority, be they executives, managers, or supervisors, have a board. The board consists of their immediate supervisor, their immediate reports, and themselves. In this circular organization, anyone who has authority over others is subject to the collective authority of those others.

Ackoff's ingenious prescription has been tried in several corporations and government agencies, including the White House Office of Communications, but it has not really caught on in any wider way.[22] This lack of acceptance presumably stems from the difficulty of implementing the systemic, rather than piecemeal, initiative that Ackoff's design requires. For these circular organizations demand much more than simply changing one part of one system. Rather, they call for internal systemwide change within an entire organization and then similar change introduced across a broad spectrum of organizations.

If innovative, broad-scale remedies like Ackoff's are difficult to pull off, less drastic measures nonetheless can still make a difference. As we have seen, for example, coalitions composed of like-minded employees can help to redirect or change a toxic leader. If that fails, a group's refusal to work for such a leader can make a serious difference.

A case in point: Francis Moore, the brilliant, radical surgeon who reigned as chief of surgery at the Peter Brent Brigham Hospital in Boston during the 1950s, insisted upon performing daring experimental procedures on terminal patients. The surgical residents who assisted him came to regard Moore's experimental surgery as nothing short of murder.[23] According to Atul Gawande, "Moore did not hesitate to expose his patients to suffering and death if a new idea made scientific sense to him."[24] Eventually, these surgeons-in-training, whose very careers depended upon Moore, courageously refused to assist him in those radical operations. Despite Moore's rationale that what they learned from these procedures would help less seriously ill patients, the residents' implacable refusal forced Moore to rethink his flawed vision. Eventually Moore, himself, began to take a far more conservative approach. In time, in a stunning turnaround, Moore became an active proponent of review boards with authority to control such experimental procedures.

Perhaps resistance to Ackoff's circular organizations also stems from the inherent conflict in business organizations between order and purpose, on one hand, and true democracy, on the other. But that tension occurs in other types of organizations as well. Business organizations face a far more critical conflict: between the democratic processes that serve as the greatest bulwark against toxicity and the necessity of making a profit to stay in business. This, I believe, is the crux of the matter. By contrast, to maintain themselves, government agencies do not need to make money, but to get money through the budget process. Admittedly, this need can pose its own difficulties. While totally eliminating an existing government agency is virtually impossible, those government organizations that limp along starved of funding rarely do great things. Nonetheless, they stand in sharp contrast to unprofitable business organizations, which have an exceedingly short lease on life. Government agencies can maintain themselves for long periods of time, despite considerable ineptitude, as long as they have the backing of a powerful constituency or congressional sponsor.

Consequently, in business organizations, a greater sense of urgency and competition commonly fuels the operation. The crisis that arises when the bottom line begins to waver all too frequently prompts us to cling anxiously to the leader who promises to keep us safe. Let's remember, even as Enron's stock was nosediving, Ken Lay was reassuring his employees that it was a great buy for them and their families, so they bought.

That critical need to "make the numbers" can also prompt us to overlook or simply deny the toxic behavior of leaders. Yet when business organizations are not in crisis mode, acting through advisory coalitions that either work constructively to help the toxic leader change or simply advise the nontoxic leader to keep him or her on an even keel can be an effective organizational strategy. At one highly respected business school, the dean organized a rotating Faculty Advisory Board (FAB), composed of associate deans and faculty members from all levels. Through the monthly meetings of the FAB, problems were aired before crises could provide the pretext for toxic action. The FAB gave that dean and his successors a vehicle for testing new initiatives and tapping into the perceptions and concerns of the faculty and associate deans. Toxicity, like truffles, grows best in the dark. Examining plans in this quasi-public forum led to a healthy transparency that discouraged toxicity from germinating.

Business leaders wield immense power, despite considerable toxicity, as the plethora of recent corporate scandals has made painfully clear. And as we have also seen, toxic corporate leaders often manage to control the very groups—their boards of governors and the media—who are meant to oversee and keep them in check. This is another key distinction between business and nonbusiness organizations that poses special challenges.

CEOs and their minions in senior management also command institutional resources that they can use to keep themselves in power. Heads of government agencies are more restricted in how they can use their organization's resources to sustain their power. With the exception of immense nonprofit organizations such as the International and U.S. Olympic Committees, the Red Cross, and various large foundations, so are the nonprofits.

A third and thornier problem in business organizations involves the selection of leaders. Ordinarily, the board of directors, commonly consisting of the current CEO, various vice presidents, and outside directors, performs this duty. Midlevel employees rarely sit on the search committee for the new CEO. In other countries, like the former Yugoslavia and Bulgaria, where lower-level employees constituted the board or selected the leader, their lack of education and experience usually doomed their efforts. Yet the seed of a possible solution lies here. For example, employees working in the middle levels of an organization usually have a pretty accurate picture of what the organization does and needs. Enron's two CEOs, Ken Lay and Jeffrey Skilling, both denied they had any knowledge of the financial malfeasance rampant in Enron. Nonetheless, on the very day that Skilling resigned, still presumably ignorant of improper Enron dealings, Sherron Watkins, an accountant in Enron's finance group, was sufficiently aware of the firm's fraudulent practices to send chairman Ken Lay an anonymous memo detailing the grave difficulties that beset the energy giant.

Individuals in the waistline of a business organization, as well as those in government agencies and other not-for-profit organizations, usually have a very clear idea of what kind of leaders their organization needs. Having worked in close proximity to numerous toxic leaders, they frequently have effective "toxicity detectors." Again, they need support from their peers. Sitting as token employees on a selection committee is usually futile. Adding a sufficient number of their savvy voices to those of the usual board members, including the outside directors, would probably help to reduce the likelihood of selecting a toxic CEO.

Choosing the Nontoxic Leader

How shall we think about selecting nontoxic leaders, not just in businesses but in all kinds of organizations? What will convince the sometimes reluctant, more inclusive nontoxic leaders to step forward? How can we accustom ourselves to the nontoxic leaders' refusal to offer us reassuring illusions? How do we learn to respond to the demands they make upon us to accept our own responsibilities as leaders?

At a minimum, we can recognize these nontoxic leaders by their even-handed attitude toward others, by the expression of *ubuntu* in their daily lives. We also recognize nontoxic leaders by their insistence that we accept the *valuable inconvenience of leadership.* They call us to commit ourselves to life-expanding enterprises, which entail at least six major, albeit hard-earned and interconnected, rewards.

First, these life-expanding experiences liberate us from our own narrow egos that badger us to enhance ourselves and those we hold dear. Rather, they push us to think beyond ourselves to a much larger, unfinished world, where the needs of the Other, writ large, call for satisfaction.

Second, such life-expanding experiences teach us to develop empathy, to view the Other not as alien and threatening but as a peculiar, precious part of ourselves for whom no sacrifice could ever be too great. Such experiences require and inspire *ubuntu* and connective leadership. Octavio Paz, winner of the Nobel prize for literature in 1990, caught this notion in his mystical epic *Sunstone* when he wrote about "the other side of this night, where I am you, we are us, the kingdom where pronouns are intertwined."[25]

Third, when we learn to take up the immense cause of the Other, we inevitably learn to lay down the smallness of ourselves. In fact,

> by unreservedly devoting ourselves to causes greater than ourselves, we free ourselves from the narrow quarrels of life, from the tyranny of egotism, and from the need to be more perfect than we can ever be. Paradoxically, in the act of immersing ourselves in the greatest expression of Other, that is, some larger purpose, we emerge as our most unique [and best] selves.[26]

Noted educator and social pioneer Horace Mann advised, "Be ashamed to die until you have won some victory for humanity."[27] When we accept the nontoxic leader's invitation to engage in such enterprises, be they discovering a cure for cancer, peacemaking or freedom seeking, mentoring a new employee, designing green housing, regularly visiting a lonely nursing home resident, or assisting at the local homeless shelter, we create new meaning for others and ourselves. Then

> we can . . . open ourselves to purposes beyond our narrow egoistic needs, new purposes in which we find our most important identity. In our search for meaning, we are finally prepared to commit ourselves, even sacrifice ourselves if necessary, to broad, supra-egoistic, perhaps, even universal, purposes. The serious ills of the world—war, poverty, disease, homelessness, environmental hazards, and the violation of human rights—now seem to beckon our wholehearted dedication.[28]

Fourth, these life-expanding experiences, by definition, make us grow. We do so in the shadow of our own mortality, where our symbolic nature, our truest identity, is evoked. They are the loam in which our self-esteem can grow to its fullest potential without metastasizing into cancerous, competitive overgrowth.

> By calling forth our most heroic, altruistic, noble selves willing to dedicate, perhaps sacrifice ourselves, to larger societal causes, we distinguish our symbolic from our physical being. In this way, we separate the egoistic self, so caught in the personal well-being of ego and body, family and career, from the supra-egoistic beings that we now yearn to be. In this way, we also try symbolically to conquer death and transcend our own mortality.[29]

That growth, of course, may bring pleasure or pain, often both. On some occasions it can force us to look deeply, more deeply than ever before, into ourselves. And at other times it makes us move out into the wide, unknown, chaotic world. In both places—deep within and far beyond ourselves—we discover the myriad lessons we must learn before we can call ourselves complete or claim that we have reduced the world's incompleteness by any measure.

Fifth, these life-expanding enterprises offer us the chance to glimpse coherence in a confusing, chaotic world. That coherence and meaning may, in the end, prove more important to us than the security we seek from strong leaders, human or divine, for it may help still our existential angst.

Sixth, these journeys may also put us on the path to autonomy and freedom. In an unfinished world, where a long-held truth may be blown away by the next scientific discovery, the search for truth embodies its own limitations and disappointments. That is not to suggest that truth is unimportant, for whatever truth we perceive at a given moment is all we have to guide our decision.

Yet when we direct at least some substantial portion of our efforts toward autonomy and freedom—our own and others—we create more enduring benefits and opportunities for the many. Autonomy and freedom liberate us from dependency on tyrants as well as on authoritarian and incompetent leaders. Freedom and autonomy, frequently braced by recognized anxiety, give us the courage to act, even in the face of death. It is then that we reach our true heroic potential. Our yearning for self-esteem is satiated. We are calling forth the leader within. Finding the leader within and winning those "victories for humanity" take us beyond our physical, creaturely selves to the expression of our noblest being.

Under these circumstances, we may also freely and fearlessly draft reluctant leaders, who have little need to enslave us. We can support and collaborate with these leaders to meet complex challenges in business, in politics, and in global enterprises. With autonomy and freedom, we can also insist intrepidly that toxic leaders purge themselves of their toxic ways. We can assist them in this task. Or, if necessary, we can join forces with others to oust incorrigible toxic leaders. Those, too, are acts of heroism.

When we have taken these steps, our existential terror of death can subside. We can gird ourselves to cope confidently and courageously with the situational anxieties that the uncertainties and stress of daily life provoke. We can loosen our grip on illusions, break the headlock of control myths, and thereby free ourselves from the bondage of toxic leaders. Building democratic institutions, where freedom exists and everyone has a voice, helps us take another critical step.

Developing a complex understanding of our self and our world moves us further along this essential path to constructive, Other-oriented leadership. Less driven by endless anxieties, overweening competitiveness, insatiable egos, endless needs for self-esteem, a pernicious achievement ethic, and calls to false heroics, we finally can assert our autonomy and set ourselves free. Then, through autonomy and freedom, we can find the inner strength not simply to escape, but to reject—resolutely and repeatedly—the allure of the toxic leader.

Notes

Chapter 1

1. Shakespeare portrayed the initial relationship between the young, recalcitrant Prince Hal and the comic Falstaff as one of mutual infatuation. Early on, it is almost difficult to discern who is leading whom. Eventually, after Prince Hal ascends to the throne, forsaking his youthful toxicity, he rejects Falstaff.

2. Some accounts use the date 1903. Curiously reflecting Mayor Curley's "colorful" life, most of the "factual" information about Curley, including dates of his political and prison terms, varies considerably across sources.

3. Mike Ryan, "Boston's Irrepressible James Michael Curley," *Boston Irish Reporter*, November 1999, available at http://web.archive.org/web/20021021195940 /http://www.bostonirish.com/jmcurley.html.

4. Jack Beatty, *The Rascal King: The Life and Times of James Michael Curley (1874–1958)* (Cambridge, MA: DaCapo Press, 2000).

5. Associated Press, "Corruption Trial Starts for Mayor of Providence," *New York Times*, April 24, 2002, A16.

6. Associated Press, "What's Providence Like Without Buddy?" June 24–25, 2003, available at http://www.turnto10.com/news/2290095/detail.html.

7. Alan Ehrenhalt, "The Paradox of Corrupt Yet Effective Leadership," *New York Times*, September 30, 2002, A23.

8. W. Zachary Malinowski, "Cianci Found Guilty of Racketeering Charge," *Providence Journal*, June 25, 2002, A1.

9. Pankaj Mishra, "Ex-Father of the Nation," *New York Times Book Review*, April 15, 2001, 12.

10. Robert Gellately, *Backing Hitler: Consent and Coercion in Nazi Germany* (New York: Oxford University Press, 2001), 3.

11. Christopher Hitchens, *The Missionary Position: Mother Teresa in Theory and Practice* (New York: Verso, 1995).

12. Matthew Sinclair, "William Aramony Is Back on the Streets," *NonProfit Times*, March 1, 2002.

13. Tim Dahlberg, "Top USOC Leaders Seek Mankamyer's Resignation," *Scoreboard*, January 21, 2003, available at http://www.evaa.nu/document/dunton/ 2003/jan22.html.

14. Gordon Witkin, "Can Jim and Tammy Make a Comeback?" *U.S. News and World Report*, October 19, 1987, 21.

15. Frank Bruni, "Italian Leader, in a First, Testifies at His Own Bribery Trial," *New York Times*, May 6, 2003, A6.

16. Ibid.

17. BBC News, "Vivendi's Messier Steps Down," July 2, 2002, available at http://news.bbc.co.uk/1/hi/business/2075948.stm.

18. John L. Allen Jr., "Italian Church Rocked by Its Own Scandals," *National Catholic Reporter*, May 31, 2002.

19. Slam! Cycling, "Killy Report to IOC on Tour de France Scandals," August 20, 1998, available at http://www.canoe.ca/TourDeFrance/aug20_kil.html.

20. BBC Online Network, "Cleaning Up the Problem," June 27, 1999, available at http://news.bbc.co.uk/2/hi/sport/tour_de_france/371200.stm.

21. Ibid.

22. Associated Press, "French Twist: Skating Judge Denies She Made a Deal for Scores," February 18, 2002, available at http://sportsillustrated.cnn.com/olympics/2002/figure_skating/news/2002/02/18/french_judge_ap/.

23. Curt Gentry, *J. Edgar Hoover: The Man and the Secrets* (New York: W. W. Norton, 1991).

24. Joseph Salvati served thirty years in prison for murder after an FBI agent deliberately testified falsely against him. Documents that would prove Salvati's innocence had been hidden by FBI agents. J. Edgar Hoover's initials appear on documents in Salvati's file, indicating that the FBI director was aware of the details. See Brian McGrory, "For Feds, It's All Hard Time," *Boston Globe*, June 24, 2003, B1.

25. See, for example, Anthony Summers, *Official and Confidential: The Secret Life of J. Edgar Hoover* (New York: Orion, 1993). See also Gentry, *J. Edgar Hoover*.

26. Paul Krugman, "The Good Guys," *New York Times*, December 24, 2002, 23.

27. Mimi Swartz with Sherron Watkins, *Power Failure: The Inside Story of the Collapse of Enron* (New York: Doubleday, 2003), 345.

28. Amanda Ripley and Maggie Sieger, "The Special Agent," *Time*, December 30, 2002–January 6, 2003, 37.

29. Anthony Bianco, William Symonds, and Nanette Byrnes, with David Polek, "The Rise and Fall of Dennis Kozlowski: A Revealing Look at the Man Behind the Tyco Scandal," *Business Week*, December 23, 2002, 65–77.

30. John A. Byrne, *Chainsaw: The Notorious Career of Al Dunlap in the Era of Profit-at-Any-Price* (New York: HarperCollins, 1999), 20.

31. "New MBAs: "Nasty by Nature," *Fortune*, February 17, 1997, 127.

32. Floyd Norris, "S.E.C. Accuses Former Sunbeam Official of Fraud," *New York Times*, May 16, 2001, A1.

33. James MacGregor Burns, *Leadership* (New York: Harper and Row, 1978).

34. See, for example, Neil Baldwin, *Henry Ford and the Jews: The Mass Production of Hate* (New York: Public Affairs, 2001).

35. Erich Fromm, *Escape from Freedom* (New York: Holt, 1991).

36. Ernest Becker, *Escape from Evil* (New York: Free Press, 1975).

37. Solomon E. Asch, "Effects of Group Pressure Upon the Modification and Distortion of Judgments," in Harold Guetzkow, ed., *Groups, Leadership, and Men* (Pittsburgh: Carnegie Press, 1951); Solomon E. Asch, "Studies on Independence and Conformity: A Minority of One Against a Unanimous Majority," *Psychological Monographs* 70, 9 (1956).

38. L. Festinger, H. W. Riecken, and S. Schacter, *When Prophecy Fails* (Minneapolis: University of Minnesota Press, 1956).

39. Muzafer Sherif, *The Psychology of Social Norms* (New York: Harper and Brothers, 1936).

40. T. W. Adorno, Else Frenkel-Brunswik, D. J. Levinson, and R. N. Sanford, *The Authoritarian Personality* (New York: Harper and Brothers, 1950).

41. Stanley Milgram, *Obedience to Authority: An Experimental View* (New York: Harper and Row, 1974).

42. Hannah Arendt, *Eichmann in Jerusalem: A Report on the Banality of Evil* (New York: Viking, 1963).

43. Daniel Jonah Goldhagen, *Hitler's Willing Executioners: Ordinary Germans and the Holocaust* (New York: Vintage, 1997).

44. Robert Gellately, *Backing Hitler: Consent and Coercion in Nazi Germany* (New York: Oxford University Press, 2001).

45. Peter Frost and Sandra Robinson, "The Toxic Handler: Organizational Hero—and Casualty," *Harvard Business Review*, July–August 1999, 96–106.

46. Adel Darwish, "Iraq: The Secret of the Palaces," December 2, 2001, available at http://web.archive.org/web/20030610105519/http://www.foreignwire.com/palaces.html.

47. In a study of 6,500 employees at seventy-six Holiday Inn hotels in the United States and Canada, the estimated cost of hotel employees' awareness of their managers' lack of integrity was calculated at $250,000 per hotel. Tony Simons, "The High Cost of Lost Trust," *Harvard Business Review*, September 2002, 18–19.

48. Connie Bruck, *The Predators' Ball* (New York: Penguin, 1988).

49. Piers Brendon, *Winston Churchill: A Brief Life* (London: Pimlico, 2001); Dennis Kavanagh, *Crisis, Charisma and British Political Leadership: Winston Churchill as the Outsider*, Sage Professional Papers in Contemporary Political Sociology, 06-001 (London and Beverly Hills: Sage, 1974).

50. James Allen, *As a Man Thinketh* (Camarillo, CA: De Vorss, 1983).

Chapter 2

1. Daniel Liechty, *Transference and Transcendence: Ernest Becker's Contribution to Psychotherapy* (Northvale, NJ: Jason Aronson, 1995).

2. Stanley Milgram, *Obedience to Authority: An Experimental View* (New York: Harper and Row, 1974).

3. Jean Lipman-Blumen, *Gender Roles and Power* (Englewood Cliffs, NJ: Prentice Hall, 1984).

4. For the distinction between micro and macro manipulation, see Lipman-Blumen, *Gender Roles and Power*.

5. See Robert K. Merton, *Social Theory and Social Structure* (Glencoe, IL: Free Press, 1957) for an early articulation of the functions of positive role models. For more recent work on positive and negative role models, see Penelope Lockwood, Christian H. Jordan, and Ziva Kunda, "Motivation by Positive or Negative Role Models: Regulatory Focus Determines Who Will Best Inspire Us," *Journal of Personality and Social Psychology* 83, 4 (2002): 854–64. See also the large body of work by E. T. Higgins, including "Beyond Pleasure and Pain," *American Psychologist* 52 (1997): 1280–300; "Making a Good Decision: Value from Fit," *American Psychologist* 55 (2000): 1217–30; E. T. Higgins and I. Silberman, "Development of Regulatory Focus: Promotion and Prevention as Ways of Living," in J. Heckhausen and C. S. Dweck, eds., *Motivation and Self-Regulation Across the Life Span* (New York: Cambridge University Press, 1998), 78–113.

6. C. Haney, C. Banks, and P. Zimbardo, "Interpersonal Dynamics in a Simulated Prison," *International Journal of Criminology and Penology* 1 (1973): 69–97.

See also Philip G. Zimbardo, "The Stanford Prison Experiment: A Simulation Study of the Psychology of Imprisonment," 1999, available at http://www.prisonexp.org, 1.

7. Maureen E. Olmsted, "Parental Alcoholism or Alcoholism in the Current Relationship: A Special Case?" paper presented at the biennial meeting of the Society for Research in Child Development, Albuquerque, NM, April 15–18, 1999. See also M. A. Schuckit, J. E. Tipp, and E. Kelner, "Are Daughters of Alcoholics More Likely to Marry Alcoholics?" *American Journal of Drug and Alcohol Abuse* 20 (1994): 237–45.

8. CNN, "Julian Lennon: Stepfather Knew Best," May 25, 1999, available at http://www.cnn.com/SHOWBIZ/News/9905/25/showbuzz/.

9. Erich Fromm, *Escape from Freedom* (New York: Holt, 1991); Robert N. Bellah, Richard Madsen, William M. Sullivan, Ann Swidler, and Steven M. Tipton, *Habits of the Heart: Individualism and Commitment in American Life* (Berkeley: University of California Press, 1985).

10. Fromm, *Escape from Freedom*.

11. Ibid.

12. Ibid.

13. Elias Canetti, *Crowds and Power* (London: Gollancz, 1962), quoted in Ernest Becker, *The Denial of Death* (New York: Basic Books, 1973), 106.

14. Ernest Becker, *Escape from Evil* (New York: Free Press, 1975), 64; Otto Rank, *Psychology of the Soul* (New York: Perpetua Books, 1961), 87.

15. Stanley Crouch, "Picking Up Where Faulkner Left Off," *Los Angeles Times Book Review*, January 26, 2003, R3.

16. Mark Muraven and Roy F. Baumeister, "Sex, Terror, Paralysis, and Other Pitfalls of Reductionist Self-Preservation Theory," *Psychological Inquiry* 8, 1 (1997): 36–40.

17. Roy F. Baumeister and D. M. Tice, "Anxiety and Social Exclusion," *Journal of Social and Clinical Psychology* 9 (1991): 165–95.

18. Plato, *The Republic of Plato*, trans. Francis MacDonald Cornford (New York: Oxford University Press, 1950).

19. Amanda Ripley and Maggie Sieger, "The Special Agent," *Time*, December 30, 2002–January 6, 2003, 37.

20. Ibid.

21. Curt Gentry, *J. Edgar Hoover: The Man and the Secrets* (New York: W. W. Norton, 1991).

22. Judith Lorber, "Outsiders Within: Comment on *Time* Persons of the Year 2002," essay sent via LISTSERV to author, December 25, 2002.

23. C. Fred Alford, *Whistleblowers: Broken Lives and Organizational Power* (Ithaca, NY: Cornell University Press, 2001), 23–24; Philip Jos, Mark Tompkins, and Steven Hays, "In Praise of Difficult People: A Portrait of the Committed Whistleblower," *Public Administration Review* 49 (1989): 552–61.

24. Although in these three prominent cases women stepped forward, there is no clear evidence that women are more likely than men to blow the whistle, despite their more structured marginality within organizations.

25. Alford, *Whistleblowers*.

26. Charles Haddad, "A Whistle-Blower Rocks an Industry," *Business Week*, June 4, 2002, 130.

27. Aspen Institute Business and Society Program, *Where Will They Lead: 2003 MBA Student Attitudes About Business and Society* (Aspen, CO: Aspen Institute, 2003).

28. Solomon E. Asch, "Studies on Independence and Conformity: A Minority of One Against a Unanimous Majority," *Psychological Monographs* 70, 9 (1956).

29. Muzafer Sherif, "Experiments on Norm Formation," in Edwin P. Hollander and Raymond G. Hunt, eds., *Classic Contributions to Social Psychology* (New York: Oxford University Press, 1972), 329; Solomon E. Asch, "Group Forces in the Modification and Distortion of Judgments," in Edwin P. Hollander and Raymond G. Hunt, eds., *Classic Contributions to Social Psychology* (New York: Oxford University Press, 1972), 330–39.

30. Sigmund Freud, *Group Psychology and the Analysis of the Ego*, trans. and ed. James Strachey (New York: W. W. Norton, 1959).

31. Gentry, *J. Edgar Hoover*, 28.

32. Ronald D. Cohen and Dave Samuelson, liner notes for *Songs for Political Action*, 1996, Bear Family Records BCD 15730 JL, 85.

33. Alexis de Tocqueville, *Democracy in America* (New York: Vintage Books, 1959).

Chapter 3

1. For earlier existential approaches, see Søren Kierkegaard, *Fear and Trembling: Dialectical Lyric by Johannes de Silentio* (London: Penguin, 1985); Otto Rank, *Art and Artist: Creative Urge and Personality Development* (New York: W. W. Norton, 1932); and Ernest Becker, *The Denial of Death* (New York: Free Press, 1973). See also Sigmund Freud, *The Problem of Anxiety* (New York: Psychoanalytic Quarterly Press and W. W. Norton, 1936). While I do not presume to include my own work at the level of these scholars, some of my earlier work, from *Gender Roles and Power* (Englewood Cliffs, NJ: Prentice Hall, 1984) to *The Connective Edge: Leading in an Interdependent World* (San Francisco: Jossey-Bass, 1996; paperback edition, *Connective Leadership: Managing in a Changing World* [New York: Oxford University Press, 2000]) and "Why Do We Tolerate Bad Leaders?" in Warren Bennis, Gretchen M. Spreitzer, and Tom G. Cummings, eds., *The Future of Leadership: Today's Top Leadership Thinkers Speak to Tomorrow's Leaders* (San Francisco: Jossey-Bass, 2001) also dealt with these issues.

2. John O'Hara, *Appointment in Samarra* (New York: Harcourt Brace, 1934).

3. Ernest Becker, *Escape from Evil* (New York: Free Press, 1975).

4. Sigmund Freud, *Group Psychology and the Analysis of the Ego*, trans. and ed. James Strachey (New York: W. W. Norton, 1959), 16.

5. Cultural anthropologist Ernest Becker suggests that "the real world is simply too terrible to admit; it tells man that he is a small, trembling animal who will decay and die. Illusion changes all this, makes man seem important, vital to the universe, immortal in some way.... The masses look to the leaders to give them just the untruth that they need; the leader continues the illusions ... and magnifies them into a truly heroic victory" (*Denial of Death*, 133).

6. F. G. Bailey, *Humbuggery and Manipulation: The Art of Leadership* (Ithaca, NY: Cornell University Press, 1988).

7. John Leavitt, "The Language of the Gods: Mythic Song and Divine Speech in the Central Himalayas," manuscript, 2001.

8. Elemér Hankiss, *Fears and Symbols: An Introduction to the Study of Western Civilization* (Budapest: Central European University Press, 2001), 26.

9. Ibid.

10. Becker, *The Denial of Death*.

11. Mimi Swartz with Sherron Watkins, *Power Failure: The Inside Story of the Collapse of Enron* (New York: Doubleday, 2003), 3.

12. Ibid., 15.

13. Daniel Liechty, *Transference and Transcendence: Ernest Becker's Contribution to Psychotherapy* (Northvale, NY: Jason Aronson, 1995).

14. Frank Bruni, "Berlusconi, in a Rough Week, Says Only He Can Save Italy," *New York Times*, May 10, 2003, A1, available at http://www.nytimes.com/2003/05/10/international/europe/10ITAL.html.

15. Katrina Brooker, "The Un-CEO," *Fortune*, September 16, 2002, 88.

16. David Rynecki, "Can Stan O'Neal Save Merrill?" *Fortune*, September 30, 2002, 76.

17. Betsy Morris, "Can Ford Save Ford?" *Fortune*, November 30, 2002, 52.

18. Devin Leonard, "Songs in the Key of Steve," *Fortune*, May 12, 2003, 52.

19. Anthony Bianco and Tom Lowry, "Can Dick Parsons Rescue AOL Time Warner?" *Business Week*, May 19, 2003, 86.

20. Kathy Gannon, "Ban on Poppy Farming Virtually Wipes Out Opium," *State Journal-Register* (IL), February 16, 2001, available at http://www.cannabisnews.com/news/thread8717.shtml.

21. Maggie Farley and Paul Watson, "Annan Asks Taliban to Reject ID Tags for Afghanistan Hindus," *Los Angles Times*, May 24, 2001, A5.

22. Pamela Constable, "Afghan Poppies Sprout Again," *Washington Post*, November 10, 2003, A16.

23. Clifford Geertz, "Centers, Kings, and Charisma: Reflections on the Symbolics of Power," in *Local Knowledge: Further Essays in Interpretive Anthropology* (New York: Basic Books, 1983), 122–23. See also Edward Shils, "Charisma, Order, and Status," *American Sociological Review*, April 30, 1965, 199–213.

24. Micha Popper, *Hypnotic Leadership: Leaders, Followers, and the Loss of Self* (Westport, CT: Praeger, 2001), xv.

25. Ibid., 12.

26. Thomas Kuhn, *The Structure of Scientific Revolutions*, 2nd ed. (Chicago: University of Chicago Press, 1970).

27. Human Genome Project Information home page, available at http://www.ornl.gov/sci/techresources/Human_Genome/home.shtml.

28. Jerry Useem, "The 25 Most Powerful People in Business," *Fortune*, August 11, 2003, 57–84.

29. Robert W. Fuller, *Somebodies and Nobodies: Overcoming the Abuse of Rank* (Gabriola Island, BC: New Society, 2003), 74.

30. Neil Baldwin, *Henry Ford and the Jews: The Mass Production of Hate* (New York: Public Affairs, 2001).

31. Becker, *Escape from Evil*, 63.

32. Australian Broadcasting Corporation Science Online, "The Genes for Megalomania," May 10, 2002, available at http://www.abc.net.au/science/news/stories/s552984.htm.

33. David Bank, "Larry Ellison Has a Science Project: Courting Biologists," *Wall Street Journal*, January 9, 2003, A1–A2.

34. Ibid., A1.

35. Søren Kierkegaard, *The Concept of Dread* (Princeton, NJ: Princeton University Press, 1944); Karl Jaspers, *Philosophie* (Heidelberg: Springer, 1948); Martin Heidegger, *Being and Time* (London: SCM, 1962).

36. Susan Pulliam, "Ordered to Commit Fraud, a Staffer Balked, Then Caved," *Wall Street Journal*, June 23, 2003, 1.

37. Ibid.

38. Ibid.
39. Swartz with Watkins, *Power Failure*, 14.
40. Added here for clarification.
41. Swartz with Watkins, *Power Failure*, 9.
42. Ibid., 11.
43. Irving Janis, *Victims of Groupthink: A Psychological Study of Foreign-Policy Decisions and Fiascoes* (Boston: Houghton Mifflin, 1972).
44. Quoted in Gordon W. Allport, "Preface," in Viktor E. Frankl, *Man's Search for Meaning* (New York: Washington Square Press, 1983), 12.
45. Swartz with Watkins, *Power Failure*, 12.
46. Ibid.
47. Ibid., 13.
48. *Business Week*, "The 25 Top Executives of the Year," January 11, 1999, available at http://www.businessweek.com/1999/02/b3611001.htm.
49. William C. Symonds, "Basic Training for CEOs," *Business Week*, June 11, 2001, 103.
50. Anthony Bianco, William Symonds, and Nanette Byrnes, with David Polek, "The Rise and Fall of Dennis Kozlowski: A Revealing Look at the Man Behind the Tyco Scandal," *Business Week*, December 23, 2002, 65–77.
51. Ibid.
52. Neil A. Lewis and David Johnston, "A Nation Challenged: The Investigation; Document That May Have Been Used to Prepare for Attacks Is Reported Found," *New York Times*, September 28, 2001, B4.
53. Becker, *Escape from Evil*, particularly Chapter 5; Otto Rank, *Psychology and the Soul* (New York: Perpetua, 1961), 87–91.
54. Leon Festinger and John Thibaut, "Interpersonal Communication in Small Groups," *Journal of Abnormal and Social Psychology* 46 (1951): 92–99; see also Leon Festinger, Stanley Schacter, and Kurt Back, *Social Pressures in Informal Groups: A Study of Human Factors in Housing* (Stanford: Stanford University Press, 1950).
55. Ernest Becker, *Escape from Evil* (New York: Free Press, 1973), 115.
56. Simone de Beauvoir, *The Second Sex* (New York: Vintage, 1974).
57. Becker, *Escape from Evil*, 115.
58. Lewis Mumford, *The Myth of the Machine: Technics and Human Development* (New York: Harcourt, Brace and World, 1966), 185–86.

Chapter 4

1. Elemér Hankiss, *Fears and Symbols: An Introduction to the Study of Western Civilization* (Budapest: Central European University Press, 2001). Hankiss argues that human beings created Western civilization in all its manifestations—governments, laws, religion, science, symbols, myths and beliefs, norms, traditions, communities, families, schools, and art, for starters—in direct response to our existential fears and anxieties stemming from our awareness of death. He contends that we experience the world as an "alien" environment, with unknown dangers that provoke our "situational fear."
2. Charles Perrow, *Normal Accidents: Living with High-Risk Technologies* (New York: Basic Books, 1984).
3. John A. Byrne, *Chainsaw: The Notorious Career of Al Dunlap in the Era of Profit-at-Any-Price* (New York: HarperCollins, 1999).
4. Lawrence Ferlinghetti, "The World Is a Beautiful Place," in *Pictures of the Gone World* (San Francisco: City Light Books, 1955).
5. But even within the many organizations that make up a democratic society,

leaders are commonly appointed by small, elite oversight bodies, such as boards of directors. These appointed leaders serve at the "pleasure of the board" without fixed terms. When they "displease" the rest of us who didn't select them, they may prove more difficult to remove.

6. Erik H. Erikson, *Childhood and Society*, 2nd ed. (New York: W. W. Norton, 1963), 268.

7. Ed Magnuson, "Earthquake," *Time*, October 30, 1989, 36.

8. Ibid.

9. Robert A. Page, Peter H. Stauffer, and James W. Hendley II, "Progress Toward a Safer Future Since the 1989 Loma Prieta Earthquake," U.S. Geological Survey Fact Sheet, 1999, available at http://geopubs.wr.usgs.gov/fact-sheet/fs151-99/.

10. Department of Conservation, State of California, "Will a Major Earthquake Interrupt the World Series? State Experts Say It's Unlikely, Though Not Impossible," NR 2002-45, October 17, 2002, available at http://www.consrv.ca.gov/index/news/2002%20News%20Releases/NR2002–45%20World%20Series%20Earthquake.htm.

11. Harold J. Leavitt, "Technology and Organizations: Where's the Off Button?" *California Management Review* 44, 2 (2002).

12. Perrow, *Normal Accidents*.

13. Leavitt, "Technology and Organizations."

14. CNN, "World Trade Center Death Toll Drops by Two," November 2, 2002, available at http://www.cnn.com/2002/US/Northeast/11/02/wtc.death.toll/.

15. Roy F. Baumeister, Ellen Bratslavsky, Catrin Finkenauer, and Kathleen D. Vohs, "Bad Is Stronger Than Good," *Review of General Psychology* 5, 4 (2001): 323–70.

16. We are ineluctably interconnected on every level—economically, environmentally, organizationally, politically, sociologically, and psychologically. In large technical systems, interdependence and tight coupling lead to unforeseen interactions that, in turn, cause normal accidents, according to Perrow, *Normal Accidents*. Interdependence has similar consequences for the organizational world. A downturn on the New York Stock Exchange ripples through financial markets around the globe. Events witnessed on television have worldwide reverberations, from Gdansk to East Berlin. The killings in Columbine trigger three thousand copycat incidents across the land in one year.

17. Erich Fromm, *Escape from Freedom* (New York: Avon, 1941), 52.

18. Ibid.

19. For a discussion of the impact of living in a world of increasing diversity, coupled with interdependence, see Jean Lipman-Blumen, *The Connective Edge: Leading in an Interdependent World* (San Francisco: Jossey-Bass, 1996).

20. John M. Glionna, "Inmate Didn't Get Life, So He Chose Death at 92," *Los Angeles Times*, July 11, 2002, A1. See also Evelyn Nieves, "Freed from Jail Despite His Pleas, 92-Year-Old Is Found Dead in a River," *New York Times*, July 12, 2002, A12, available at http://www.nytimes.com/2002/07/12/national/12INMA.html.

21. Edgar H. Schein with Inge Schneier and Curtis H. Barker, *Coercive Persuasion: A Socio-psychological Analysis of the "Brainwashing" of American Civilian Prisoners by the Chinese Communists* (New York: W. W. Norton, 1961).

22. Otto Rank, *Art and Artist: Creative Urge and Personality Development* (New York: W. W. Norton, 1932); Ernest Becker, *The Denial of Death* (New York: Basic Books, 1973).

23. Lipman-Blumen, *The Connective Edge*.

24. Becker, *The Denial of Death*.

25. Hankiss, *Fears and Symbols*.

26. Neil J. Smelser, *The Theory of Collective Behavior* (New York: Free Press, 1962); Malcolm Gladwell, *The Tipping Point* (Boston: Little, Brown, 2002).

27. See Howard E. Gardner, *Leading Minds: An Anatomy of Leadership* (New York: Basic Books, 1996).

28. William J. Holstein, "A Culture Turned Against Itself at Andersen," review of Barbara Ley Toffler, *Final Accounting, New York Times*, February 23, 2003, Section 3, 6.

29. Barbara Ley Toffler, *Final Accounting: Ambition, Greed, and the Fall of Arthur Andersen* (New York: Broadway Books, 2003), 34.

Chapter 5

1. Bob Herbert, "The Right Answer," *New York Times*, September 20, 2001, A31.

2. Art Boulay, "Leadership Focus: Malden Mills: A Study in Leadership," *Quality Monitor Newsletter,* October 1996, available at http://www.opi-inc.com/malden.htm.

3. For a treatment of how anxiety, uncertainty, and meaning are related to our tolerance for toxic leaders, see Jean Lipman-Blumen, "Why Do We Tolerate Bad Leaders? Magnificent Uncertitude, Anxiety, and Meaning," in Warren Bennis, Gretchen M. Spreitzer, and Thomas G. Cummings, eds., *The Future of Leadership: Today's Top Leadership Thinkers Speak to Tomorrow's Leaders* (San Francisco: Jossey-Bass, 2001).

4. This point and the remainder of this section draw heavily on Jean Lipman-Blumen, "Role De-Differentiation as a System Response to Crisis," *Sociological Inquiry* 43, 2 (1973): 105–29.

5. Ibid.

6. Héctor Tobar, "Pomp, Not Panic, During Argentine Leader's Inaugural," *Los Angeles Times*, May 26, 2003, A3.

7. John A. Byrne, *Chainsaw: The Notorious Career of Al Dunlap in the Era of Profit-at-Any-Price* (New York: HarperBusiness, 1999), 11.

8. Ibid., 4.

9. Ibid., 4–5.

10. Max Weber, *Max Weber: The Theory of Social and Economic Organization*, trans. A. M. Henderson and Talcott Parsons (New York: Free Press of Glencoe, 1947).

11. Lipman-Blumen, "Role De-Differentiation."

12. F. Cohen, S. Solomon, M. Maxfield, T. Pyszczynski, and J. Greenberg, "Fatal Attraction: The Effects of Mortality Salience on Evaluations of Charismatic, Task-Focused, and Relationship-Focused Leaders," in preparation.

13. Max Weber, "The Sociology of Charismatic Authority," in *From Max Weber: Essays in Sociology*, eds. H. H. Gerth and C. Wright Mills (New York: Oxford University Press, 1946), 245–52.

14. Piers Brendon, *The Dark Valley: A Panorama of the 1930s* (New York: Alfred A. Knopf, 2000), 281.

15. David Aberbach, "Charisma and Attachment Theory: A Cross-Disciplinary Interpretation," *International Journal of Psychoanalysis* 76 (1995): 845–55.

16. Micha Popper, *Hypnotic Leadership: Leaders, Followers, and the Loss of Self* (Westport, CT: Praeger, 2001), describing Aberbach, "Charisma and Attachment Theory."

17. Warren Bennis and Robert J. Thomas, *Geeks and Geezers: How Era, Values*

and Defining Moments Shape Leaders (Boston: Harvard Business School Press, 2003).

18. Aberbach, "Charisma and Attachment Theory."

19. F. G. Bailey, *Humbuggery and Manipulation: The Art of Leadership* (Ithaca, NY: Cornell University Press, 1988).

20. Bob Herbert, "Rudy's No-Exit Strategy," *New York Times*, October 1, 2001, A23.

21. For a discussion of how well-done graphical representations can help decision makers, see Edward Rolf Tufte, *Visual Explanations* (Cheshire, CT: Graphics Press, 1997).

22. For a discussion of groupthink, see Irving I. Janis, *Victims of Groupthink: A Psychological Study of Foreign-Policy Decisions and Fiascoes* (Boston: Houghton Mifflin, 1972). For a discussion of the political and bureaucratic difficulties that impede a leader's access to trustworthy information in times of crisis, see Graham T. Allison, *Essence of Decision: Explaining the Cuban Missile Crisis* (Boston: Little, Brown, 1971).

23. Steven Sample, *The Contrarian's Guide to Leadership* (San Francisco: Jossey-Bass, 2001).

24. Dale L. Watson, statement for the record of Dale L. Watson, executive assistant director, counterterrorism and counterintelligence, FBI, on "The Terrorist Threat Confronting the United States," before the Senate Select Committee on Intelligence, Washington, DC, February 6, 2002, available at http://www.fbi.gov/congress/congress02/watson020602.htm.

25. Carol Hymowitz, "Companies Experience Major Power Shifts as Crises Continue," *Wall Street Journal*, October 9, 2001, B1.

26. George W. Bush, address to Joint Session of the U.S. Congress, September 20, 2001.

27. John A. Byrne and Heather Timmons, "Tough Times: How Ken Chenault of AmEx Is Being Tested in Ways Few Could Have Imagined," *Business Week*, October 29, 2001, 66.

28. Sidney Hook, *The Hero in History: A Study in Limitation and Possibility* (Boston: Beacon, 1943).

29. Larry Celona, "Cop Is Shot with Own Gun—Just as Khalid Urged," *New York Post*, September 8, 1998, 16.

30. Martin Niemöller in the *Congressional Record*, October 14, 1968, 31636.

31. Benjamin Franklin, 1759, quoted in John Bartlett, *Familiar Quotations*, 14th ed., ed. Emily Morison Beck (Boston: Little, Brown, 1968), 422.

32. Mark Lasswell, "The Controversy over CBS' Hitler," *TV Guide*, April 12–18, 2003, 33.

33. Howard Rosenberg, "He Fought Our Fear, and the Fear Won," *Los Angeles Times*, April 14, 2003, E1.

34. James Glanz and John Schwartz, "Dogged Engineer's Effort to Assess Shuttle Damage," *New York Times*, September 26, 2003, A1, available at http://www.nytimes.com/2003/09/26/national/nationalspecial/26ENGI.html.

35. Ibid.

36. Daniel Webster, from a speech at the foundation of the Bunker Hill monument commemorating the soldiers of the American Revolution, June 17, 1825.

37. Eric Lichtblau, "U.S. Uses Terror Law to Pursue Crimes from Drugs to Swindling," *New York Times*, September 28, 2003, 1.

38. Ibid.

39. Lisa Guernsey, "Living Under an Electronic Eye," *New York Times*, September 27, 2001, G1.

40. Ibid.

41. Janis, *Victims of Groupthink.*

42. Terence Hunt, "Clinton Pledges Turkey Quake Aid; President Visits Chilly Tent Camp, Consoles Victims," *Lexington Herald-Leader*, November 17, 1999, A3.

43. Paul Shrivastava, *Bhopal: Anatomy of a Crisis* (Cambridge, MA: Ballinger, 1987).

Chapter 6

1. Available at http://elib.zib.de / pub / UserHome / Groetschel / Predictions / Predictions/tsld007.htm.

2. Sharon Begley, "Science's Big Query: What Can We Know, and What Can't We?" *Wall Street Journal* Science Journal, May 30, 2003, B1.

3. Kurt Godel (1906–1978), available at http://www.exploratorium.edu / complexity/CompLexicon/godel.html.

4. Begley, "Science's Big Query."

5. Judy Jones and William Wilson, *An Incomplete Education* (New York: Ballantine, 1995).

6. Katsuhiro Kohara, "The Future of Bioethics and Christianity," *Echoes of Peace* 64, 1 (2003), available at http://theology.doshisha.ac.jp:8008/kkohara/works.nsf/ 626e6035eadbb4cd85256499006b15a6/3aa47576a4a0d93c49256cbf005c9546?Open Document.

7. Donald Trump and Kate Bonher, *The Art of the Comeback* (New York: Times Books, 1997).

8. D. C. McClelland, J. W. Atkinson, R. A. Clark, and E. L. Lowell, *The Achievement Motive* (New York: Appleton-Century-Crofts, 1953); D. C. McClelland, *The Achieving Society* (Princeton, NJ: Van Nostrand, 1961); R. A. Le-Vine, *Dreams and Deeds: Achievement Motivation in Nigeria* (Chicago: University of Chicago Press, 1966); B. C. Rosen and R. G. D'Andrade, "The Psychosocial Origins of Achievement Motivation," *Sociometry* 22, 3 (1959): 185–218; H. J. Kornandt, L. H. Eckensberger, and W. B. Emminghaus, "Cross-cultural Research on Motivation and Its Contribution to a General Theory of Motivation," in H. C. Triandis and W. Lonner, eds., *Handbook of Cross-Cultural Psychology*, vol. 3: *Basic Processes* (Boston: Allyn and Bacon, 1980).

9. Erica Goode, "A Boy Genius? Mother Says She Faked Tests," *New York Times*, March 2, 2002, A1.

10. David D. Kirkpatrick, "Historian Says Borrowing Was Wider Than Known," *New York Times*, February 23, 2002, A10, available at http://www .nytimes.com/2002/02/23/books/23BOOK.html.

11. Marjorie Garber, "Our Genius Problem," *The Atlantic*, December 2002.

12. Ibid.

13. Philip Anson, "Dutoit: A Glance Back," *La Scena Musicale*, LSM Online, April 18, 2002.

14. Thierry C. Pauchant and Associates, *In Search of Meaning: Managing for the Health of Our Organizations, Our Communities, and the Natural World* (San Francisco: Jossey-Bass, 1995); Thomas J. Peters and Robert H. Waterman Jr., *In Search of Excellence: Lessons from America's Best-Run Companies* (New York: Harper and Row, 1982).

15. Ernest Becker, *Escape from Evil* (New York: Free Press, 1975).

16. Ibid., 81

17. Ibid.

18. Max Weber, *The Protestant Ethic and the Spirit of Capitalism* (New York: Charles Scribner's Sons, 1958).

19. George Horton Cooley, *Human Nature and the Social Order* (New York: Scribner's, 1902), particularly 179–85.

20. Abraham H. Maslow, *Motivation and Personality* (New York: Harper and Brothers, 1954).

21. Ernest Becker, *The Denial of Death* (New York: Basic Books, 1973).

22. "They Said What?" *The Observer,* April 21, 2002, available at http://observer.guardian.co.uk/comment/story/0,6903,688077,00.html.

23. Piers Brendon, *Winston Churchill: A Brief Life* (London: Pimlico, 2001).

24. Alexander L. George and Juliette L. George, *Woodrow Wilson and Colonel House: A Personality Study* (New York: Dover, 1989), 8–9.

25. Vincent Bugliosi with Curt Gentry, *Helter Skelter* (New York: Bantam Books, 1974), 349.

26. Jean Lipman-Blumen, *The Connective Edge: Leading in an Interdependent World* (San Francisco: Jossey-Bass, 1996).

27. James March, "Information Technology, Decision Making and the Human Condition," paper presented at the 24th International Federation of Training and Development Organizations (IFTDO) World Conference on Personal Renewal, Helsinki, Finland, 1995.

28. Ibid., 3.

Chapter 7

1. J. A. Byrne, *Chainsaw: The Notorious Career of Al Dunlap in the Era of Profit-at-Any Price* (New York: HarperBusiness, 1999), 25.

2. Jodie Morse and Amanda Bower, "Persons of the Year: The Party Crasher," *Time,* December 30, 2002–January 6, 2003, 54.

3. R. Schoenberg, *Geneen* (New York: Norton, 1985).

4. This section draws from my earlier work: Jean Lipman-Blumen, "Why Do We Tolerate Bad Leaders? Magnificent Uncertitude, Anxiety, and Meaning," in Warren Bennis, Gretchen M. Spreitzer, and Thomas G. Cummings, eds., *The Future of Leadership: Today's Top Leadership Thinkers Speak to Tomorrow's Leaders* (San Francisco: Jossey-Bass, 2001), 125–38. For an earlier conceptualization of control myths, see Jean Lipman-Blumen, *Gender Roles and Power* (Englewood Cliffs, NJ: Prentice Hall, 1984).

5. Abraham Maslow, *Motivation and Personality* (New York: Harper, 1954); Abraham Maslow, *The Farther Reaches of Human Nature* (New York: Viking, 1971).

6. Maslow, *Motivation and Personality*, 98–101.

7. Ibid., especially 206–29.

8. Maslow, *The Farther Reaches of Human Nature*.

9. In *Motivation and Personality*, Maslow talked about the "desires to know and to understand" but chose not to include them officially in the hierarchy at that time. His reason was that not enough was known about the more nuanced dynamics of cognitive impulses. The lack of knowledge about cognitive needs arose, he argued, because they escaped the notice of most clinicians who focused primarily on eliminating psychopathology. According to Maslow, "cognitive psychopathology is pale, subtle, and easily overlooked, or defined as normal" (93).

10. Maslow, *The Farther Reaches of Human Nature*, 271. Maslow's concept of transcendence subsumes thirty-five well-delineated dimensions, including the capacity to transcend time, culture, one's past, the we/they dichotomy, and death,

plus many other facets too numerous to be detailed here. See particularly Chapter 21, 269–79.

11. Ibid., 269.

12. Ibid., 275.

13. Maslow, *Motivation and Personality*, 91.

14. Maslow, *The Farther Reaches of Human Nature*, 269.

15. This term was suggested to me by Robert Fisher in a personal communication.

16. Kenneth Cloke and Joan Goldsmith, *The End of Management and the Rise of Organizational Democracy* (San Francisco: Jossey-Bass, 2002), 180.

17. Robert W. Fuller, *Somebodies and Nobodies: Overcoming the Abuse of Rank* (Gabriola Island, BC: New Society, 2003).

Chapter 8

1. Ernest Becker, *Denial of Death* (New York: Free Press, 1973); Ernest Becker, *Escape from Evil* (New York: Free Press, 1975); Otto Rank, *Art and Artist: Creative Urge and Personality Development* (New York: W. W. Norton, 1932); Otto Rank, *Truth and Reality* (New York: W. W. Norton, 1936); E. James Lieberman, *Acts of Will* (New York: Free Press, 1985); Robert Kramer, *A Psychology of Difference: The American Lectures* (Princeton, NJ: Princeton University Press, 1996); Tom Pyszczynski, Sheldon Solomon, and Jeff Greenberg, *In the Wake of 9/11: The Psychology of Terror* (Washington, DC: American Psychological Association, 2003); Elemér Hankiss, *Fear and Symbols: An Introduction to the Study of Western Civilization* (Budapest: Central European University Press, 2001); Thomas J. Peters and Robert H. Waterman Jr., *In Search of Excellence: Lessons from America's Best-Run Companies* (New York: Harper and Row, 1982).

2. Elizabeth Mehren, "Father's Mind-Set Is Liberated," *Los Angeles Times*, April 14, 2003, A1.

3. Ira Sager, "Lou Gerstner on Catching the Third Wave," *Business Week*, October 30, 1995.

4. Lou Gerstner, speech at Uniforum Conference, San Francisco, February 14, 1996.

5. Lou Bertin, "The Observer: Gerstner's Gift to IBM," *Information Week*, December 2, 2002, available at http://www.informationweek.com/story/show Article.jhtml?articleID=6503961.

6. Robert Worth, "What Lou Gerstner Could Teach Bill Clinton: Lessons for Government from IBM's Dramatic Turnaround," *Washington Monthly*, September 1999.

7. James C. Thomson Jr., 1968 "How Could Vietnam Happen?—An Autopsy," *Atlantic Monthly*, April 1968, 47–53.

8. Harrison E. Salisbury, *The New Emperors: China in the Era of Mao and Deng* (New York: Avon, 1993).

9. Martin Niemöller in the *Congressional Record*, October 14, 1968, 31636.

10. See http://www.sprucegoose.org/; http://www.wikipedia.org/wiki/Spruce _Goose.

11. A. D. Hopkins and K. J. Evans, eds., *The First 100: Portraits of Men and Women Who Shaped Las Vegas* (Las Vegas: Huntington Press, 2000).

12. Dan Bilefsky and Anita Raghavan, "How 'Europe's GE' and Its Star CEO Tumbled to Earth," *Wall Street Journal*, January 23, 2003, A1, A8.

13. Ibid.

14. Ibid.

15. Sophocles, *Antigone*, rev. and updated by Paul Roche (London: Meridian, 1996), 205.

16. Mimi Swartz with Sherron Watkins, *Power Failure: The Inside Story of the Collapse of Enron* (New York: Doubleday, 2003), 5.

17. Ibid., 35.

18. For an intriguing, if somewhat cynical, discussion of the role of the entourage, see F. G. Bailey, *Humbuggery and Manipulation: The Art of Leadership* (Ithaca, NY: Cornell University Press, 1988).

19. Richard Reeves, *President Kennedy: Profile of Power* (New York: Simon and Schuster, 1993), 103–4.

20. Ibid., 104.

21. James MacGregor Burns, *Roosevelt: The Lion and the Fox* (New York: Harcourt Brace Jovanovich, 1956), particularly 370–75.

22. Bailey, *Humbuggery and Manipulation*, 123.

Chapter 9

1. Jack Miles, "Corporate Leadership and the Media: Trouble Marriage or Cold War?" interpretive report on the conference "Media and Corporate Leadership: The Challenge and Courage to Lead," cosponsored by the Institute for Advanced Studies in Leadership, Peter F. Drucker Graduate School of Management, Claremont Graduate University; The Leadership Institute, Marshall School of Business, University of Southern California; and the Annenberg School for Communication, University of Southern California, held in Los Angeles, May 1999, 19.

2. Ibid., 15–16.

3. Ibid., 11.

4. Ibid., 10.

5. Peter Wyden, *The Bay of Pigs: The Untold Story* (New York: Simon and Schuster, 1979), 155n.

6. For a bibliography of the most important work on boards of all descriptions prior to 1990, see the bibliography in Cyril O. Houle, *Governing Boards: Their Nature and Nurture* (San Francisco: Jossey-Bass, 1989), 185–93. See also John Carver, *Boards That Make a Difference* (San Francisco: Jossey-Bass, 1990); John Carver and Caroline Oliver, *Corporate Boards That Create Value* (New York: John Wiley and Sons, 2002); Ram Charan, *Boards at Work: How Corporate Boards Create Competitive Advantage* (San Francisco: Jossey-Bass, 1998); John Nirenberg, *Destroy the Illusion—Make Responsible Corporate Governance a Reality* (Louisville: Brown Herron, 2002).

7. Available at http://www.sarbanes-oxley.com/displaypcaob.php?level=2&pub _id=SEC-Rules&chap_id=SEC2&message_id=92.

8. Micheline Maynard, "AMR Chair to Quit Boards," *International Herald Tribune*, April 29, 2003, 12.

9. CNNmoney, "American Drops Exec Bonus," April 18, 2003, available at http://money.cnn.com/2003/04/18/news/companies/amr_friday/.

10. Gretchen Morgenson, "Good Governance, Good Business," *International Herald Tribune*, April 29, 2003, 9.

11. See particularly the research of Solomon Asch, "Effects of Group Pressure upon the Modification and Distortion of Judgment," in H. Guetzkow, ed., *Groups,*

Leadership, and Men (Pittsburgh: Carnegie Press, 1951), 177–90; Muzafer Sherif, *The Psychology of Social Norms* (New York: Harper, 1936).

12. F. I. Nye, *Role Structure and Analysis of the Family* (Beverly Hills, CA: Sage, 1976); L. S. Cottrell, "The Adjustment of the Individual to His Age and Sex Roles," *American Sociological Review* 7 (1942): 617–20; J. Jackson, "A Conceptual and Measurement Model for Norms and Roles," *Pacific Sociological Review* 9 (1966): 35–47; T. R. Sarbin and V. R. Allen, "Role Theory," in G. Lindsey and E. Aronson, eds., *The Handbook of Social Psychology*, 2nd ed., vol. 1 (Reading, MA: Addison-Wesley, 1968), 488–567; J. W. Thibaut and H. H. Kelley, *The Social Psychology of Groups* (New York: Wiley, 1959).

13. Morgenson, "Good Governance, Good Business," 9.

14. Ibid.

15. Louis Lavelle, "The Best and Worst Boards: A Special Report," *Business Week*, October 7, 2002, 104–5.

16. Testimony of Herbert S. Winokur Jr. before the Subcommittee on Oversight and Investigations, Committee on Energy and Commerce, U.S. House of Representatives, February 7, 2002, 5, available at http://energycommerce.house .gov/107/hearings/02072002Hearing485/Winokur799.htm.

17. Associated Press, "Citigroup's Weill Gives Up CEO Job," July 16, 2002.

18. Ibid.

19. Ben McGrath, "Talk of the Town: Business as Usual," *The New Yorker*, August 4, 2003, 22.

20. Michelle Gabrielle, "Outside Board Members Earning Record Sums," February 8, 2001, available at http://www.cfo.com/article/1,5309,2085,00.html?f= related.

21. Testimony of Robert K. Jaedicke before the Subcommittee on Oversight and Investigations, Committee on Energy and Commerce, U.S. House of Representatives," February 7, 2002, 3–4, available at http://energycommerce.house .gov/107/hearings/02072002Hearing485/Jaedicke798.htm.

22. Ibid., 5.

23. Ibid., 11.

Chapter 10

1. Jean Lipman-Blumen, *The Connective Edge: Leading in an Interdependent World* (San Francisco: Jossey-Bass, 1996); see also Jean Lipman-Blumen and Harold J. Leavitt, *Hot Groups: Seeding Them, Feeding Them, and Using Them to Ignite Your Organization* (New York: Oxford University Press, 1999).

2. Lipman-Blumen, *The Connective Edge*.

3. Robert K. Merton, *Social Theory and Social Structure* (Glencoe, IL: Free Press, 1957), 302.

4. Penelope Lockwood, Christian H. Jordan, and Ziva Kunda, "Motivation by Positive or Negative Role Models: Regulatory Focus Determines Who Will Best Inspire Us," *Journal of Personality and Social Psychology* 83, 4 (2002): 854–64. See also the large body of work by E. T. Higgins, including "Beyond Pleasure and Pain," *American Psychologist* 52 (1997): 1280–300; "Making a Good Decision: Value from Fit," *American Psychologist* 55 (2000), 1217–30; E. T. Higgins and I. Silberman, "Development of Regulatory Focus: Promotion and Prevention as Ways of Living," in J. Heckhausen and C. S. Dweck, eds., *Motivation and Self-Regulation Across the Life Span* (New York: Cambridge University Press, 1998), 78–113.

5. Lockwood, Jordan, and Kunda, "Motivation by Positive or Negative Role Models."

6. Leon Festinger and John Thibaut, "Interpersonal Communication in Small Groups," *Journal of Abnormal and Social Psychology* 46 (1951): 92–99; see also Leon Festinger, Stanley Schacter, and Kurt Back, *Social Pressures in Informal Groups: A Study of Human Factors in Housing* (Stanford: Stanford University Press, 1950).

Chapter 11

1. Craig Lambert, "Traits of Gibraltar? Introversion Unbound," *Harvard Magazine*, July-August 2003, 12–13.

2. Peter Frost and Sandra Robinson, "The Toxic Handler: Organizational Hero—and Casualty," *Harvard Business Review*, July–August 1999, 96–106.

3. *Fred Korematsu v. United States*, 323 U.S. 214, 65 S. Ct 193 89 L. Ed 194, argued October 11, 1944, decided December 18, 1944, available at http://www.law.uh.edu/teacher/korematsu.

4. Kurt Lewin, *The Complete Social Scientist: A Kurt Lewin Reader*, ed. Martin Gold (Washington, DC: American Psychological Association, 1999).

5. Michael Beschloss, *The Conquerors: Roosevelt, Truman and the Destruction of Hitler's Germany 1941–1945* (New York: Simon and Schuster, 2002).

6. Associated Press, "Harry Truman's 'Lost' Diary," July 11, 2003, available at http://www.cbsnews.com/stories/2003/07/11/national/main562742.shtml.

7. Special Committee to the Board of Directors of Westar Energy, "Report of the Special Committee to the Board of Directors," April 29, 2003, available at http://media.corporate-ir.net/media_files/NYS/wr/reports/custom_page/Westar Energy.pdf. See also Rebecca Smith, "Westar Panel Says Ex-Chairman Exploited Job for Personal Gain," *Wall Street Journal*, May 16, 2003, C9.

8. David J. Garrow, *Bearing the Cross: Martin Luther King, Jr., and the Southern Baptist Leadership Conference* (New York: William Morrow, 1986). See, in Garrow, the description of how the early strategists decided against using as a test case an earlier incident in which a fifteen-year-old high school student, Claudette Colvin, had refused to go to the rear of the bus and had been removed forcibly by the police. The decision not to use Colvin was based on two factors. First, Colvin's resistance to being removed from the bus had led to charges filed against her for assault and battery, in addition to violating segregation status. Second, Colvin allegedly was several months pregnant (15–16).

9. Keith Bradsher, "Bending to Protests, Hong Kong Leader Will Revisit Security Bill," *New York Times*, July 18, 2003, A5.

10. For an analysis of the impact of the reputation for gaining even small but consistent wins on would-be challengers, see Thomas J. Peters, "Patterns of Winning and Losing: Effects on Approach and Avoidance by Friends and Enemies," Ph.D. dissertation, Stanford Graduate School of Business, 1977.

11. Jorge I. Dominguez, "The Country Castro Will Leave Behind," *New York Times*, July 25, 2003, A23.

12. Cullen Murphy, "The Rogues of Academe," *Atlantic Monthly*, December 2002, 20.

13. Alan Ehrenhalt, "The Paradox of Corrupt Yet Effective Leadership," *New York Times*, September 30, 2002, A25.

14. Robert W. Fuller, *Somebodies and Nobodies: Overcoming the Abuse of Rank* (Gabriola Island, BC: New Society, 2003).

15. This term was brought to my attention by Robert Fisher.

Chapter 12

1. Wilfred Owen, "Dulce et Decorum Est," in David Roberts, ed., *Out in the Dark: Poetry of the First World War in Context and with Basic Notes* (Philadelphia: Trans-Atlantic Publications, 1998).

2. Jean Lipman-Blumen and Harold J. Leavitt, *Hot Groups: Seeding Them, Feeding Them, and Using Them to Ignite Your Organization* (New York: Oxford University Press, 1999).

3. Mihaly Csikszentmihalyi, *Flow: The Psychology of Optimal Experience* (New York: Harper and Row, 1990).

4. Tom Pyszczynski, Sheldon Solomon, and Jeff Greenberg, *In the Wake of 9/11: The Psychology of Terror* (Washington, DC: American Psychological Association, 2003).

5. Helen Keller, *Let Us Have Faith* (Garden City, NY: Doubleday Doran, 1940); quote available at http://www.usachcs.army.mil/TACarchive/ACTNG/Brinkley.htm.

6. Heinrich Himmler, quoted from Alexander Mitscherlich and Margarete Mitscherlich, *The Inability to Mourn* (New York: Grove, 1975), in Elemér Hankiss, *Fears and Symbols: An Introduction to the Study of Western Civilization* (Budapest: Central European University Press, 2001), 195.

7. "The Golden Mean (or Golden Section), represented by the Greek letter phi, is one of those mysterious natural numbers, like *e* or pi, that seem to arise out of the basic structure of our cosmos. Unlike those abstract numbers, however, phi appears clearly and regularly in the realm of things that grow and unfold in steps, and that includes *living* things," Vashti.net, http://www.vashti.net/mceinc/grgolden.htm.

8. Max DePree, *Leadership Is an Art* (New York: Dell, 1989).

9. CNN, "Giuliani Recalls 'Tremendous Courage of All Those People,' " March 11, 2002, available at http://www.cnn.com/2002/US/03/11/giuliani.cnna/.

10. Sigmund Freud, *The Problem of Anxiety*, trans. Henry Alden Bunker (New York: Psychoanalytic Quarterly Press and W. W. Norton, 1936).

11. Elemér Hankiss, *Fears and Symbols: An Introduction to the Study of Western Civilization* (Budapest: Central European University Press, 2001), 26.

12. Ronald A. Heifetz, *Leadership Without Easy Answers* (Cambridge, MA: Belknap, 1994).

13. Warren G. Bennis and Robert J. Thomas, *Geeks and Geezers: How Era, Values, and Defining Moments Shape Leaders* (Boston: Harvard Business School Press, 2002).

14. Hugh S. Moorhead, ed., *The Meaning of Life* (Chicago: Chicago Review Press, 1988), 155.

15. Eric Voegelin, *Order and History*, vol. 1: *Israel and Revelation* (Baton Rouge: Louisiana State University Press, 1956), 1.

16. Hankiss, *Fears and Symbols*, 89.

17. Voegelin, *Order and History*, 1:1–3.

18. James Campbell Quick and Joanne H. Gavin, "The Next Frontier: Edgar Schein on Organizational Therapy," *Academy of Management Executive* 14, 1 (2000): 31–48.

19. Jean Delumeau, *Sin and Fear: The Emergence of a Western Guilt Culture, 13th–18th Centuries* (New York: St. Martin's Press, 1990).

20. Hankiss, *Fears and Symbols*, 45n.

21. This definition of courage was suggested by my colleague Neil Elgee, M.D.

Chapter 13

1. Sigmund Freud, *Group Psychology and the Analysis of the Ego*, trans. and ed. James Strachey (New York: W. W. Norton, 1959); Otto Rank, *Art and Artist: Creative Urge and Personality Development* (New York: W. W. Norton, 1968); and Ernest Becker, *The Denial of Death* (New York: Basic Books, 1973).

2. Rank, *Art and Artist*; Becker, *Denial of Death*; Ernest Becker, *Escape from Evil* (New York: Free Press, 1975); Otto Rank, *Truth and Reality* (New York: W. W. Norton, 1936).

3. The following section draws heavily on my previous work, which laid out the general outline of this book: Jean Lipman-Blumen, "Why Do We Tolerate Bad Leaders? Magnificent Uncertitude, Anxiety, and Meaning," in Warren Bennis, Gretchen M. Spreitzer, and Thomas G. Cummings, eds., *The Future of Leadership: Today's Top Leadership Thinkers Speak to Tomorrow's Leaders* (San Francisco: Jossey-Bass, 2001), 125–38.

4. Søren Kierkegaard, *The Concept of Dread*, trans. Walter Lowrie (Princeton, NJ: Princeton University Press, 1957), 144.

5. Kurt Lewin, "Group Decision and Social Change," in Guy E. Swanson, Theodore M. Newcomb, and Eugene L. Hartley, eds., *Readings in Social Psychology*, rev. ed. (New York: Henry Holt, 1952), 459–73.

6. Harold J. Leavitt, *Managerial Psychology*, 4th ed (Chicago: University of Chicago Press), 131.

7. Warren Bennis, "Followership," in *Managing the Dream* (Reading, MA: Perseus, 2000), 270.

8. For a more in-depth discussion of this point, see Jean Lipman-Blumen, *The Connective Edge: Leading in an Interdependent World* (San Francisco: Jossey-Bass, 1996), Chapter 3.

9. Chester Barnard, *The Functions of the Executive* (Cambridge, MA: Harvard University Press, 1938).

10. Diane Coutu, "How Resilience Works," *Harvard Business Review*, May 2002, 46–55.

11. Søren Kierkegaard, *Either/Or* (New York: Anchor, 1959), 1:129; Søren Kierkegaard, *The Gospel of Sufferings* (Minneapolis: Augsburg, 1948), 92; Martin Heidegger, *Being and Time* (London: SCM, 1962); Karl Jaspers, *Philosophie* (Heidelberg: Springer, 1948).

12. Thomas Szasz, *Second Sin* (London: Routledge, Kegan and Paul, 1974).

13. Stanley Crouch, "Picking Up Where Faulkner Left Off," *Los Angeles Times Book Review*, January 26, 2003, R3.

14. Albert Nolan, "Spiritual Growth and the Option for the Poor," speech given to the Catholic Institute of International Relations, London, at its annual meeting, June 29, 1984.

15. South African Government, "South African Governmental White Paper on Welfare," *Government Gazette* 16943, February 2, 1996, 18, paragraph 18.

16. For a more extended discussion of *ubuntu*, see http://web.archive.org/web/20030621124054/http://www.ivow.net/ubuntu.html; Michael Jesse Battle and Desmond Mpilo Tutu, *Reconciliation: The Ubuntu Theology of Desmond Tutu* (Cleveland: Pilgrim, 1997).

17. Lipman-Blumen, *The Connective Edge*.

18. Clifford C. Geertz, *The Interpretation of Cultures* (New York: Basic Books, 1973). See also Clifford C. Geertz, *Myth, Symbol, and Culture* (New York: W. W.

Norton, 1974). Geertz considers anthropology's task as the "thick description" of various cultures.

19. Kenneth C. Cole, "Mind Over Matter: When Competition and Cooperation Collide," *Los Angeles Times*, August 6, 2001.

20. For a more in-depth discussion of these two leadership perspectives, a politics of differences and a politics of commonalities, see Lipman-Blumen, *The Connective Edge*, 19–20, 190–91, 335, 339–40.

21. Harold J. Leavitt, *Top Down: Why Hierarchies Are Here to Stay and How to Manage Them More Effectively* (Boston: Harvard Business School Press, in press).

22. Russell L. Ackoff, *The Democratic Corporations: A Radical Prescription for Recreating Corporate America and Rediscovering Success* (New York: Oxford University Press, 1994).

23. Atul Gawande, "Annals of Medicine: Desperate Measures," *The New Yorker*, May 5, 2003, 70–81.

24. Ibid., 75.

25. Octavio Paz, *Sunstone*, trans. Eliot Weinberger (New York: New Dimensions, 1991).

26. Lipman-Blumen, *The Connective Edge*, 334.

27. This famous quotation was the parting words of Antioch's first president, Horace Mann, in his last Baccalaureate Sermon to Antioch students in 1859. Mann died several months later.

28. Lipman-Blumen, *The Connective Edge*, 330.

29. Ibid.

Bibliography

Aberbach, David. "Charisma and Attachment Theory: A Cross-Disciplinary Interpretation." *International Journal of Psychoanalysis* 76 (1995): 845–55.

Ackoff, Russell L. *The Democratic Corporations: A Radical Prescription for Recreating Corporate America and Rediscovering Success.* New York: Oxford University Press, 1994.

Adorno, T. W., Else Frenkel-Brunswik, D. J. Levinson, and R. N. Sanford. *The Authoritarian Personality.* New York: Harper and Brothers, 1950.

Alford, C. Fred. *Whistleblowers: Broken Lives and Organizational Power.* Ithaca: Cornell University Press, 2001.

Allen, James. *As a Man Thinketh.* Camarillo, CA: De Vorss, 1983.

Allen, John L., Jr. "Italian Church Rocked by Its Own Scandals." *National Catholic Reporter,* May 31, 2002.

Allison, Graham T. *Essence of Decision: Explaining the Cuban Missile Crisis.* Boston: Little, Brown, 1971.

Allport, Gordon W. "Preface." In Viktor E. Frankl, *Man's Search for Meaning.* New York: Washington Square Press, 1983.

Anson, Philip. "Dutoit: A Glance Back." *La Scena Musicale,* LSM Online, April 18, 2002.

Arendt, Hannah. *Eichmann in Jerusalem: A Report on the Banality of Evil.* New York: Viking Press, 1963.

Asch, Solomon E. "Effects of Group Pressure Upon the Modification and Distortion of Judgments." In *Groups, Leadership, and Men,* edited by Harold Guetzkow. Pittsburgh: Carnegie Press, 1951.

———. "Group Forces in the Modification and Distortion of Judgments." In *Classic Contributions to Social Psychology,* edited by Edwin P. Hollander and Raymond G. Hunt. New York: Oxford University Press, 1972.

———. "Studies on Independence and Conformity: A Minority of One Against a Unanimous Majority." *Psychological Monographs* 70, 9 (1956).

Aspen Institute Business and Society Program. *Where Will They Lead: 2003 MBA Student Attitudes about Business and Society.* Aspen: Aspen Institute, 2003.

Associated Press. "Citigroup's Weill Gives Up CEO Job." *MSNBC News,* July 16, 2003.

———. "Corruption Trial Starts for Mayor of Providence." *New York Times,* April 24, 2002, A16.

———. "French Twist: Skating Judge Denies She Made a Deal for Scores." *Sports Illustrated,* February 18, 2002.

———. "Harry Truman's 'Lost' Diary." *CBS News,* July 11, 2003.

———. "What's Providence Like Without Buddy?" News Channel 10 (NBC, Providence/New Bedford), June 24–25, 2003.

Australian Broadcasting Corporation Science Online. "The Genes for Megalomania." *ABC Science Online*, May 10, 2002.

Bailey, F. G. *Humbuggery and Manipulation: The Art of Leadership*. Ithaca, NY: Cornell University Press, 1988.

Baldwin, Neil. *Henry Ford and the Jews: The Mass Production of Hate*. New York: Public Affairs, 2001.

Bank, David. "Larry Ellison Has a Science Project: Courting Biologists." *Wall Street Journal*, January 9, 2003, A1–A2.

Barnard, Chester. *The Functions of the Executive*. Cambridge, MA: Harvard University Press, 1938.

Bartlett, John. *Familiar Quotations*. 14th ed. Edited by Emily Morison Beck. Boston: Little, Brown, 1968.

Battle, Michael Jesse, and Desmond Mpilo Tutu. *Reconciliation: The Ubuntu Theology of Desmond Tutu*. Cleveland: Pilgrim Press, 1997.

Baumeister, Roy F., Ellen Bratslavsky, Catrin Finkenauer, and Kathleen D. Vohs. "Bad Is Stronger Than Good," *Review of General Psychology* 5, 4 (December 2001): 323–70.

Baumeister, Roy F., and D. M. Tice. "Anxiety and Social Exclusion." *Journal of Social and Clinical Psychology* 9 (1991): 165–95.

BBC News. "Vivendi's Messier Steps Down." *BBC News*, July 2, 2002.

BBC Online Network, "Cleaning Up the Problem." June 27, 1999.

Beatty, Jack. *The Rascal King: The Life and Times of James Michael Curley (1874–1958)*. Cambridge, MA: DaCapo Press, 2000.

Beauvoir, Simone de. *The Second Sex*. New York: Vintage Books, 1974.

Becker, Ernest. *Escape from Evil*. New York: Free Press, 1975.

———. *The Denial of Death*. New York: Basic Books, 1973.

Begley, Sharon. "Science's Big Query: What Can We Know, and What Can't We?" *Wall Street Journal* Science Journal, May 30, 2003, B1.

Bellah, Robert N., Richard Madsen, William M. Sullivan, Ann Swidler, and Steven M. Tipton. *Habits of the Heart: Individualism and Commitment in American Life*. Berkeley: University of California Press, 1985.

Bennis, Warren. *Managing the Dream*. Reading: Perseus Books, 2000.

Bennis, Warren G., and Robert J. Thomas. *Geeks and Geezers: How Era, Values, and Defining Moments Shape Leaders*. Boston: Harvard Business School Press, 2002.

Bertin, Lou. "The Observer: Gerstner's Gift to IBM." *InformationWeek*, December 2, 2002.

Beschloss, Michael. *The Conquerors: Roosevelt, Truman and the Destruction of Hitler's Germany 1941–1945*. New York: Simon and Schuster, 2002.

Bianco, Anthony, and Tom Lowry. "Can Dick Parsons Rescue AOL Time Warner?" *Business Week*, May 19, 2003, 86.

Bianco, Anthony, William Symonds, and Nanette Byrnes, with David Polek. "The Rise and Fall of Dennis Kozlowski: A Revealing Look at the Man Behind the Tyco Scandal." *Business Week*, December 23, 2002, 65–77.

Bilefsky, Dan, and Anita Raghavan. "How 'Europe's GE' and Its Star CEO Tumbled to Earth." *Wall Street Journal*, January 23, 2003, A1, A8.

Boulay, Art. "Leadership Focus: Malden Mills: A Study in Leadership." *Quality Monitor Newsletter*, October 1996.

Bradsher, Keith. "Bending to Protests, Hong Kong Leader Will Revisit Security Bill." *The New York Times,* July 18, 2003, A5.

Brendon, Piers. *The Dark Valley: A Panorama of the 1930s.* New York: Alfred A. Knopf, 2000.

———. *Winston Churchill: A Brief Life.* London: Pimlico, 2001.

Brooker, Katrina. "The Un-CEO." *Fortune,* September 16, 2002, 88.

Bruck, Connie. *The Predators' Ball.* New York: Penguin Books, 1988.

Bruni, Frank. "Berlusconi, in a Rough Week, Says Only He Can Save Italy." *New York Times,* May 10, 2003.

———. "Italian Leader, in a First, Testifies at His Own Bribery Trial." *New York Times,* May 6, 2003.

Bugliosi, Vincent, with Curt Gentry. *Helter Skelter.* New York: Bantam Books, 1974.

Burns, James MacGregor. *Leadership.* New York: Harper and Row, 1978.

———. *Roosevelt: The Lion and the Fox.* New York: Harcourt Brace Jovanovich, 1956.

Bush, George W. "Address to Joint Session of the U.S. Congress," September 20, 2001.

Business Week. "The 25 Top Executives of the Year," *Business Week,* January 11, 1999.

Byrne, John A. *Chainsaw: The Notorious Career of Al Dunlap in the Era of Profit-At-Any-Price.* New York: HarperCollins, 1999.

Byrne, John A., and Heather Timmons. "Tough Times: How Ken Chenault of AmEx is Being Tested in Ways Few Could Have Imagined." *Business Week,* October 29, 2001, 66.

Canetti, Elias. *Crowds and Power.* London: Gollancz, 1962.

Carver, John. *Boards That Make a Difference.* San Francisco: Jossey-Bass, 1990.

Carver, John, and Caroline Oliver. *Corporate Boards That Create Value.* New York: John Wiley and Sons, 2002.

Celona, Larry. "Cop Is Shot with Own Gun—Just as Khalid Urged." *New York Post,* September 8, 1998.

Charan, Ram. *Boards at Work: How Corporate Boards Create Competitive Advantage.* San Francisco: Jossey-Bass, 1998.

Cloke, Kenneth, and Joan Goldsmith. *The End of Management and the Rise of Organizational Democracy.* San Francisco: Jossey-Bass, 2002.

CNN. "Giuliani Recalls 'Tremendous Courage of All Those People.' " March 11, 2002.

———. "Julian Lennon: Stepfather Knew Best." May 25, 1999.

———. "World Trade Center Death Toll Drops by Two." November 2, 2002.

CNNmoney. "American Drops Exec Bonus." April 18, 2003.

Cohen, F., S. Solomon, M. Maxfield, T. Pyszczynski, and J. Greenberg. "Fatal Attraction: The Effects of Mortality Salience on Evaluations of Charismatic, Task-Focused, and Relationship-Focused Leaders." Manuscript in preparation.

Cohen, Ronald D., and Dave Samuelson. Liner notes for *Songs for Political Action.* Bear Family Records BCD 15730 JL, 1996, 85.

Cole, Kenneth C. "Mind Over Matter: When Competition and Cooperation Collide." *Los Angeles Times,* August 6, 2001.

Constable, Pamela "Afghan Poppies Sprout Again." *Washington Post,* November 10, 2003, A16.

Cooley, George Horton. *Human Nature and the Social Order*. New York: Scribner's, 1902.

Cottrell, L. S. "The Adjustment of the Individual to His Age and Sex Roles." *American Sociological Review* 7 (1942): 617–20.

Coutu, Diane. "How Resilience Works." *Harvard Business Review*, May 2002: 46–55.

Crouch, Stanley. "Picking Up Where Faulkner Left Off." *Los Angeles Times Book Review*, January 26, 2003, R3.

Csikszentmihalyi, Mihaly. *Flow: The Psychology of Optimal Experience*. New York: Harper and Row, 1990.

Dahlberg, Tim. "Top USOC Leaders Seek Mankamyer's Resignation." *Scoreboard*, January 21, 2003.

Darwish, Adel. "Iraq: The Secret of the Palaces." *Foreign Wire*, December 2, 2001.

Delumeau, Jean. *Sin and Fear: The Emergence of a Western Guilt Culture, 13th–18th Centuries*. New York: St. Martin's Press, 1990.

Department of Conservation, State of California. "Will a Major Earthquake Interrupt the World Series? State Experts Say It's Unlikely, Though Not Impossible." NR 2002–45. Sacramento, CA.

DePree, Max. *Leadership Is an Art*. New York: Dell, 1989.

Dominguez, Jorge I. "The Country Castro Will Leave Behind." *New York Times*, July 25, 2003, A23.

Ehrenhalt, Alan. "The Paradox of Corrupt Yet Effective Leadership." *New York Times*, September 30, 2002, A23.

Erikson, Erik H. *Childhood and Society*. 2nd ed. New York: W. W. Norton, 1963.

Farley, Maggie, and Paul Watson. "Annan Asks Taliban to Reject ID Tags for Afghanistan Hindus." *Los Angles Times*, May 24, 2001, A5.

Ferlinghetti, Lawrence. "The World Is a Beautiful Place." In *Pictures of the Gone World*. San Francisco: City Light Books, 1955.

Festinger, L., H. W. Riecken, and S. Schacter. *When Prophecy Fails*. Minneapolis: University of Minnesota Press, 1956.

Festinger, Leon, Stanley Schacter, and Kurt Back. *Social Pressures in Informal Groups: A Study of Human Factors in Housing*. Stanford: Stanford University Press, 1950.

Festinger, Leon, and John Thibaut. "Interpersonal Communication in Small Groups." *Journal of Abnormal and Social Psychology* 46 (1951): 92–99.

Freud, Sigmund. *Group Psychology and the Analysis of the Ego*. Translated and edited by James Strachey. New York: W. W. Norton, 1959.

———. *The Problem of Anxiety*. Translated by Henry Alden Bunker, M.D. New York: The Psychoanalytic Quarterly Press and W. W. Norton, 1936.

Fromm, Erich. *Escape from Freedom*. New York: Avon, 1941; Holt, 1991.

Frost, Peter, and Sandra Robinson. "The Toxic Handler: Organizational Hero—and Casualty." *Harvard Business Review*, July–August 1999, 96–106.

Fuller, Robert W. *Somebodies and Nobodies: Overcoming the Abuse of Rank*. Gabriola Island: New Society Publishers, 2003.

Gabrielle, Michelle. "Outside Board Members Earning Record Sums." *CFO.com*, February 8, 2001.

Gannon, Kathy. "Ban on Poppy Farming Virtually Wipes Out Opium." *State Journal-Register* (IL), February 16, 2001.

Garber, Marjorie. "Our Genius Problem." *The Atlantic*, December 2002.

Gardner, Howard E. *Leading Minds: An Anatomy of Leadership*. New York: Basic Books, 1996.

Garrow, David J. *Bearing the Cross: Martin Luther King, Jr., and the Southern Baptist Leadership Conference.* New York: William Morrow, 1986.

Gawande, Atul. "Annals of Medicine: Desperate Measures." *The New Yorker*, May 5, 2003.

Geertz, Clifford. *Local Knowledge: Further Essays in Interpretive Anthropology.* New York: Basic Books,1983.

———. *Myth, Symbol, and Culture.* New York: W. W. Norton, 1974.

———. *The Interpretation of Cultures.* New York: Basic Books, 1973.

Gellately, Robert. *Backing Hitler: Consent and Coercion in Nazi Germany.* New York: Oxford University Press, 2001.

Gentry, Curt. *J. Edgar Hoover: The Man and the Secrets.* New York: W. W. Norton, 1991.

George, Alexander L., and Juliette L. George. *Woodrow Wilson and Colonel House: A Personality Study.* New York: Dover Publications, 1989.

Gerstner, Lou. Speech at Uniforum Conference, San Francisco, February 14, 1996.

Gladwell, Malcolm. *The Tipping Point.* Boston: Little, Brown, 2002.

Glanz, James, and Schwartz, John. "Dogged Engineer's Effort to Assess Shuttle Damage." *New York Times*, September 26, 2003, A1.

Glionna, John M. "Inmate Didn't Get Life, So He Chose Death at 92." *Los Angeles Times*, July 11, 2002, A1.

"The Golden Mean." Vashti.net. Available at http://www.vashti.net/mceinc/grgolden.htm.

Goldhagen, Daniel Jonah. *Hitler's Willing Executioners: Ordinary Germans and the Holocaust.* New York: Vintage Books, 1997.

Goode, Erica. "A Boy Genius? Mother Says She Faked Tests." *New York Times*, March 2, 2002.

Guernsey, Lisa. "Living Under an Electronic Eye." *New York Times*, September 27, 2001, G1.

Haddad, Charles. "A Whistle-Blower Rocks an Industry." *Business Week*, June 4, 2002, 130.

Haney, C., C. Banks, and P. Zimbardo. "Interpersonal Dynamics in a Simulated Prison." *International Journal of Criminology and Penology* 1 (1973): 69–97.

Hankiss, Elemér. *Fears and Symbols: An Introduction to the Study of Western Civilization.* Budapest: Central European University Press, 2001.

Heidegger, Martin. *Being and Time.* London: SCM, 1962.

Heifetz, Ronald A. *Leadership Without Easy Answers.* Cambridge: Belknap, 1994.

Herbert, Bob. "Rudy's No-Exit Strategy." *New York Times*, October 1, 2001.

———. "The Right Answer." *New York Times*, September 20, 2001.

Higgins, E. T. "Beyond Pleasure and Pain." *American Psychologist* 52 (1997): 1280–300.

———. "Making a Good Decision: Value from Fit." *American Psychologist* 55 (2000): 1217–30.

Higgins, E. T., and I. Silberman. "Development of Regulatory Focus: Promotion and Prevention as Ways of Living." In *Motivation and Self-Regulation Across the Life Span*, edited by J. Heckhausen and C. S. Dweck. New York: Cambridge University Press, 1998, 78–113.

Hitchens, Christopher. *The Missionary Position: Mother Teresa in Theory and Practice.* New York: Verso, 1995.

Holstein, William J. "Book Value: A Culture Turned Against Itself at Andersen." *New York Times*, February 23, 2003, sec. 3, 6.

Hook, Sidney. *The Hero in History: A Study in Limitation and Possibility.* Boston: Beacon Press, 1943.

Hopkins, A. D., and K. J. Evans, eds. *The First 100: Portraits of Men and Women Who Shaped Las Vegas.* Las Vegas: Huntington Press, 2000.

Houle, Cyril O. *Governing Boards: Their Nature and Nurture.* San Francisco: Jossey-Bass, 1989.

Hunt, Terence. "Clinton Pledges Turkey Quake Aid; President Visits Chilly Tent Camp, Consoles Victims." *Lexington Herald-Leader,* November 17, 1999, A3.

Hymowitz, Carol. "Companies Experience Major Power Shifts as Crises Continue." *Wall Street Journal,* October 9, 2001, B1.

Irving, I. Janis. *Victims of Groupthink: A Psychological Study of Foreign-Policy Decisions and Fiascoes.* Boston: Houghton Mifflin, 1972.

Jackson, J. "A Conceptual and Measurement Model for Norms and Roles." *Pacific Sociological Review* 9 (1966): 35–47.

Jaedicke, Robert K. Testimony before the Subcommittee on Oversight and Investigations, Committee on Energy and Commerce, U.S. House of Representatives, February 7, 2002.

Jaspers, Karl. *Philosophie.* Heidelberg: Springer, 1948.

Jones, Judy, and William Wilson. *An Incomplete Education.* New York: Ballantine Books, 1995.

Jos, Philip, Mark Tompkins, and Steven Hays. "In Praise of Difficult People: A Portrait of the Committed Whistleblower." *Public Administration Review* 49 (1989): 552–61.

Kavanagh, Dennis. *Crisis, Charisma and British Political Leadership: Winston Churchill as the Outsider.* Sage Professional Papers in Contemporary Political Sociology, 06–001. London and Beverly Hills: Sage, 1974.

Keller, Helen. *Let Us Have Faith.* Garden City: Doubleday Doran, 1940.

Kierkegaard, Søren. *Either/Or.* New York: Anchor Books, 1959.

———. *Fear and Trembling: Dialectical Lyric by Johannes de Silentio.* London: Penguin, 1985.

———. *The Concept of Dread.* Princeton: Princeton University Press, 1944.

———. *The Gospel of Sufferings.* Minneapolis: Augsburg Publishing House, 1948.

Kirkpatrick, David D. "Historian Says Borrowing Was Wider Than Known." *New York Times,* February 23, 2002, A10.

Kohara, Katsuhiro. "The Future of Bioethics and Chrisianity," *Echoes of Peace* 64, 1 (2003).

Kornandt, H. J., L. H. Eckensberger, and W. B. Emminghaus. "Cross-Cultural Research on Motivation and Its Contribution to a General Theory of Motivation." In *Handbook of Cross-Cultural Psychology,* vol. 3: *Basic Processes,* edited by H. C. Triandis and W. Lonner. Boston: Allyn and Bacon, 1980.

Kramer, Robert. *A Psychology of Difference: The American Lectures.* Princeton: Princeton University Press, 1996.

Krugman, Paul. "The Good Guys." *New York Times,* December 24, 2002, 23.

Kuhn, Thomas. *The Structure of Scientific Revolutions,* 2nd ed. Chicago: University of Chicago Press, 1970.

"Kurt Godel (1906–1978)." San Francisco: Exploratorium, 1996.

Lambert, Craig. "Traits of Gibraltar? Introversion Unbound." *Harvard Magazine,* July–August 2003, 12–13.

Lasswell, Mark. "The Controversy Over CBS' Hitler." *TV Guide,* April 12–18, 2003, 33.

Lavelle, Louis. "The Best and Worst Boards: A Special Report," *Business Week*, October 7, 2002, 104–5.

Leavitt, Harold J. *Managerial Psychology*. 4th ed. Chicago: University of Chicago Press, 1978.

———. "Technology and Organizations: Where's the Off Button?" *California Management Review* 44, 2 (2002).

———. *Top Down: Why Hierarchies Are Here to Stay and How to Manage Them More Effectively*. Boston: Harvard Business School Press, in press.

Leavitt, John. "The Language of the Gods: Mythic Song and Divine Speech in the Central Himalayas." Manuscript, 2001.

Leonard, Devin. "Songs in the Key of Steve." *Fortune*, May 12, 2003, 52.

LeVine, R. A. *Dreams and Deeds: Achievement Motivation in Nigeria*. Chicago: University of Chicago Press, 1966.

Lewin, Kurt. "Group Decision and Social Change." In *Readings in Social Psychology*, rev. ed., edited by Guy E. Swanson, Theodore M. Newcomb and Eugene L. Hartley. New York: Henry Holt, 1952.

Lewin, Kurt, and Martin Gold, ed. *The Complete Social Scientist: A Kurt Lewin Reader*. Washington, D.C.: American Psychological Association, 1999.

Lewis, Neil A., and David Johnston. "A Nation Challenged: The Investigation: Document That May Have Been Used to Prepare for Attacks Is Reported Found." *New York Times*, September 28, 2001, B4.

Lichtblau, Eric. "U.S. Uses Terror Law to Pursue Crimes from Drugs to Swindling," *New York Times*, September 28, 2003, 1.

Lieberman, E. James. *Acts of Will*. New York: Free Press, 1985.

Liechty, Daniel. *Transference and Transcendence: Ernest Becker's Contribution to Psychotherapy*. Northvale: Jason Aronson Press, 1995.

Lipman-Blumen, Jean. *Connective Leadership: Managing in a Changing World*. New York: Oxford University Press, 2000.

———. *Gender Roles and Power*. Englewood Cliffs, NJ: Prentice-Hall, 1984.

———. "Role De-Differentiation as a System Response to Crisis." *Sociological Inquiry* 43, 2 (1973): 105–29.

———. *The Connective Edge: Leading in an Interdependent World*. San Francisco: Jossey-Bass, 1996.

———. "Why Do We Tolerate Bad Leaders? Magnificent Uncertitude, Anxiety, and Meaning." In *The Future of Leadership: Today's Top Leadership Thinkers Speak to Tomorrow's Leaders*, edited by Warren Bennis, Gretchen M Spreitzer, and Thomas G. Cummings. San Francisco: Jossey-Bass, 2001.

Lipman-Blumen, Jean, and Harold J. Leavitt. *Hot Groups: Seeding Them, Feeding Them, and Using Them to Ignite Your Organization*. New York: Oxford University Press, 1999.

Lockwood, Penelope, Christian H. Jordan, and Ziva Kunda. "Motivation by Positive or Negative Role Models: Regulatory Focus Determines Who Will Best Inspire Us." *Journal of Personality and Social Psychology* 83, 4 (2002): 854–64.

Lorber, Judith. "Outsiders Within: Comments on *Time* Persons of the Year 2002." Essay sent to author via LISTSERVE, December 25, 2002.

Magnuson, Ed. "Earthquake." *Time*, October 30, 1989, 36.

Malinowski, Zachary. "Cianci Found Guilty of Racketeering Charge." *Providence Journal*, June 25, 2002.

March, James. "Information Technology, Decision Making and the Human Condition." Paper presented at the 24th International Federation of Training and Development Organizations (IFTDO) World Conference on Personal Renewal, Helsinki, Finland, 1995.

Maslow, Abraham. *Motivation and Personality*. New York: Harper and Brothers, 1954.

———. *The Farther Reaches of Human Nature*. New York: Viking Press, 1971.

Maynard, Micheline. "AMR Chair to Quit Boards." *International Herald Tribune*, April 29, 2003, 12.

McClelland, D. C. *The Achieving Society*. Princeton: Van Nostrand, 1961.

McClelland, D. C., J. W. Atkinson, R. A. Clark, and E. L. Lowell. *The Achievement Motive*. New York: Appleton-Century-Crofts, 1953.

McGrath, Ben. "Talk of the Town: Business As Usual." *The New Yorker*, August 4, 2003, 22.

McGrory, Brian. "For Feds, It's All Hard Time." *Boston Globe*, June 24, 2003, B1.

Mehren, Elizabeth. "Father's Mind-Set Is Liberated." *Los Angeles Times*, April 14, 2003, A1.

Merton, Robert K. *Social Theory and Social Structure*. Glencoe: Free Press, 1957.

Miles, Jack. *Corporate Leadership and the Media: Trouble Marriage or Cold War?* Interpretive report on the conference "Media and Corporate Leadership: The Challenge and Courage to Lead," cosponsored by the Institute for Advanced Studies in Leadership, Peter F. Drucker Graduate School of Management, Claremont Graduate University; The Leadership Institute, Marshall School of Business, University of Southern California; and the Annenberg School for Communication, University of Southern California, held in Los Angeles, May, 1999.

Milgram, Stanley. *Obedience to Authority: An Experimental View*. New York: Harper and Row, 1974.

Mishra, Pankaj. "Ex-Father of the Nation." *New York Times Book Review*, April 15, 2001, 12.

Mitscherlich, Alexander, and Margarete Mitscherlich. *The Inability to Mourn*. New York: Grove, 1975.

Moorhead, Hugh S., ed. *The Meaning of Life*. Chicago: Chicago Review Press, 1988.

Morgenson, Gretchen. "Good Governance, Good Business." *International Herald Tribune*, April 29, 2003, 9.

Morris, Betsy. "Can Ford Save Ford?" *Fortune*, November 30, 2002, 52.

Morse, Jodie, and Amanda Bower. "Persons of the Year: The Party Crasher." *Time*, December 30, 2002/January 6, 2003, 53–56.

Mumford, Lewis. *The Myth of the Machine: Technics and Human Development*. New York: Harcourt, Brace and World, 1966.

Muraven, Mark, and Roy F. Baumeister. "Sex, Terror, Paralysis, and Other Pitfalls of Reductionist Self-Preservation Theory." *Psychological Inquiry* 8, 1 (1997): 36–40.

Murphy, Cullen. "The Rogues of Academe." *Atlantic Monthly*, December 2002, 20.

"New MBAs: Nasty by Nature." *Fortune*, February 17, 1997, 127.

Nieves, Evelyn. "Freed from Jail Despite His Pleas, 92-Year-Old Is Found Dead in a River." *New York Times*, July 1, 2002, A12.

Nirenberg, John. *Destroy the Illusion—Make Responsible Corporate Governance a Reality*. Louisville: BrownHerron, 2002.

Nolan, Albert. "Spiritual Growth and the Option for the Poor," speech given to the Catholic Institute of International Relations, London, annual meeting, June 29, 1984.

Norris, Floyd. "S.E.C. Accuses Former Sunbeam Official of Fraud." *New York Times*, May 16, 2001, A1.

Nye, F. I. *Role Structure and Analysis of the Family*. Beverly Hills: Sage, 1976.

O'Hara, John. *Appointment in Samarra*. New York: Harcourt Brace, 1934.

Olmsted, Maureen E. "Parental Alcoholism or Alcoholism in the Current Relationship: A Special Case?" Paper presented at the biennial meeting of the Society for Research in Child Development, Albuquerque, NM, April 15–18, 1999.

Owen, Wilfred. "Dulce et Decorum Est." In *Out in the Dark: Poetry of the First World War in Context and with Basic Notes*, edited by David Roberts. Philadelphia: Trans-Atlantic Publications, 1998.

Page, Robert A., Peter H. Stauffer, and James W. Hendley II. "Progress Toward a Safer Future Since the 1989 Loma Prieta Earthquake." U.S. Geological Survey Fact Sheet 151–99, Washington, DC, 1999.

Pauchant, Thierry C., et al. *In Search of Meaning: Managing for the Health of Our Organizations, Our Communities, and the Natural World*. San Francisco: Jossey-Bass, 1995.

Paz, Octavio. *Sunstone*. Translated by Eliot Weinberger. New York: New Dimensions, 1991.

Perrow, Charles. *Normal Accidents: Living with High-Risk Technologies*. New York: Basic Books, 1984.

Peters, Thomas J. "Patterns of Winning and Losing: Effects on Approach and Avoidance by Friends and Enemies." Ph.D. dissertation, Stanford: Stanford Graduate School of Business, 1977.

Peters, Thomas J., and Robert H. Waterman, Jr. *In Search of Excellence: Lessons from America's Best-Run Companies*. New York: Harper and Row, 1982.

Plato. *The Republic of Plato*. Translated by Francis MacDonald. New York: Oxford University Press, 1941/50.

Popper, Micha. *Hypnotic Leadership: Leaders, Followers, and the Loss of Self*. Westport: Praeger Publishers, 2001.

"Predictions about Computers." Zuse Institute Berlin online.

Pulliam, Susan. "Ordered to Commit Fraud, A Staffer Balked, Then Caved." *Wall Street Journal*, June 23, 2003, 1.

Pyszczynski, Tom, Sheldon Solomon, and Jeff Greenberg. *In the Wake of 9/11: The Psychology of Terror*. Washington, DC: American Psychological Association, 2003.

Quick, James Campbell, and Joanne H. Gavin. "The Next Frontier: Edgar Schein on Organizational Therapy." *Academy of Management Executive* 14, 1 (2000): 31–48.

Rank, Otto. *Art and Artist: Creative Urge and Personality Development*. New York: W. W. Norton, 1932, 1968.

———. *Psychology and the Soul*. New York: Perpetua Books, 1961.

———. *Truth and Reality*. New York: W. W. Norton, 1936.

Reeves, Richard. *President Kennedy: Profile of Power*. New York: Simon and Schuster, 1993.

Ripley, Amanda, and Maggie Sieger. "The Special Agent." *Time*, December 30, 2002–January 6, 2003, 34–40.

Rosen, B. C., and R. D'Andrade. "The Psychological Origins of Achievement Motivation." *Sociometry* 22 (1959): 185–218.

Rosenberg, Howard. "He Fought Our Fear, and the Fear Won." *Los Angeles Times*, April 14, 2003, E1.

Ryan, Mike. "Boston's Irrepressible James Michael Curley." *Boston Irish Reporter*, November 1999.

Rynecki, David. "Can Stan O'Neal Save Merrill?" *Fortune*, September 30, 2002, 76.

Salisbury, Harrison E. *The New Emperors: China in the Era of Mao and Deng*. New York: Avon, 1993.

Sample, Steven. *The Contrarian's Guide To Leadership*. San Francisco: Jossey-Bass, 2001.

Sarbin, T. R., and V. R. Allen. "Role Theory." In *The Handbook of Social Psychology*, 2nd ed., edited by G. Lindsey and E. Aronson. Reading: Addison-Wesley, 1968, 488–567.

Sager, Ira. "Lou Gerstner on Catching the Third Wave." *Business Week*, October 30, 1995.

Schein, Edgar H., with Inge Schneier, and Curtis H. Barker. *Coercive Persuasion: A Socio-Psychological Analysis of the "Brainwashing" of American Civilian Prisoners by the Chinese Communists*. New York: W. W. Norton, 1961.

Schoenberg, R. *Geneen*. New York: Norton, 1985.

Schuckit, M. A., J. E. Tipp, and E. Kelner. "Are Daughters of Alcoholics More Likely to Marry Alcoholics?" *American Journal of Drug and Alcohol Abuse* (1994): 20, 237–45.

Securities and Exchange Commission. "Final Rule: Improper Influence on Conduct of Audits." Sarbanes-Oxley Online, July 3, 2003.

Sherif, Muzafer. "Experiments on Norm Formation." In *Classic Contributions to Social Psychology*, edited by Edwin P. Hollander and Raymond G. Hunt. New York: Oxford University Press, 1972.

———. *The Psychology of Social Norms*. New York: Harper and Brothers, 1936.

Shils, Edward. "Charisma, Order, and Status." *American Sociological Review* 30, 2 (1965): 199–213.

Shrivastava, Paul. *Bhopal: Anatomy of a Crisis*. Cambridge: Ballinger, 1987.

Simons, Tony. "The High Cost of Lost Trust." *Harvard Business Review*, September 2002, 18–19.

Sinclair, Matthew. "William Aramony Is Back on the Streets." *The NonProfit Times*, March 1, 2002.

Slam! Sports. "Killy Report to IOC on Tour de France Scandals." August 20, 1998.

Smelser, Neil. J. *The Theory of Collective Behavior*. Toronto: Free Press, 1962.

Smith, Rebecca. "Westar Panel Says Ex-Chairman Exploited Job for Personal Gain." *Wall Street Journal*, May 16, 2003, C9.

Sophocles. *Antigone*. Revised and updated by Paul Roche. London: Meridian, 1996.

South African Government. "South African Governmental White Paper on Welfare." *Government Gazette* No.16943, February 2, 1996, 18, paragraph 18.

Summers, Anthony. *Official and Confidential: The Secret Life of J. Edgar Hoover*. New York: Orion Publishing Group, 1993.

Swartz, Mimi, with Sherron Watkins. *Power Failure: The Inside Story of the Collapse of Enron*. New York: Doubleday, 2003.

Symonds, William C. "Basic Training for CEOs." *Business Week*, June 11, 2001, 103.

Szasz, Thomas. *Second Sin*. London: Routledge Kegan and Paul, 1974.

"They Said What?" *The Observer,* April 21, 2002.

Thibaut, J. W., and H. H. Kelley. *The Social Psychology of Groups.* New York: Wiley, 1959.

Thomson, James C., Jr. "How Could Vietnam Happen? An Autopsy." *Atlantic Monthly,* April 1968, 47, 53.

Tobar, Héctor. "Pomp, Not Panic, During Argentine Leader's Inaugural." *Los Angeles Times,* May 26, 2003, A3.

Tocqueville, Alexis de. *Democracy in America.* New York: Vintage Books, 1959.

Toffler, Barbara Ley. *Final Accounting: Ambition, Greed, and the Fall of Arthur Andersen.* New York: Broadway Books, 2003.

Trump, Donald, and Bonher, Kate. *The Art of the Comeback.* New York: Times Books, 1997.

Tufte, Edward Rolf. *Visual Explanations.* Cheshire: Graphics Press, 1997.

U.S. Department of Energy, Office of Science. Human Genome Project Information Homepage. Available at http://www.ornl.gov/sci/techresources/Human _Genome/home.shtml.

Useem, Jerry. "The 25 Most Powerful People in Business." *Fortune,* August 11, 2003, 57–84.

Voegelin, Eric. *Order and History,* vol. 1: *Israel and Revelation.* Baton Rouge: Louisiana State University Press, 1956.

Watson, Dale L. Statement before the Senate Select Committee on Intelligence, Washington, D.C., Feb. 6, 2002.

Weber, Max. *Max Weber: The Theory of Social and Economic Organization.* Translated by A. M. Henderson and Talcott Parsons. New York: Free Press of Glencoe, 1947.

———. *The Protestant Ethic and the Spirit of Capitalism.* New York: Charles Scribner's Sons, 1958.

———. "The Sociology of Charismatic Authority." In *From Max Weber: Essays in Sociology,* edited by H. H. Gerth and C. Wright Mills. New York: Oxford University Press, 1946. 245–52.

Webster, Daniel. From a speech at the foundation of the Bunker Hill monument commemorating the soldiers of the American Revolution, June 17, 1825.

Westar Energy. *Report of the Special Committee to the Board of Directors,* April 29, 2003.

Winokur, Herbert S., Jr. Testimony before the Subcommittee on Oversight and Investigations, Committee on Energy and Commerce, U.S. House of Representatives, February 7, 2002.

Witkin, Gordon. "Can Jim and Tammy Make a Comeback?" *U.S. News and World Report,* October 19, 1987, 21.

Worth, Robert. "What Lou Gerstner Could Teach Bill Clinton: Lessons for Government from IBM's Dramatic Turnaround." *Washington Monthly,* September 1999.

Wyden, Peter. *The Bay of Pigs: The Untold Story.* New York: Simon and Schuster, 1979.

Zimbardo, Philip G. "The Stanford Prison Experiment: A Simulation Study of the Psychology of Imprisonment." Stanford Prison Experiment Online, 1999.

Index

Note: Page numbers in **bold** refer to entire chapters.

Obama ?